THE COMPLETE GUIDE TO
Origami & Papercraft

THE COMPLETE GUIDE TO

Origami &
Papercraft

Oceana

AN OCEANA BOOK

This book is produced by
Quantum Publishing Ltd
6 Blundell Street
London N7 9BH

ISBN 0-681-28866-3

QUMCGTO

Manufactured in Singapore by
Pica Digital Pte. Ltd

Printed in Singapore by
Star Standard Industries Pte. Ltd

CONTENTS

Above INTRICATE PAPER-CUT

This extremely intricate pattern dates from 1855. The image is an ingenious reflection of Swiss rural and town life. Note the contrast between the well at the top and the water pumps at the bottom.

Below PATTERNED PAPER-CUT

Black makes an effective background for these surreal figures. The decorated papers mirror the title of the piece (Earth, Wind, Water, Fire, Cynthia Gale).

INTRODUCTION

One of the most familiar forms of paper arts is origami. It is debatable whether origami originated in Japan, Korea, or China. However, we do know that the Japanese were producing sophisticated forms some 1,200 years ago. The word itself is Japanese, from *ori* (to fold) and *kami* (paper). The popularity of the art died out until the 1930s, when a young Japanese, Akira Yoshizawa, began to develop new forms based on old designs. Unlike the traditional form, which let the paper to be cut as well as folded, the newer forms demanded that all shapes be created from a single piece of paper using folds only. The popularity of origami spread to the West and was confirmed by the publication in 1956 of a British book called *Paper Magic* by the South African Robert Harbin.

Paper Sculpture and Pop-ups

It is believed that modern paper sculpture originated in Poland. Subsequently, the works of Polish artists influenced English and American artists. In the 1940s and 1950s, department stores adopted paper sculpture as an exciting new means of creating window displays. Advertising agencies too used paper sculpture in campaigns.

Another paper art form exploited by the advertising and graphic arts industry is pop-ups. These were first used in children's books during the latter half of the 19th century. Soon greetings-card manufacturers began to use pop-ups, and the medium was developed to create a variety of complex and ingenious designs.

Today, paper artists can draw on traditional techniques, and either practise them in their pure forms, or adapt them using modern design values and style. And never before has there been a greater range of paper types, weights, colours and textures available.

Although there is a lot of choice available in the shops for you to buy, paper actually comes in just three basic types: handmade, mould-made, and machinemade. And when purchasing paper there are two basic qualities for you to consider – weight and grain. Handmade papers, which often incorporate long fibres, have four deckle edges (a deckle is the rough edge of the paper) but no grain (the direction in which the fibres lie). Mould-made papers are manufactured by machine. These have two deckle edges and longer fibres than in machinemade papers. Mould-made and machinemade papers both have a grain.

Other frequently used paper terms are 'laid', 'wove' and 'sized'. 'Laid' paper is made on a mould that has wire, or sometimes wooden, bars laid across the frame. These bars allow a thinner deposit of pulp to be laid and leave an impression on the sheet of paper. This impression may be visible only against the light. Watermarks are formed similarly. Paper without these lines is called 'wove', from the woven mesh on which the pulp is poured. Paper can be 'sized', which means that it is coated with a glue substance (usually gelatine or starch), or it can be 'unsized'. Sized paper is less absorbent and therefore ink or paint do not bleed when drawn or painted on it. Unsized paper is known as 'waterleaf'.

Paper Weight

Paper is often measured in terms of grammes per square metre, expressed as g/m^2 or gsm^2. Where the weight is given in pounds, it refers to pounds per ream (a ream comprises 500 sheets). It is possible to convert pounds per ream to grammes per square metre.

Left *Decorated origami and gift-wrapping papers are printed as part of their manufacturing process. Some are printed on one side only, which increases their versatility in papercrafts.*

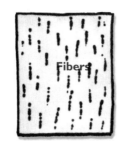

1 *A sheet of paper with the grain running from top to bottom.*

2 *The sheet will bend easily when the lefthand edge is brought over to the right, because the bend follows the direction of the grain.*

3 *The sheet will not bend as easily when the top edge is brought down to the bottom, because the bend runs across the direction of the grain.*

4 *A torn edge is straighter when it follows the direction of the grain, than when it runs across the grain.*

An average paper, such as the writing paper you us every day, weighs between 80 and 120 gsm^2. Paper weighing more than 225 gsm^2 is card; it becomes board when it weighs 500 gsm^2 and more.

Paper Grain

The grain of paper is pronounced in machinemade papers because the mould on which they are made is a moving belt and the fibres settle in the direction of the movement of the belt. This allows the paper to fold, curve, tear and crease more easily along its grain. But it also has drawbacks: when wetted, the fibres swell widthways but not lengthways, and although they compress again when dry, if two surfaces are being joined, you may end up with a curved surface. To prevent this from happening, one tip is to try dampening both sheets of paper.

To find out which way the grain runs, curl the paper in both directions and, while pressing gently with one hand, feel which way bends more easily. Another way is to tear two strips from the paper, one in each direction. The tear will be much cleaner along the grain. Find the grain in card and board by flexing the sheet between your hands and then turning it through 90° and flexing it the other way; it will flex more readily in the direction of the grain.

DIRECTORY OF PAPERS

The type, texture, finish, weight and colour of paper affect suitability for each art form, so it is important to know which types of paper to use for different projects. Handmade papers can be hot-pressed, cold-pressed, or rough. Hot-pressed paper is fairly smooth; cold-pressed has a slight texture, or 'tooth'; and rough paper has a distinct texture.

Paper can be categorised into the following four groups:

Uncoated papers comprise the majority of machine-made papers used in the printing industry. They include white and coloured papers in plain and embossed finishes.

Coated papers have smooth surfaces and are found in gloss or dull finishes of various brightness. The coloured papers are good for torn sculptural effects because they reveal an attractive white edge when torn.

Handmade papers are generally made from cotton or linen rags. Their sculptural qualities are superb because the fibres occur in a random pattern.

Speciality papers include crêpe, tracing and corrugated papers.

Commercial Uncoated

COVER PAPER
The kind of paper used for booklets and folders. Available in white and a wide range of colours, including bright primaries. Suitable for weaving, collage, paper-cuts, pop-ups, papermaking and paper sculpture. Weight: medium.

BOND PAPER
Everyday paper, available as office and home stationery. Supplied mainly in shades of white, cream and pale grey or blue. Suitable for weaving, collage, paper-cuts, origami, papermaking, papier mâchè and paper sculpture. Weight: medium.

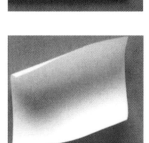

ART PAPER
Fine paper sold for use by artists, available in various colours. Suitable for weaving, collage, paper-cuts, pop-ups, papermaking and paper sculpture. Weight: white, heavy; colours, medium.

DRAWING PAPER
A strong, more opaque bond of the kind used in sketchbooks, available in white and a range of bright and pale colours. Suitable for collage, pop-ups, papermaking and paper sculpture. Weight: medium.

BRISTOL
Good-quality, fairly heavy paper, ideal for constructional purposes. Supplied in white and various colours. Suitable for collage, pop-ups, papermaking and paper sculpture. Weight: heavy.

RECYCLED
Machine-made recycled papers are available in white and mainly pale colours. Suitable for weaving, collage, paper-cuts, pop-ups, papermaking, papier mâchè and paper sculpture. Weight: medium.

SCORED

CURLED

CRUMPLED

TORN

Commercial Uncoated: continued

PARCHMENT
Fine-quality artwork paper available in unusual shades, such as peach and antique gold. Suitable for weaving, collage, paper-cuts, pop-ups, papermaking, papier mâché and paper sculpture.
Weight: medium.

KRAFT
Strong, low-cost wrapping paper, ribbed and unbleached. Suitable for weaving, collage, paper-cuts, papermaking, papier mâché and paper sculpture.
Weight: medium.

PASTEBOARD
Stiff and relatively thick unlined grey board. Suitable for collage, pop-ups and papermaking. Weight: heavy.

NEWSPRINT
Coarse, weak paper used for newspapers and also sold for rough sketching. Usually white. Suitable for weaving, collage, papercuts, papermaking, papier mâché and origami.
Weight: standard.

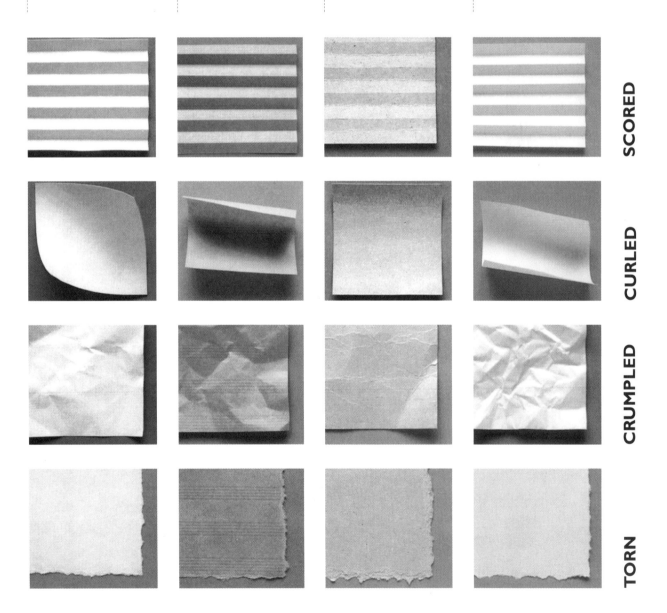

SCORED

CURLED

CRUMPLED

TORN

Commercial Coated Papers

Handmade Papers

ART AND PRINTING PAPER

High-quality papers coated in gloss or dull finishes in a variety of colours. Suitable for weaving, collage, paper-cuts, pop-ups and paper sculpture. Weight: heavy.

COVER PAPER

Firm, light, flexible coated card in a wide range of colours. Suitable for weaving, collage, paper-cuts, pop-ups and paper sculpture. Weight: heavy.

HANDMADE RAG LIGHT

Fine-quality, strong, durable white paper, available in cold-pressed, hot-pressed and rough finishes. Suitable for weaving, collage, paper-cuts, papermaking, papier mâchè and paper sculpture. Weight: heavy.

HANDMADE RAG HEAVY

A heavier version of light rag paper with the same qualities and availability. Suitable for collage, pop-ups, papermaking and paper sculpture. Weight: heavy.

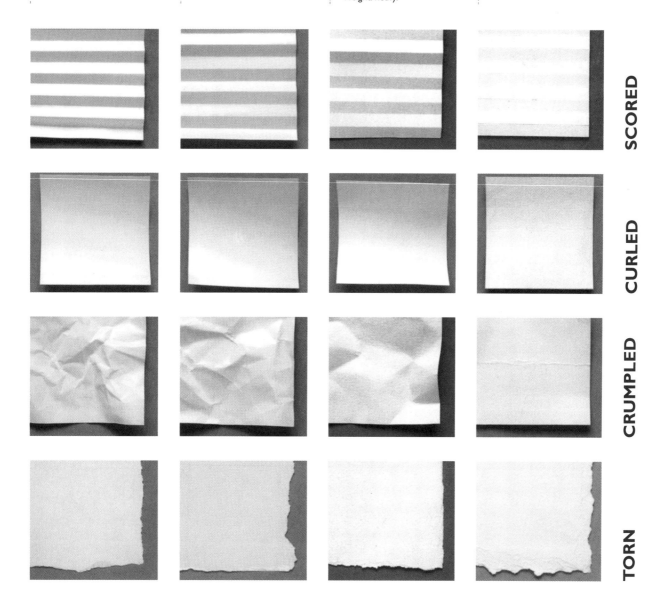

SCORED

CURLED

CRUMPLED

TORN

Handmade Papers: continued

Speciality Papers

CHINESE HANDMADE

Superior paper suitable for weaving, collage, paper-cuts, papermaking, papier mâchè, origami and paper sculpture. Weight: variable.

HANDMADE WITH EMBEDDED OBJECTS

A variety of unusual effects and colours is possible with papers containing embedded items. Suitable for weaving, collage, paper-cuts, papier mâchè and paper sculpture. Weight: variable.

CRÊPE

Thin crinkled paper in white and various colours. Suitable for weaving, collage, papermaking and papier mâchè. Weight: standard.

TISSUE

Fine, easily crumpled paper, available in white and various colours. Suitable for weaving, collage, papermaking, papier mâchè and paper sculpture. Weight: standard.

SCORED

CURLED

CRUMPLED

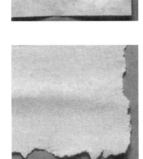

TORN

TRACING
Highly transparent plain paper with a choice of thickness. Suitable for weaving, collage, origami and paper sculpture. Weight: light and medium.

SUGAR PAPER
Inexpensive, plain paper in a variety of colours. Suitable for collage and weaving. Weight: standard.

CORRUGATED
Light but strong paper traditionally used as packing material for fragile items. Available in natural brown and various colours. Suitable for weaving, collage, pop-ups, papermaking and paper sculpture. Weight: standard.

RICE PAPER
Thin paper made from rice grass, available in natural white. Suitable for weaving, collage, papermaking and papier mâchè. Weight: standard.

SCORED

CURLED

CRUMPLED

TORN

15

TOOLS AND EQUIPMENT

The beauty and appeal of most papercrafts is that they are relatively inexpensive pastimes and require only basic tools. Measuring and marking tools include pencils, rulers, a compass and a triangle. For cutting you will require scissors and knives – or, best of all, a craft knife with a selection of interchangeable blades. A cutting mat saves wear on your knife blades and your work surface. Always use a metal rule or straightedge to guide your knife when cutting a straight line; a plastic ruler is not sturdy enough and can cause the blade to slip and cut you. Additionally, you will also want a range of tools and materials to decorate your work, such as paints, pastels, brushes and sprays.

PAINTBRUSHES
2.5 cm (1 in.) brush for painting and glazing papier mâchè and gluing collage components. Artists' brushes for finer detail.

CUTTING MAT
Self-sealing surface for smooth knife-cutting and reduction of wear on blades.

SCISSORS
Small scissors for detailed pieces and large scissors for cutting out basic shapes.

KNIVES
A knife with interchangeable blades. You can also use a craft knife with a wedge-shaped blade for cutting straight strips and another with a long fine point for cutting intricate shapes.

PENCILS
A 6H for transferring tracings and a 2B for drawing shapes on layout paper.

TRIANGLE
For drawing straight lines and for use in conjunction with a ruler to draw parallel lines horizontally and vertically.

RULERS
A 12 in. (30 cm) plastic ruler for measuring and drawing, and a 12 in. (30 cm) metal rule for straight-edge cutting.

ERASER
White nylon eraser for removing pencil lines and any other unwanted marks.

SMALL WOODEN SKEWERS
For applying small amounts of adhesive, especially useful in paper sculpture.

BASIC EQUIPMENT CHECK LIST
- ◆ **Metal rule**
- ◆ **Plastic rule**
- ◆ **Triangle**
- ◆ **Craft knife**
- ◆ **Pencils—2B and 6H**
- ◆ **Scissors, small and large**
- ◆ **Cutting mat**
- ◆ **Paintbrushes**
- ◆ **Eraser**
- ◆ **Small wooden skewers**

SPECIALIZED TOOLS

From time to time you will need to use a special piece of equipment: a hole punch to cut circles for eyes, a mould and deckle for papermaking, some polystyrene to build relief effects. These pages show some of the specialized tools that paper artists find most useful, but you can also exploit your ingenuity to discover or improvise an item that works for a particular job. Our alternatives are listed in brackets—many of these are everyday household items.

ROLLER
For pressing large pieces of paper onto a background after gluing [rolling pin, dowel].

LARGE SOFT BRUSH
For applying paste to paper [decorators' brush, paste brush].

NEEDLES
For piercing a pattern or making a small connecting hole, for example in mobiles [pins, drawing pins].

POLYSTYRENE
Available as sheets of different thicknesses, used to elevate the paper layers and create relief effects [corrugated card, polystyrene tiles].

PAPERMAKING EQUIPMENT
You must have the following pieces of equipment to make paper: mould and deckle (wooden frames for forming sheets of paper from pulped material); pressing boards (for pressing water out of freshly formed paper); and pieces of felt (to layer between freshly made sheets when pressing).

Pressing boards [any board]

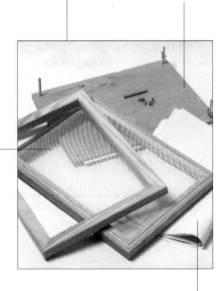

Mould and deckle [canvaswork frame]

Felt blanket [or cloth]

HOME EQUIPMENT
You may be surprised to find that you already have much of the equipment needed, particularly for the papermaking section.

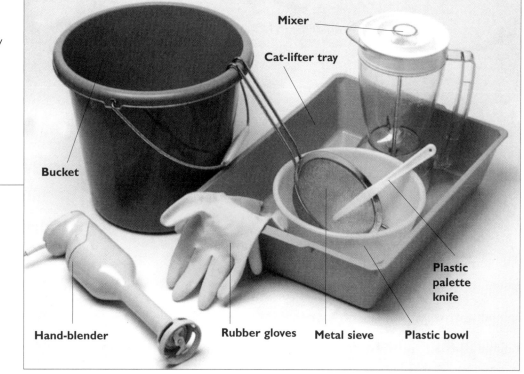

Mixer

Cat-lifter tray

Bucket

Plastic palette knife

Hand-blender

Rubber gloves

Metal sieve

Plastic bowl

STAPLER
For fastening paper instantly. Useful for making quick models of a planned sculpture [paper clips].

WOODEN DOWEL
Used for shaping and curling paper [handle of wooden spoon].

WOODEN SCULPTING TOOLS
For scoring, curling, and general shaping [knitting needles, ballpoint pens].

HOLE PUNCH/ LEATHER PUNCH
For punching small circles that would be difficult to cut out [paper punch].

BURNISHER
Ideal for flattening folds [empty ballpoint pen].

MASKING TAPE
*Useful for a variety of
purposes, but is more
temporary than glue.*

ADHESIVES

A number of strong paper glues are suitable
for projects that involve paper construction.
Polyvinyl acetate (PVA) or a quick-bonding
all-purpose adhesive is recommended for
pop-ups and sculpture, and wallpaper paste
or white plastic glue are necessary for papier
mâchè. Sellotape is useful for temporary fixing
and should always be to hand.

WALLPAPER PASTE
*Used primarily for
papier mâchè.*

POLYVINYL ACETATE (PVA)
*A good all-purpose adhesive,
particularly for paper sculpture
and pop-ups.*

VARNISH
*Make sure you use a clear
varnish to seal paper,
particularly for découpage.*

FINISHING

You will often want to add a decorative finish
to your art forms. To create a good surface,
coat your work with gesso before applying
watercolor, acrylic, or poster paints.

PAINTS
*The most useful paints
are watercolor, acrylic,
and poster paints.*

GESSO
*Available in tubs and bottles. Used to
seal papier mâchè before painting.*

MOULD-MAKING

To build an original work in papier mâchè, you will need materials for making a mould, and a releasing agent to prevent the paper from sticking to it.

SILICONE SEALANT
Used for casting paper and papier mâchè.

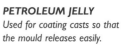

PETROLEUM JELLY
Used for coating casts so that the mould releases easily.

MODELING CLAY
Used for making models for papier mâchè.

WATERPROOF TAPE
Available in various colors and widths. Used for papermaking and casting.

FOUND OBJECTS
You can use found objects in a variety of ways for weaving, papier mâchè, origami, collage, papermaking, and paper sculpture. In addition to the items shown, you can experiment with twigs, leaves, bones, bark, seeds, wallpaper, junk mail, stones, leaflets, wrappers, washers, sand, fabric scraps—to mention just a few!

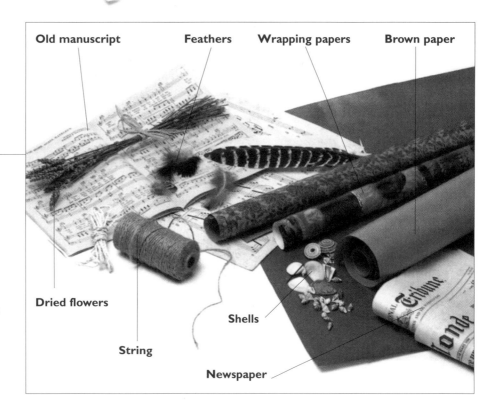

Old manuscript   **Feathers**   **Wrapping papers**   **Brown paper**

Dried flowers

Shells

String

Newspaper

ORIGAMI

INTRODUCTION TO ORIGAMI

Why do people find pleasure in folding paper? Most do so because they enjoy making something out of nothing. A sheet of paper is so ordinary to us that to transform it into a beautiful object can seem miraculous; it is a blank canvas that presents us with an infinite number of creative possibilities. Another reason is the simplicity. Folding paper needs no tools or specialist equipment. It is relaxing, involving, and rewarding, too.

The first papers capable of being folded were produced in China about 2,000 years ago, though there is no evidence to suggest that the Chinese folded paper in a decorative way back then. A few dozen ancient Japanese designs survive to the present day, but since the secret of how to produce paper did not reach Japan until several centuries after its invention in China, the exact origins of the craft are obscure.

Traditional Japanese designs have been the inspiration for the recent flood of creative work from Japan and the West, and the Japanese word for paper folding—origami— has been adopted worldwide. What must have once been a trivial diversion has proven to be a craft of extraordinary richness and enduring, universal appeal. There are now societies of paper folders in several countries around the world who organize exhibitions and courses, and publish specialist publications on the subject.

The next few pages will give you all the information you need to understand the instructions for the projects. So, good luck and happy folding!

SELECTING THE PAPER

Most papers are suitable for folding, but the trick really is matching the right paper to the right design. Avoid papers that do not crease sharply, such as newspaper or paper towels, unless these are specified as part of the design. Once you have selected the right paper, you will stand a much better chance of creating successful origami projects.

Specialist Japanese shops usually sell square origami paper in packets, but these are few and far between. In any case, origami paper is often expensive and the colors can sometimes be harsh.

Good papers for trying out a design include typing paper, writing paper, xerox paper, and computer paper. These are easily available, inexpensive, and crease very well. If nothing else is around and you want to try a design immediately, a page cut from a glossy magazine will also fold well.

For origami designs that need to be sturdy and robust, use thick artist's papers capable of absorbing moisture without warping, such as Ingres paper or watercolor paper. This will allow you to employ the so-called "wet folding" process: before folding a paper, stroke both sides with a lightly dampened cloth, then fold; the paper will dry rigid into its folded shape. Other papers, such as drawing paper, are suitable for general folding, but unfortunately they warp and shred when wet.

Some designs are best made from a sheet with different colors on its two sides. Alternatively, simply use two thin sheets of different colors and fold them back-to-back, as one layer.

Stationers often sell sheets or rolls of metallic foil backed with paper. This material, though malleable for folding, has a harsh, crude surface that can look rather unattractive. Use it selectively, perhaps for festive decorations such as the Bauble. To soften the reflective surface—but keep the folding properties of foil, try covering the foil-side with a layer of soft-colored tissue.

For many of the origami designs that follow there is advice on the best weight of paper to use. Lightweight paper is the weight of typing paper, while mediumweight is that of drawing paper. Heavy paper is the weight of watercolor paper. It is advisable to use the weight suggested. However, a paper of another weight may work equally well, so feel free to experiment. Once you have completed a few projects, you will have more of a feel of which type of paper to use for different projects.

SYMBOLS

Symbols are the core of any book about origami; they provide simple, easy-to-follow explanation to projects. They need not all be learnt at once, but it is important to know at least the symbols for valley and mountain folds. When you see an unfamiliar symbol, refer back to this page to see what it means.

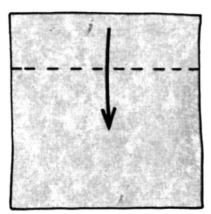

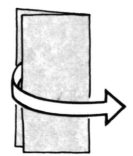

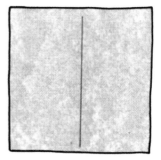

unfold or pull open

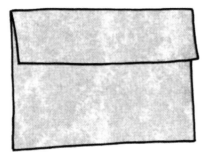

valley fold (fold to the front)

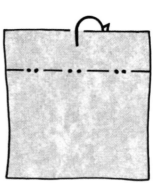

existing crease

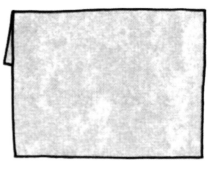

mountain fold (fold behind)

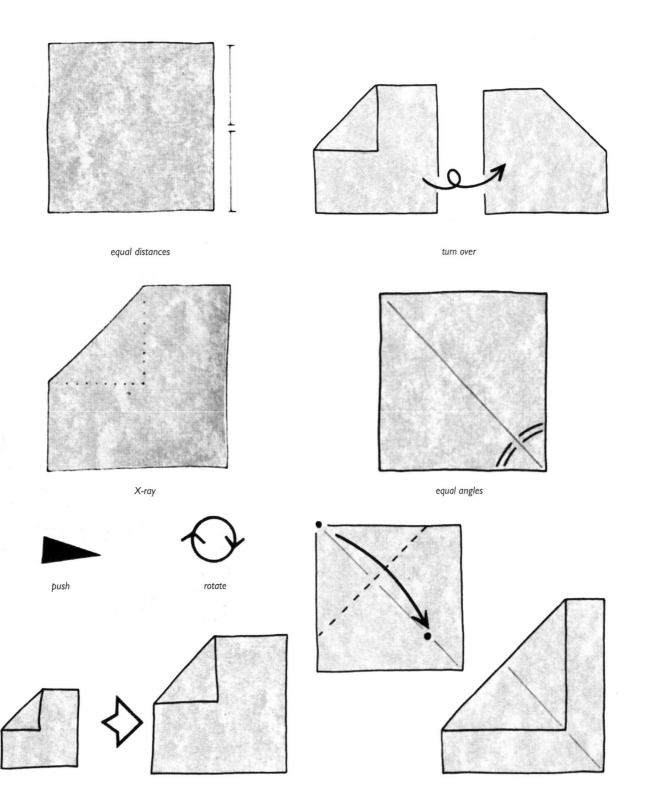

equal distances

turn over

X-ray

equal angles

push

rotate

the next drawing is bigger

fold dot to dot

TIPS ON FOLDING

Folding paper is not a difficult skill to learn, but it can become difficult if you fold in an incorrect way. To help you fold properly, here are some tips:

■ Fold against a hard, level surface such as a table top or hardback book. Experts in the art of origami fold entirely in the air, but this is very awkward for beginners. Nevertheless, there will be occasions, particularly when folding the last stages of a design, when you will need to pick up the paper and fold it in the air, but do so only when necessary.

■ Fold slowly, do not rush! Folding needs to be done carefully and neatly. A few sloppy creases here and there can throw everything else out of alignment, so it is important to check and double-check the accuracy of your folds.

■ Fold crisply and firmly.

■ Look at the diagrams and read all the instructions before embarking on an origami project. All too often, mistakes are made by looking at one without reference to the other. Look at all the symbols (see pages 26 and 27) on a step, checking whether a crease is a valley or a mountain, which corner or edge is at the top of the paper, whether you should turn the paper over, how the lettered corners move about from step to step, and so on. One careless mistake can ruin an entire project.

■ The symbols and written instructions for each step will make a shape that looks like the next illustration. So it is important to keep looking ahead to the next diagram to see what shape you are trying to make. Never look at one step in isolation from the others, but look ahead, then back, then ahead, and so on.

■ Before folding a design, check that the paper you are using is *exactly square, exactly a 2 x 1 rectangle,* or whatever the shape specified, and that it is not too small, too large, too thick, or too thin for that design.

■ Wash your hands! The last thing you want is for all your hard work to be spoilt by smudge marks.

HOW TO MAKE A SQUARE

Most bought papers are rectangular and have to be trimmed square. There are a number of methods that can be used to achieve this, but here is the best.

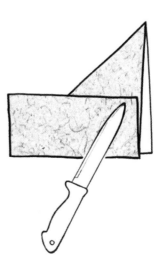

3 *Cut off the excess rectangle of paper with a non-serrated kitchen knife that has a blade at least 5 in. (12 cm) long.*

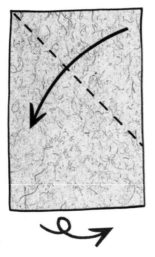

1 Fold a triangle. Turn over.

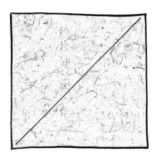

4 *Hold the paper firmly against a hard, level surface and cut along the crease with a series of smooth slicing movements.*

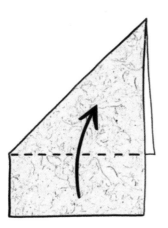

2 Fold up the rectangle exactly level with the edge of the triangle behind.

5 *The completed square. Done properly, the edge is pleasingly clean.*

HOW TO MAKE A CREASE

This may seem rather pedantic to the eager beginner, but it is important to know how to make an accurate crease. Just one inaccuracy early in a sequence will throw all the later creases out of alignment, creating a clumsy, unattractive design.

The basic rule is a very simple one to learn. Keep rotating the paper (or turning it over), so that every crease is made from left to right across your body (or right to left, if preferred), and the part of the paper that folds over when the crease is made moves away from your body, not towards it or to one side.

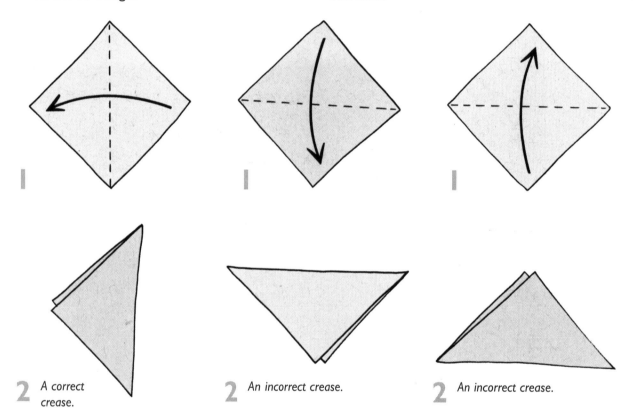

1

1

1

2 A correct crease.

2 An incorrect crease.

2 An incorrect crease.

■ When you see a crease on a diagram that does not run from left to right, *rotate the paper* so that it does.

■ When you see a mountain fold symbol, turn the paper over (or open up the inside), making a *valley* fold, and then turn back over again.

■ Creases should not be viewed as chores to be done for completing a design. Some experts believe that the pleasure of origami lies more in the making of creases and the manipulation of paper, than in achieving a final design. Take time out to *enjoy* your folding.

BASIC TECHNIQUES

The root of all paper folding is the valley fold (and its opposite, the mountain fold). Such basic creases do not require detailed explanation, but more complex ones do. The most common of these more complex techniques is the reverse fold along with its opposite, the outside-reverse fold (most techniques in origami, it seems, have an opposite). They are explained in the steps below and on the following pages, as is the squash fold. Other techniques are explained alongside the designs that they are needed for.

If you are unfamiliar with the reverse and squash folds, it is important that you take a little time to fold the basic examples and studies that follow.

REVERSE FOLD
Basic Example

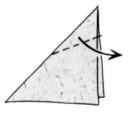

1 *Fold in half.*

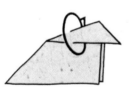

2 *Fold the corner across to the right . . .*

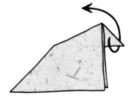

3 *. . . then fold it around the back along the same crease.*

4 *Unfold.*

5 *Hold as shown. Swing the top corner down between the layers . . .*

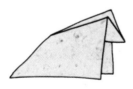

6 *. . . like this. Flatten the creases. The reverse fold is complete. The reverse fold described above is notated like this:*

1   **2** *Reverse*

■ *If you are unfamiliar with the reverse fold, prepare by folding the crease backwards and forwards as in steps 2–4 of the basic example above.*

Studies

Here are further examples. Look at them carefully before attempting them.

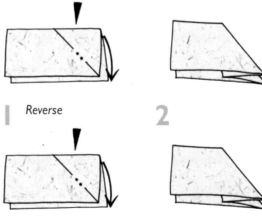

1 *Reverse*   **2**

1 *Reverse*   **2**

OUTSIDE-REVERSE FOLD
Basic Example

1   *Fold the corner across to the left . . .*

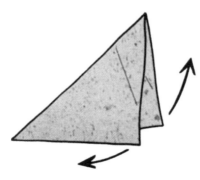

4   *Spread A and B.*

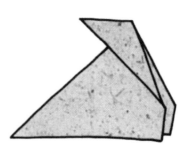

7   *The outside-reverse fold is complete.*

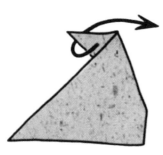

2   *. . . then fold it around the back along the same crease.*

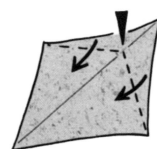

5   *Refold both short creases as valleys, lifting C.*

■ The outside-reverse fold described above is notated like this:

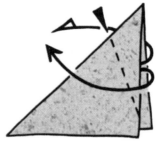

1   *Outside reverse*

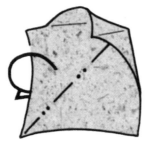

3   *Unfold.*

6   *Collapse back in half.*

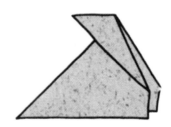

2

SQUASH FOLD
Basic Example

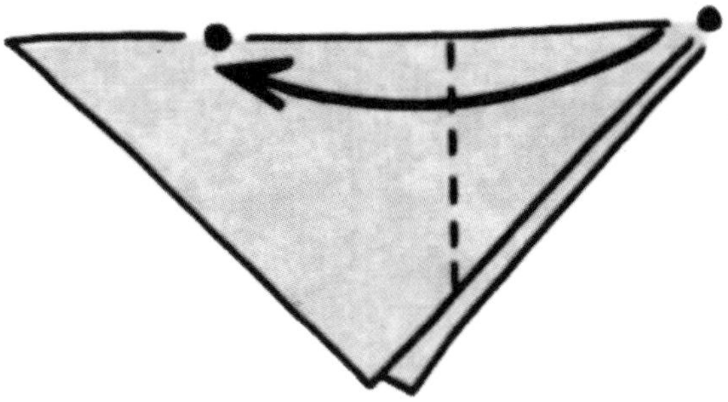

1 *Fold in half.*

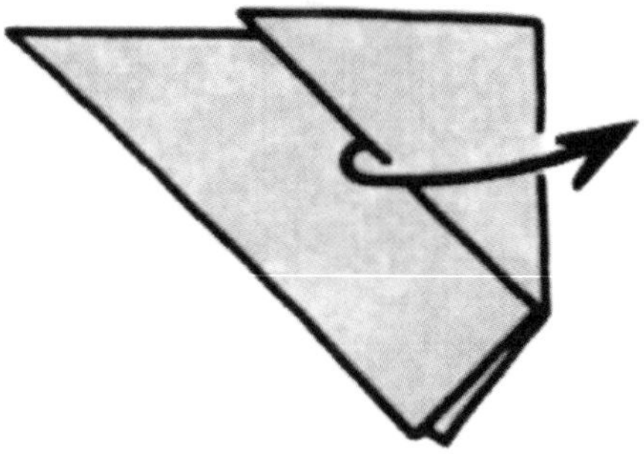

2 *Fold dot to dot.*

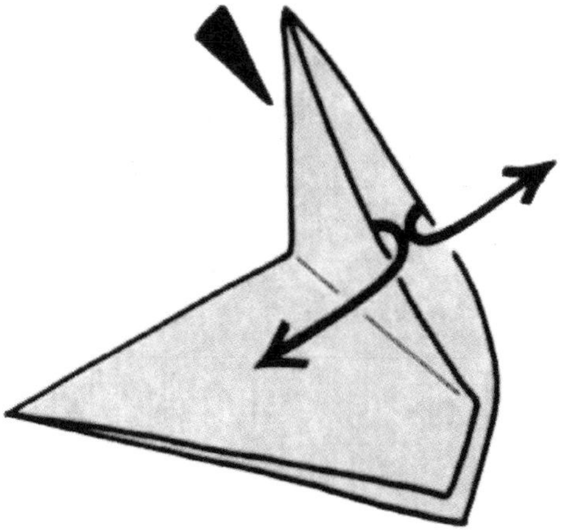

3 *Unfold, so that A stands upright.*

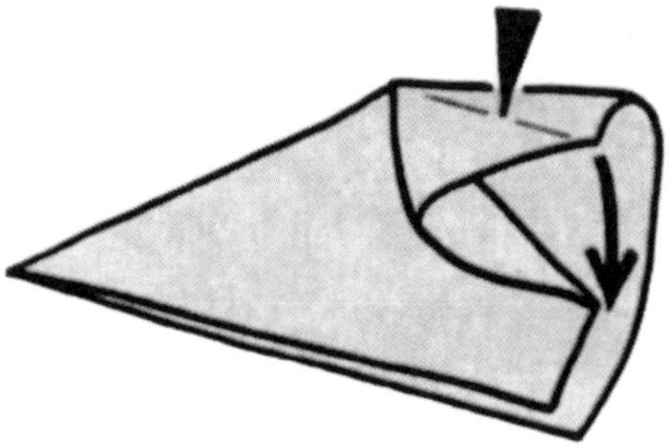

4 *Squash A flat, opening the pocket . . .*

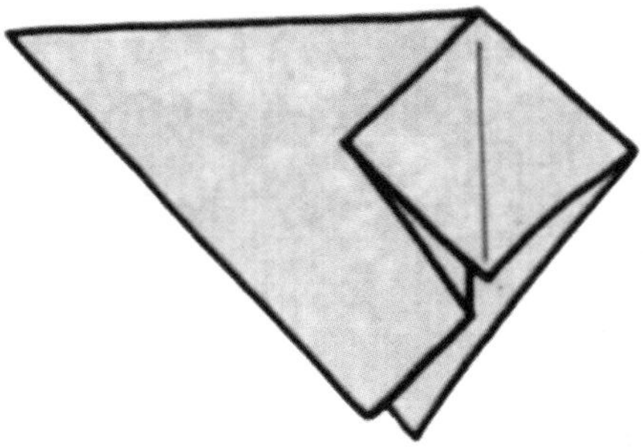

5 *. . . like this. Flatten the paper. The squash fold is complete.*

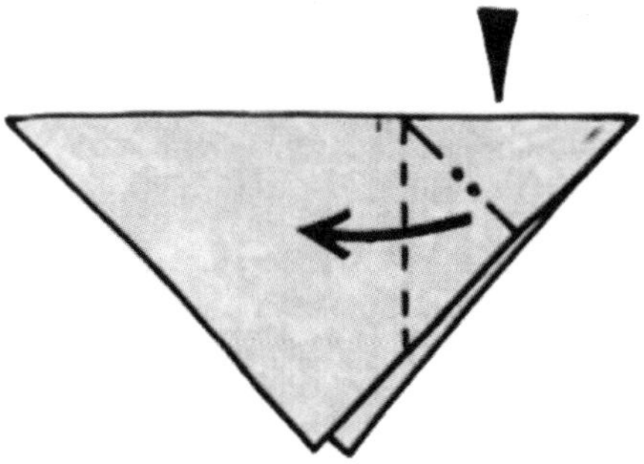

1 *Squash*

2

ORIGAMI FOR BEGINNERS

Origami is a very accessible craft for beginners. It is relatively easy to learn and does not require expensive materials and equipment. Of course, some origami designs are quite complex and should not be attempted until you have a better understanding of the principles of the craft, but the projects that follow in this chapter are a wonderful introduction to the basics of origami and will help provide you with the knowledge you will need in order to tackle more difficult designs.

EGG COSY

Paper is an excellent insulator, so this design really will help to keep eggs warm as well as adding a fun, eye-catching touch to the breakfast table.

PAPER
Use a rectangle of lightweight paper about 8 x 6 in. (20 x 15 cm).

SPECIAL NOTE
Reverse folds are explained in detail in the section on Folding Techniques (see Introduction).

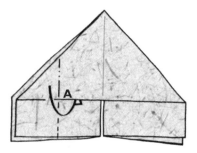

1 *See Special Note. Reverse-fold the front left layer into the middle. Note A. Repeat with the rear left layer.*

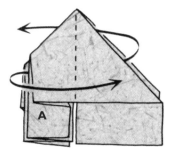

2 *Swivel the front left layer across to the right and swivel the rear right layer across to the left.*

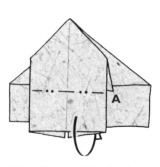

3 *See Special Note. Reverse-fold the front left layer into the middle. Note A. Repeat with the rear left layer.*

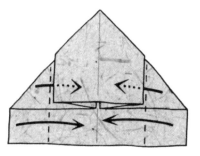

4 *Swivel the front left layer across to the right and swivel the rear right layer across to the left.*

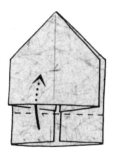

5 *See Special Note. Reverse-fold the front left layer into the middle. Note A. Repeat with the rear left layer.*

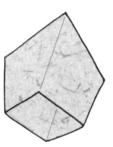

6 *Swivel the front left layer across to the right and swivel the rear right layer across to the left.*

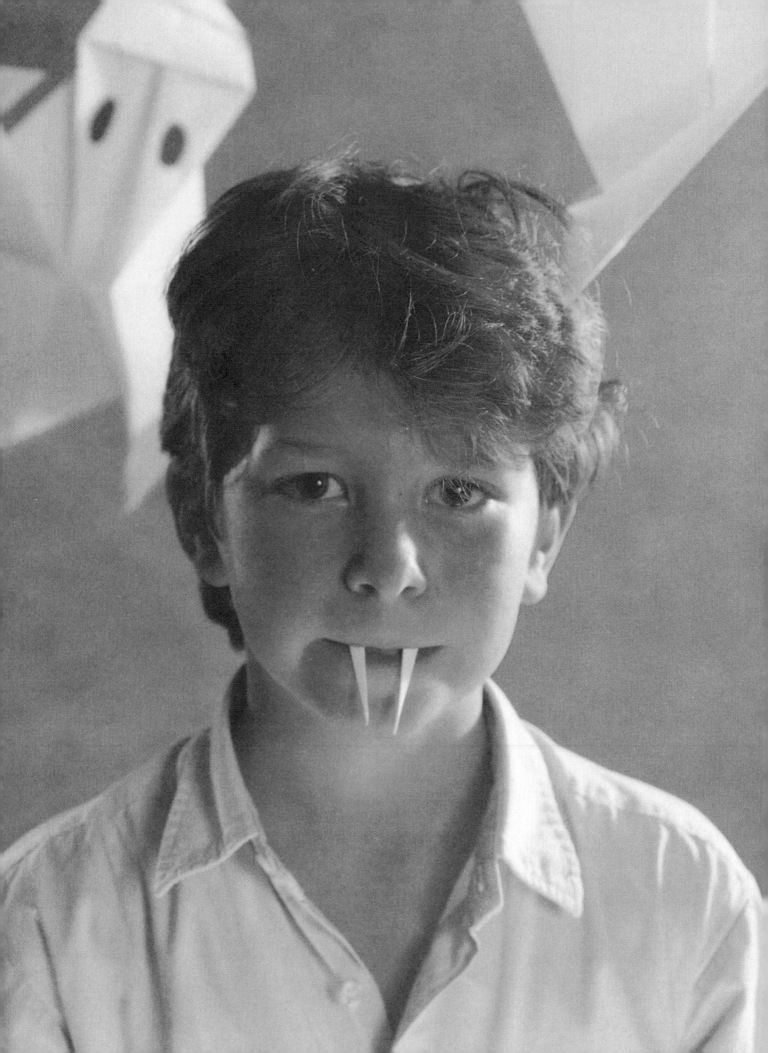

FANGS

This delightfully simple fold is great fun for th beginner, and easily within the abilities of older children. More advanced folders could develop fangs that are longer and sharper— try experimenting.

PAPER

Use a 4 x 1 in. (10 x 2½ cm) strip of lightweight paper.

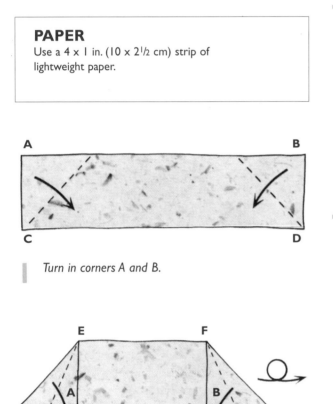

1   *Turn in corners A and B.*

2   *Fold edge EC to lie along EA, and edge FD to lie along FB. Turn over.*

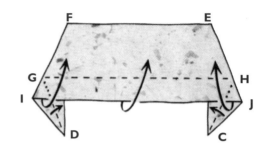

3   *Make crease GH, so that ID lies along DF and JC lies along CE . . .*

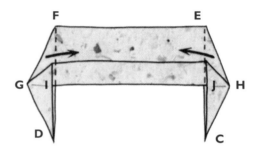

4   *. . . like this. Fold G and H towards the middle.*

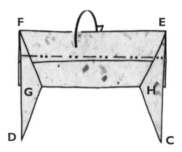

5   *Mountain-fold FE behind to lie along GH.*

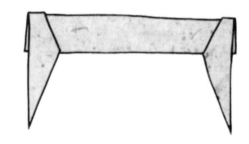

6   *The Completed Fangs.*

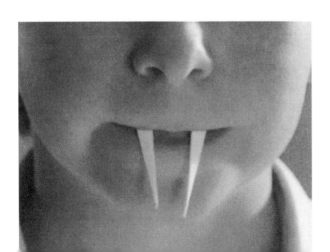

CUP

Most origami designs are purely decorative, but this designs has a practical use. Made from a waterproof material such as metallic kitchen foil or greaseproof paper, this simple design will hold a liquid without leaking through an open edge. Turned upside down, it will even make an excellent hat. Flap B can be brought down to form a visor. Use a 6-8 in. (15-20 cm) square of paper.

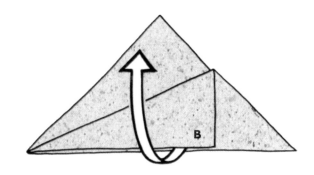

3 *. . . like this. Unfold.*

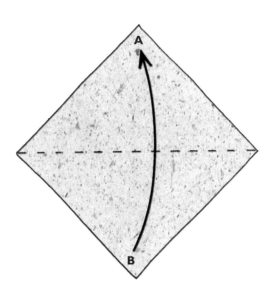

1 *Fold in half along a diagonal.*

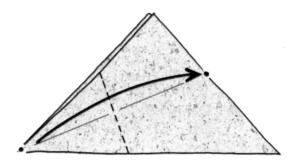

4 *Fold one dot to the other.*

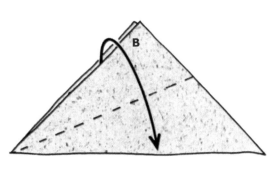

2 *Fold down corner B to the bottom edge . . .*

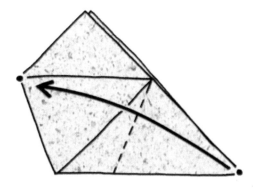

5 *Fold one dot to the other.*

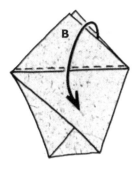

6 Fold down single layer B.

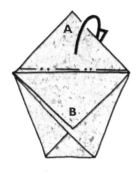

7 Fold A behind.

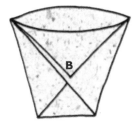

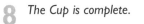

8 The Cup is complete.

CORNUCOPIA NAPKIN

Ideal for Thanksgiving or Harvest Festival meals, this is a simple but elegant folded napkin. You can use a piece of fruit to hold the napkin open.

PAPER
Use 4-ply napkins for the best results.

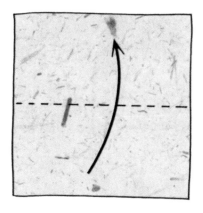

1 Fold the bottom edge of an open napkin up to the top.

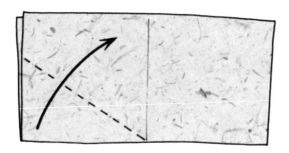

2 Fold in the bottom left-hand corner, as shown.

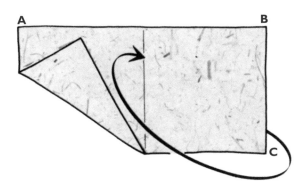

3 Without making any creases, roll BC across to the left, so that C comes to rest against the middle of the top edge . . .

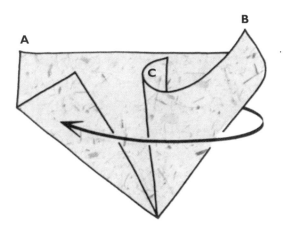

4 . . . like this. Continue to roll, so that B comes to rest in front of A.

5 To lock, fold A and B behind.

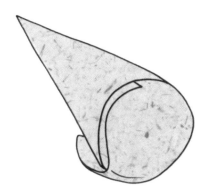

6 The Cornucopia Napkin is complete.

BANGER

This is one of the most entertaining of all paper folds and certainly the loudest! Practice Step 7, because good execution of the technique described will increase the volume of the bang. Use a rectangle of thin or medium-weight paper, at least 10 x 15 in. (25 x 37 cm). Larger sheets will produce louder noises.

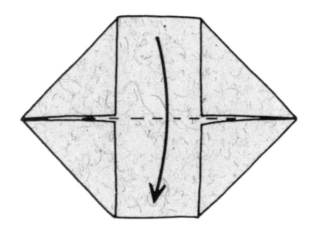

3 *Fold in half along the Step 1 crease.*

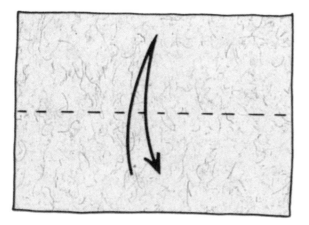

1 *Fold one long edge across to the other. Crease and unfold.*

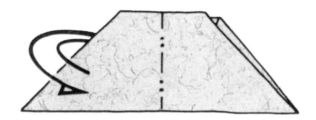

4 *Mountain-fold across the middle. Crease and unfold.*

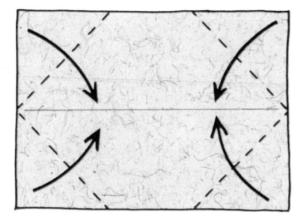

2 *Fold in the corners to the center crease.*

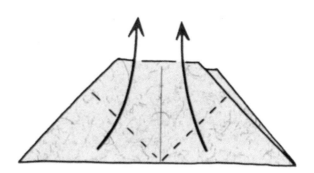

5 *Check that the center crease made in Step 1 is a mountain (if it's a valley, turn the paper over), then fold the sharp corners across to the right.*

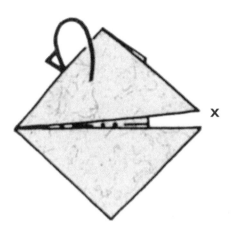

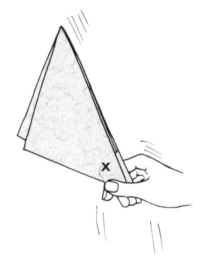

6 *Mountain-fold in half. Note the double corner at X.*

7 *Hold X as shown. Bend your elbow so that the Banger is behind your head, then whip it downwards very quickly. The paper will unfold with a loud **BANG!** If it doesn't, check that you haven't held the paper upside down and try to move your arm quicker.*

SIX-POINTED STAR

One of the simplest and most attractive of all folded decorations, the six-pointed star uses the most basic folding techniques. Steps 1-4 show how to make an equilateral triangle (one with all its sides of equal length) from a square. If you know another method of doing this, by all means use it—although the one shown here is accurate and pleasing.

Make several stars, in an array of bright colors, and hang from the Christmas tree for extra sparkle; but these great decorations can be used the whole year round.

PAPER

Use a square of paper of any weight or size. The best paper to use for this decoration is paperbacked metallic foil, which reflects the light and will make the star stand out against the dark foliage of a natural Christmas tree.

OTHER EQUIPMENT

Scissors; needle and thread.

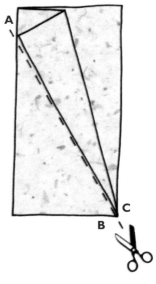

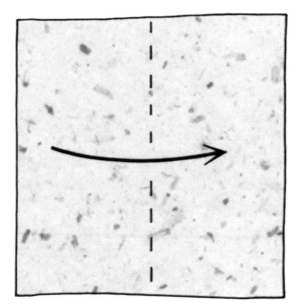

Fold in half, left to right.

2 Turn in the top layer corner to exactly touch the crease made in Step 1, at such a point that the new crease will run exactly down to the bottom corner. Take your time lining it up – this is the most important crease in the whole design. Badly placed, it will spoil the shape of the star.

3 Cut along edge BA. Open out the bottom left-hand triangle and discard the remainder of the paper. Add creases that run into corners B and C to locate the center of the triangle.

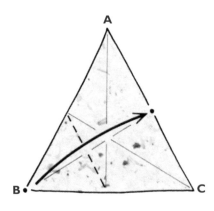

4 *Fold B across to the opposite edge.*

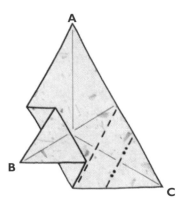

6 *Repeat Steps 4 and 5 with C.*

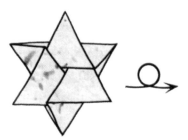

8 *. . . like this. Turn over.*

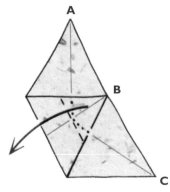

5 *Fold B back along a crease that passes over the center of the triangle.*

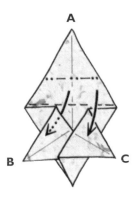

7 *Repeat Steps 4 and 5 with A. Tuck the left-hand part of the pleat under B to lock A, B and C together in a symmetrical pattern . . .*

9 *The Six-Pointed Star is complete. To suspend, attach a loop to the star with needle and thread. The star looks most effective when hung in groups.*

CROWN

Hats are a popular and enduring origami subject. This design creates a large, well-locked hat from a relatively small sheet and because of its square shape it will grip your head well. Use a square of sturdy paper 15 x 15 in. (37 x 37 cm) for a child and a little larger for an adult head.

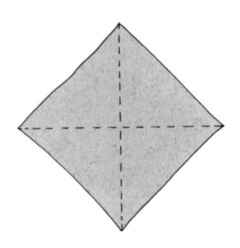

1 *Crease and unfold both diagonals.*

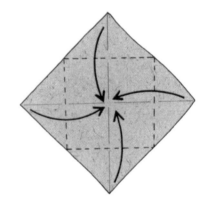

2 *Fold the corners to the center.*

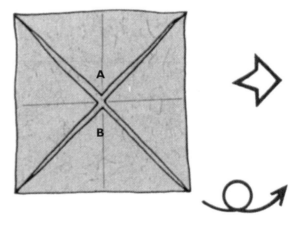

3 *Note A and B. Turn over.*

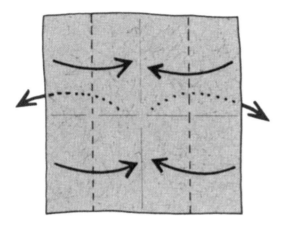

4   *Fold the top and bottom edges to the center crease, allowing corners A and B to flip out from behind . . .*

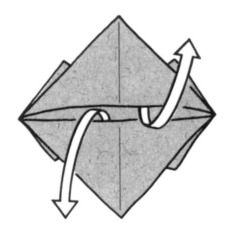

6   *Pull open the slit . . .*

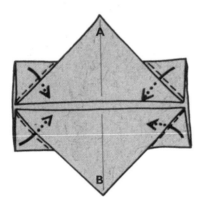

5   *. . . like this. Fold the small triangles under the large ones.*

7   *. . . to complete the Crown. Press it into shape, squaring the sides.*

GLIDER

What could be simpler—a glider with only two folds! Be careful to follow the instructions carefully, because for it to work properly it is important to hold and release it in the correct way. There is probably an even simpler glider with just one crease waiting to be designed! Use a 6 in. (15 cm) square of thin paper such as origami paper, airmail paper, or undercopy (bank) typing paper. Heavier paper will not float the design through the air.

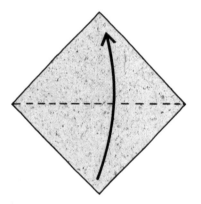

1 *Fold in half along a diagonal.*

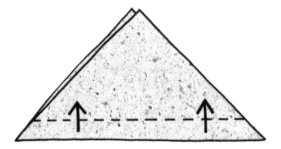

2 *Fold up the lower edge a little way. Try to keep the crease exactly parallel to the edge.*

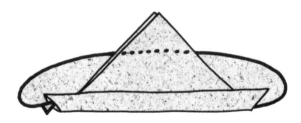

3 *Tuck one end of the hem into the pocket at the other end, bending the paper into a circle with the hem on the outside.*

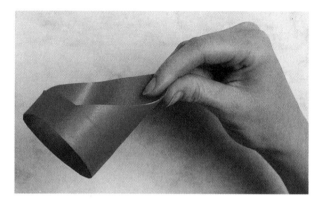

4 *The Glider is complete. Make sure that the leading edge is a neat circle.*

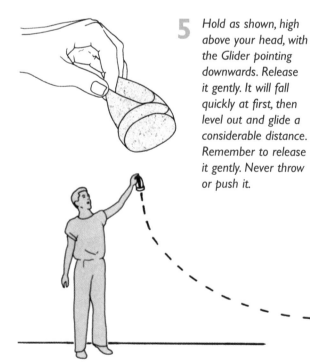

5 *Hold as shown, high above your head, with the Glider pointing downwards. Release it gently. It will fall quickly at first, then level out and glide a considerable distance. Remember to release it gently. Never throw or push it.*

YACHT

There are many origami yachts, boats, and ships, but none are as simple or as full of movement as this wonderful design by Japan's First Lady of origami, Mrs Toshie Takahama. Mrs Takahama has produced many exquisite designs, particularly of animals (see her Cat on pages 116-7) and flowers. She has written several books, some of which have recently been translated into English. Use a 6-8 in. (15-20 cm) square of origami paper.

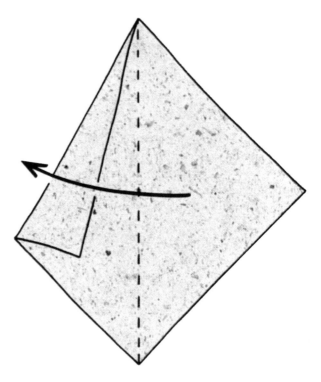

2   Fold the right-hand corner across to the left.

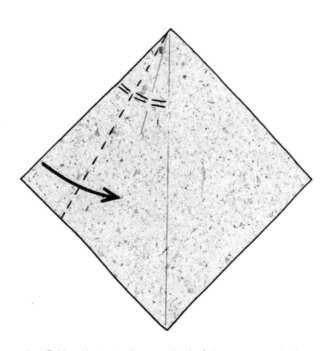

1   Fold in the top edge one-third of the way towards the diagonal crease.

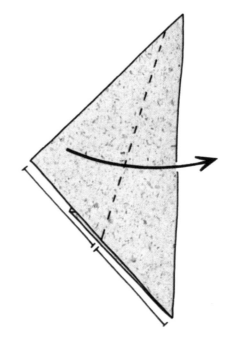

3   Fold it back along a crease that starts just to the left of the top corner and goes to the mid-point of the lower edge.

4 Fold the bottom corner across to the right.

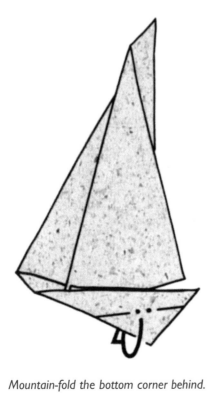

5 Mountain-fold the bottom corner behind.

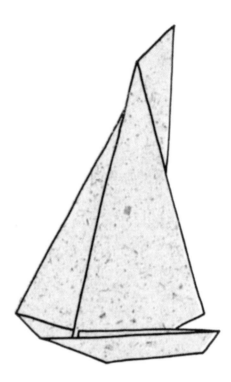

6 The Yacht is complete.

SNAP HEXAHEDRON

Hexahedrons are common in origami. This one by Edwin Corrie (England) is one of the simplest and features an interesting move at Step 5. To make the 3 x 3 grid of squares needed in Step 1, fold a 4 x 4 grid by creasing halves and quarters horizontally and vertically, then cut off a line of squares along two adjacent edges to leave a 3 x 3 grid. Use a 6 in. (15 cm) square of paper. Large squares will not "snap" at Step 7.

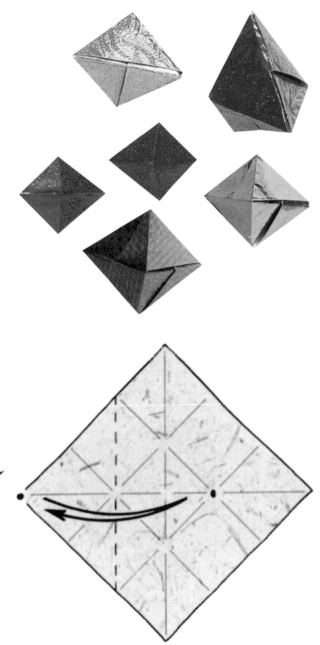

1 *Fold the vertical diagonal as a mountain and the horizontal diagonal as a valley.*

2 *Fold dot to dot. Unfold.*

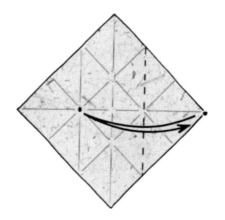

3   *Similarly, fold dot to dot. Unfold.*

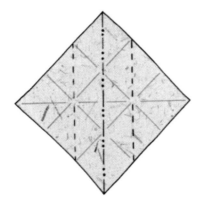

4   *Pleat as shown.*

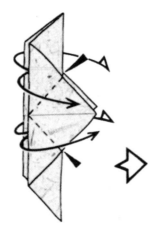

5   *Outside-reverse the top and bottom corners.*

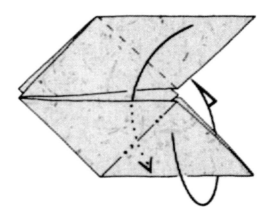

6   *Valley-fold the top corner into the pocket formed by the lower outside-reverse fold. Then, mountain the lower corner into the upper outside-reverse fold, behind.*

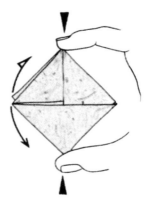

7   *Hold as shown and squeeze. The left-hand corners will separate to create a third edge around the middle, forming a 3D hexahedron.*

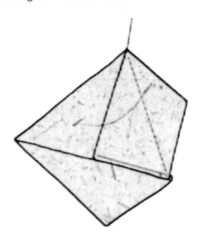

8   *The Snap Hexahedron is complete.*

ROWING BOAT

This design by Martin Wall (England) shows a simple shape. Note steps 8-9, not just for the way they lock the boat into shape, but also for the way in which the inside is kept clean. With metallic kitchen foil or greaseproof paper, it will float. Or else, use a 6-8 in. (15-20 cm) square of medium-weight paper.

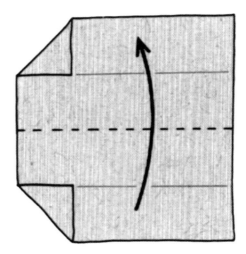

3 *Fold in half.*

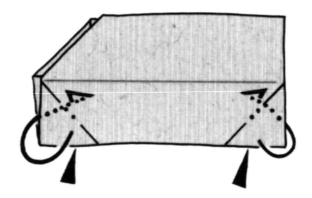

4 *Reverse the bottom corners, level with the quarter crease.*

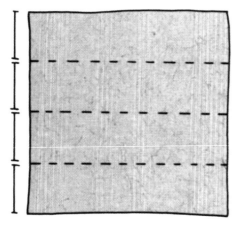

1 *Valley into quarters.*

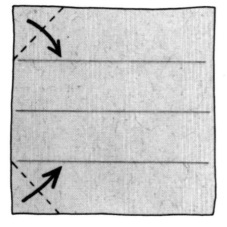

2 *Turn in the left-hand corners, top and bottom.*

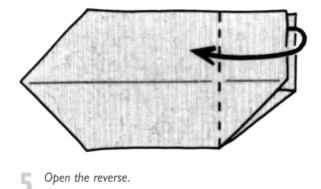

5 *Open the reverse.*

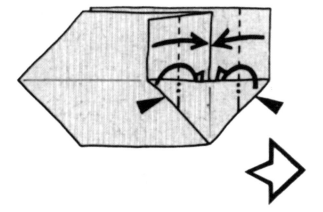

6   *Reverse twice . . .*

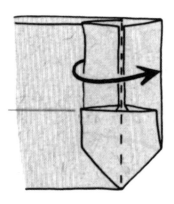

7   *. . . like this. Fold A across to the right.*

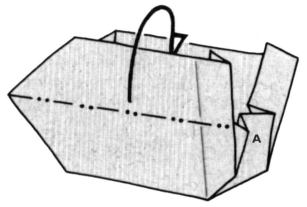

8   *Tuck the nearside top quarter into the boat. Take it over the top of A, but not over the top of the reverse-fold layers at the bow (front) . . .*

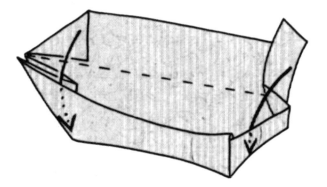

9   *. . . like this. Similarly, fold in the far-side layer, but this time also folding it over the reverse at the bow to close it shut. Flatten the bottom of the boat.*

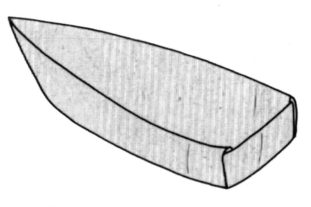

10   *The Rowing Boat is complete.*

TOOT-FLUTE

Of the few musical instruments that can be created from paper, this is perhaps the simplest design and you will be amazed by the sound it produces. A must for any children's party, get your young guests to make their own and mount a competition for the loudest "toot"!

PAPER

Use a lightweight sheet of 8½ x 11 in. (A4) paper. For deeper musical tones, use larger sheets; for higher tones, use smaller ones. The Toot-Flute can also be made from a paper drinking straw, cut to a point at one end rather like the nib of a fountain pen, and then snipped in the appropriate place to give it an arrowhead shape.

OTHER EQUIPMENT

Pencil; sticky tape; scissors (safety scissors if children are making their own toot-flutes).

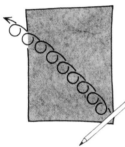

i *Wrap a corner of the paper around a pencil and roll it across the sheet at 45° to the edge.*

3 *Starting from the notch at one end, make a cut to free A . . .*

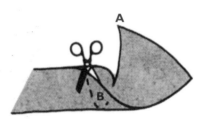

5 *Repeat at the other side of the notch, to free B.*

2 *Drop the pencil out and secure the loose corner with a piece of sticky tape.*

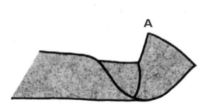

4 *. . . like this.*

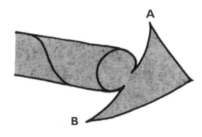

6 *Note that the triangle is joined to the tube by only a small edge. The smaller the edge, the easier the triangle will vibrate, and so the louder the flute will sound.*

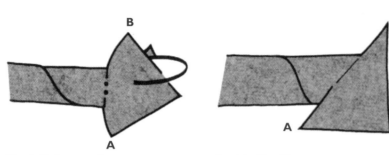

7 Fold the triangle against the tube.

8 The Toot-Flute is complete.

Below With the triangle at the bottom of the flute, suck gently and the flute will buzz! Alternatively, put the triangle into your mouth (be careful not to wet it) and blow gently to produce a buzz too.

THE UN-UNFOLDABLE BOX

Boxes are the most common subject in origami. Some are very complex and ornate, whereas this one by Ed Sullivan (USA) is particularly plain. However, the fascination of this design *is in the folding*, because once folded, it cannot then be unfolded, at least not without making extra folds or fumbling with the paper. It is unique in origami and a remarkable design, which is sure to prove a favorite of anyone who makes it. Use a large square of medium-weight paper.

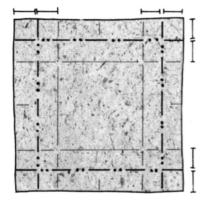

1 *Pinch the mid-points of the four edges. Use them as a guide to make four valley creases along the horizontal and vertical quarter marks.*

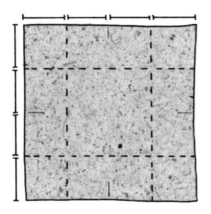

2 *Make mountain folds midway between the valley quarters and the edges.*

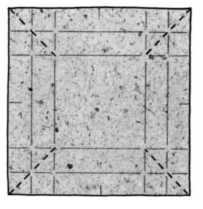

3 *Form valley diagonals at the corners, to create a box with triangular flaps.*

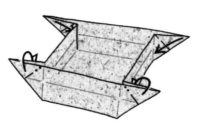

4 *Point two flaps to the left and two to the right. Fold the triangles in half by turning the loose corners inside.*

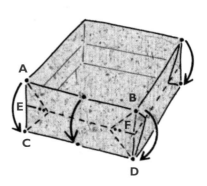

5 *Fold the triangles to the inside, flat against the box.*

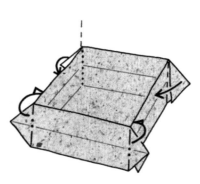

6 *Collapse, bringing A down to C and B down to D. E and F move towards the center of the front edge. Repeat behind.*

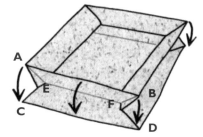

7 *This is the shape half collapsed . . .*

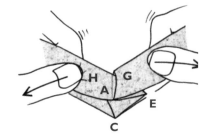

9 *Hold corner AC as shown. Pull your hands gently apart and H will slide away from G . . .*

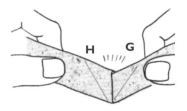

11 *. . . until the corner is fully formed. Repeat at the other corners of the box.*

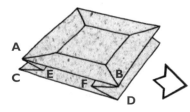

8 *. . . and here fully collapsed. Note E and F.*

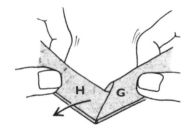

10 *. . . like this. Keep pulling . . .*

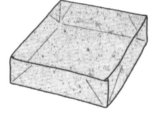

12 *The Un-unfoldable Box is complete.*

PIRATE'S HAT AND SHIRT

Many readers will be familiar with the basic triangular hat shown in Step 5, but few will know that it can be developed into the stronger Pirate's Hat at Step 10 and later torn to create the fun Shirt. Step 13 could even be a pirate ship!

Provide a Step 10 Pirate Hat for each child (or adult, if it's that sort of party!), and then choose an appropriate moment to show how the hat can become a Shirt. Stand back, and watch the chaos as everyone strives to make their own!

PAPER
Use a complete double-page leaf from a broadsheet (large format) newspaper.

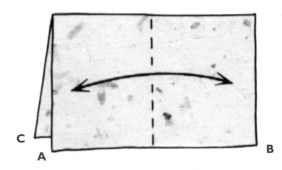

2 Fold in half, left to right. Unfold.

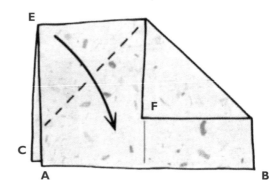

3 Fold corners E and F to the center crease. F is shown already folded.

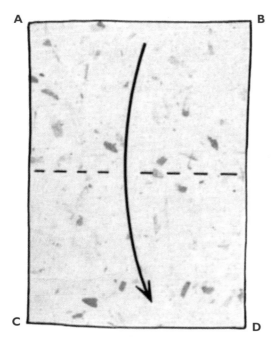

1 Fold in half from top to bottom.

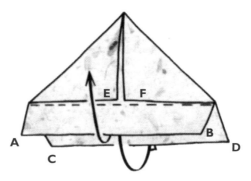

4 Fold up edge AB along a crease that runs along the bottom of triangles E and F, and similarly, fold up CD behind.

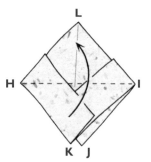

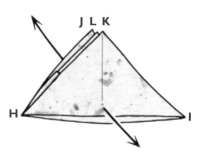

5 *This makes a simple, though rather large and floppy, hat.*

8 *Fold K up to L, and behind fold J to L.*

9 *It should look like this.*

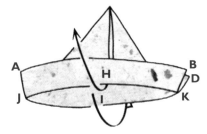

6 *Hold as shown at H and I. Pull H and I apart, so that J and K come towards each other.*

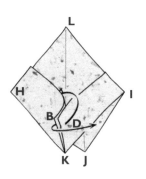

7 *This makes a diamond shape. Tuck D behind B to flatten the front. Repeat behind, tucking A under C.*

Right *To complete the Pirate's Hat and Shirt, refer to the opposite page for the remaining instructions.*

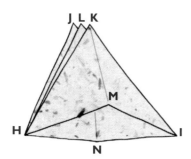

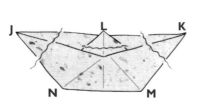

10 As you did in Step 6, open up the bottom to form the Pirate's Hat. To make the Pirate's Shirt, bring H and I together by pulling M and N apart, as in Steps 6-7.

13 Could this be a pirate ship? Tear off J, K, and L as shown. Carefully, completely unfold the remainder of the ship.

14 And here is the Pirate's Shirt!

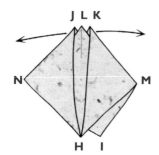

11 Hold K and J and pull them away from L . . .

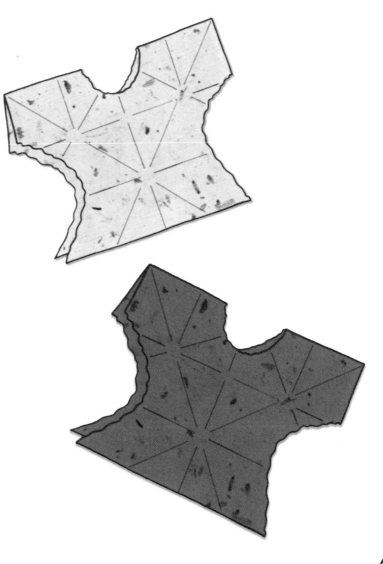

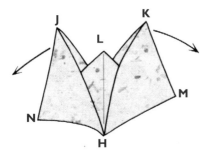

12 . . . like this. Continue to pull until Step 13 is made.

STAR RING

This project uses identical modules to create
two eye-catching designs.

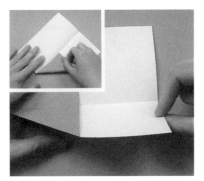

1   Fold a square of paper vertically in
half. Fold a corner in to meet the
crease (see inset). Repeat with the
maching corner on the other side
of the crease. Fold the square in
half using the existing crease.

2   Fold a short edge to lie along the
other short edge. Crease firmly and
unfold back to the beginning of
Step 2.

3   Inside reverse-fold the corner
using the creases made in the
last step.

4   The module is complete. Make
seven more units.

5   Hold one unit above the other and
lower the higher unit between the
two open edges of the lower unit
as shown.

6   Make sure it is tightly inserted,
then tuck a small overlapping
flap behind into the 'pocket' of
the second unit.

7   Repeat with the overlapping flap
from behind, keeping both units
tightly interlocked

8   Continue adding units, making sure
they they are all tightly inserted.
The final unit is a little difficult, but
perfectlytly possible if you are
careful.

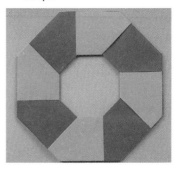

Above   The model is finished. You have two
choices: either slide all the units away from
each other to form an octagonal ring, or
slide them into each other to form an
attractive star.

MOUNT FUJI AND THE SEA

The late creator of this design, Seiryo Takegawa (Japan), specialized in producing very simple designs for children, including many wonderful action toys. This little-known masterpiece is typical of his work: simple, poetic, audacious, and charming. Perhaps it is like the traditional Bird on page 102—more a symbol than a representation. Use a 6-8 in. (15-20 cm) square. Origami paper is ideal.

1   *Fold in half. Unfold.*

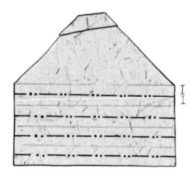

3   *Mountain-fold the top corners behind, so that the vertical edges are brought down level with the horizontal fold.*

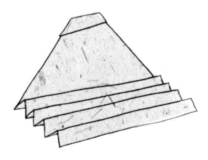

5   *Place mountains between the valleys. Pleat the creases, including the original horizontal fold.*

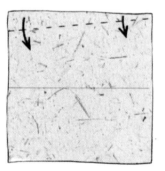

2   *Fold down the top edge a little way, more on the left than on the right.*

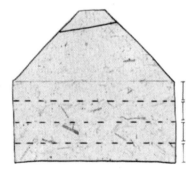

4   *Divide the lower section into quarters. All the creases must be valleys.*

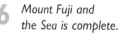

6   *Mount Fuji and the Sea is complete.*

BUFFET SERVER

This is a practical and easy-to-make design for beginners that is ideal for buffets—to pre-wrap sets of cutlery—or equally for children's parties.

PAPER

Use paper napkins; 4-ply is the best, but 3- or 2-ply are adequate. Starched linen napkins may also be used.

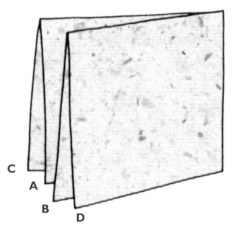

3 *Note CABD. Rotate to the Step 4 position.*

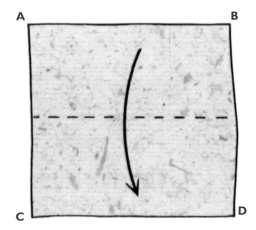

1 *If the napkin is already folded into quarters (as most are), skip forward to Step 3. Otherwise, fold AB down to CD.*

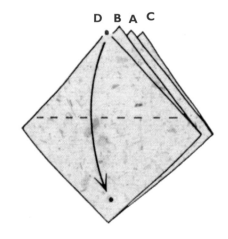

4 *Fold down D almost to the bottom corner.*

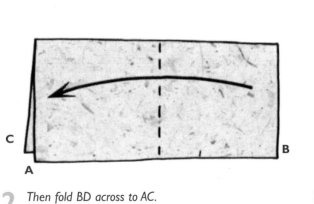

2 *Then fold BD across to AC.*

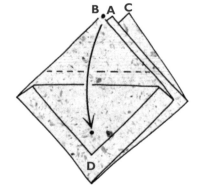

5 *Fold B almost to D.*

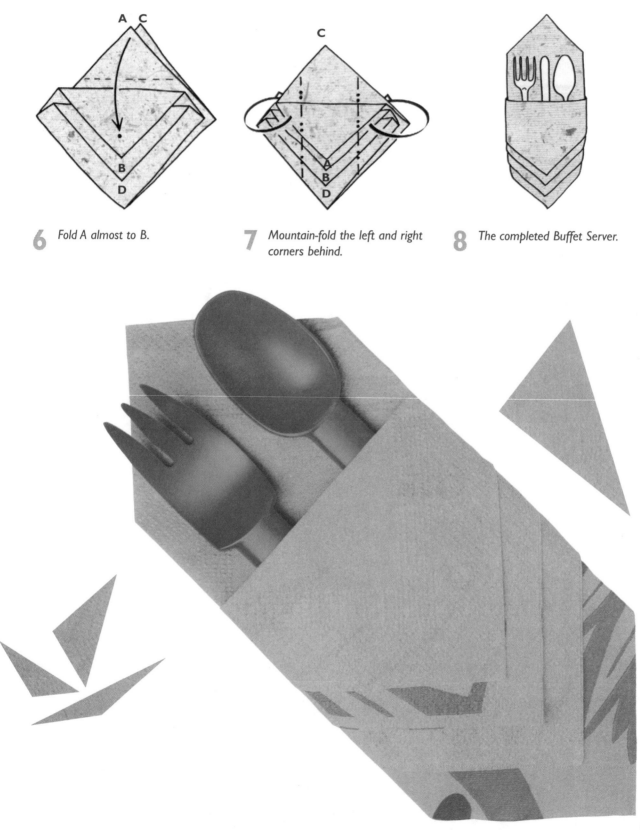

6 *Fold A almost to B.*

7 *Mountain-fold the left and right corners behind.*

8 *The completed Buffet Server.*

FESTIVE DECORATIONS

When folding a design for a festive occasion, a special paper will always make a design look more attractive. Special papers may be bought from two main sources: shops that supply materials to artists, and those that supply materials to graphic artists and designers. Large cities sometimes have shops that specialize in selling paper, but they are disappointingly few in number. Patterned giftwrap paper, sold by stationers, is useful for decorative designs.

STAR

One of the best ways to form geometric shapes is to fold a number of simple shapes that can interlock. This is commonly known as "modular origami." The Star is a simple example of this kind of folding, and is an ideal project for the beginner. To experiment, try folding six, eight, or more modules to make stars with more than four points.

PAPER
You will need four sheets of lightweight paper or foil, about 4 in. (10 cm) square, in two colors or textures that work well together. Careful choosing of complementary papers adds to the finished piece.

OTHER EQUIPMENT
To suspend the star you will need a needle and thread.

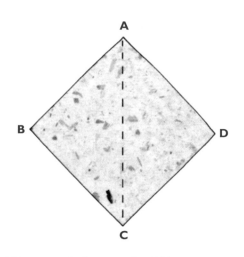

1   *Fold B over to D. Crease and unfold.*

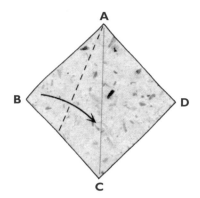

2   *Fold in edge AB to lie along crease AC.*

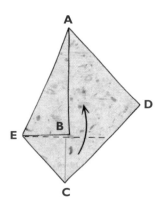

3   *Fold up C along a crease that follows edge EB, covering B.*

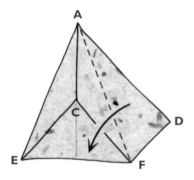

4 *Fold in edge AD to the center so that it half-covers C.*

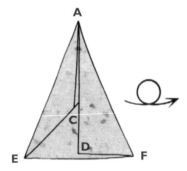

5 *The paper looks like this. Turn over.*

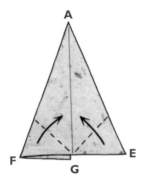

6 *Fold in F and E to lie along crease AG.*

7 *Fold F and E back out to the just-formed sloping edges that meet at G. E is shown already folded. Keep the folds neat at G.*

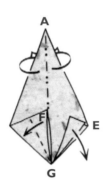

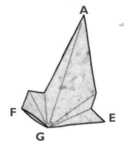

8 *Unfold the last two steps so it looks like this. This is one point of the star. Make three more sections in the same way as the first, though make two of them in another (maybe patterned) paper.*

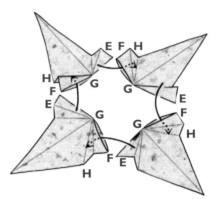

9 *Tuck corner E of one section in between the layers of another at F, and continue to push it further in until E touches H and the two Gs touch. The mountain and valley creases should line up where they overlap. In the same way, tuck in the third and fourth sections, alternating the types of paper, and finally locking the first section into the fourth. Strengthen and sharpen all the creases.*

10 *The Star is complete. To suspend, attach a loop to one point of the star with needle and thread.*

BAUBLE

Here is another stunning decoration suitable for all kinds of festive occasions. On first glance, this may seem like a complex design, but it is little more than a simple crease pattern repeated many times along the paper. The secret of success is to crease with care and accuracy.

PAPER

Use a rectangle of lightweight paper or foil, four times as long as it is wide. For a small bauble, use a piece 12 x 3 in. (30 x 7.5 cm), and for a huge one try an rectangle measuring 36 x 9 in. (90 x 22.5 cm). It is probably easier to start with a medium-sized one. Avoid using papers with a strong decorative pattern—the many facets of the bauble create a strong light-and-shade pattern of their own, which would clash with color patterns.

OTHER EQUIPMENT

To suspend the bauble you will need needle and thread, and some plasticine.

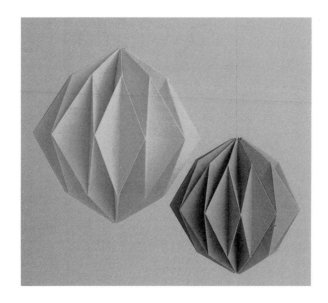

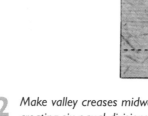

1 *With the paper right-side up, valley-fold twice to form three equal sections.*

2 *Make valley creases midway between each section, creating six equal divisions.*

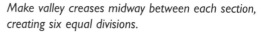

3 *Make valley creases midway between the existing creases, creating 12 equal divisions.*

4 Make valley creases midway between each of the existing creases, creating 24 equal divisions. Keep the folds accurate.

7 Look at the crease pattern so far. All the existing creases are valleys, while the new ones will be mountains.

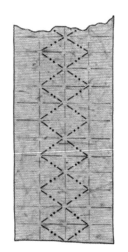

5 Fold the sheet in half along its length. Unfold.

8 Now make careful diagonal mountain folds across the middle, as shown, making sure your folds exactly connect at the intersections of existing creases. It may help to draw the line of the new folds with a pencil before creasing. This is a tricky step. Make sure the creases do not stray towards the outer edges of the sheet, and make them firm.

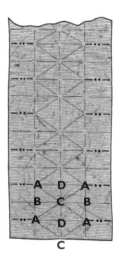

6 Fold the sides into the middle of the sheet, creasing right along its length. Unfold.

9 Along the two outer-edge sections, re-crease alternate valley creases to make them mountains as shown. This will produce a pleated effect along the edges, with diamonds across the middle. Locate As, Bs, Cs and Ds.

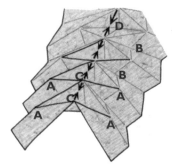

10 Now squeeze the pleats together on both edges so that the side and end points (C and A) of the diamond rise up, and the middle point (D) of the diamond and pleat (B) cave in.

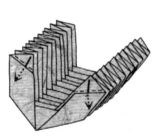

13 Valley-fold the double-layer corners on the inside edges, as shown. Repeat all the way down the row of pleats, neatly folding in each corner in turn.

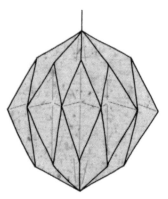

16 The Bauble is complete. To hang it, simply use a needle and thread to fix a loop to the top of the bauble. Alternatively, before locking the ends of the bauble together (see Step 15), attach a blob of plasticine to the free ends of a loop of thread and position it inside the body of the bauble, allowing the loop to issue from the top. The locking action will enclose the plasticine and hold the thread firmly in place.

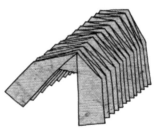

11 Compress the pleats all along the strip, concertina fashion. Press firmly to reinforce all the creases, and then turn over.

14 Bring the ends round and together to form the bauble shape.

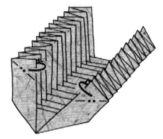

12 Mountain-fold the single-layer corners inside at both the front ends.

15 Tuck the left-hand edge under the right, as shown, locking the bauble.

STREAMER

Here is a model that can be made as long as you like! Learn the technique on one strip, fold another, and then join them together by gluing the last pleat of one to the first pleat of another. Repeat as many times as you wish, being careful to fold all sections from identical strips. The result is spectacular.

PAPER
Use a long, narrow strip of lightweight paper or foil, about 3 in. (8 cm) wide. As you get more confident, you can experiment by altering the paper width.

OTHER EQUIPMENT
Glue.

1   *With the right side of the paper facing you, mountain-fold edge AB on a diagonal, so that AB lies under the bottom edge of the strip.*

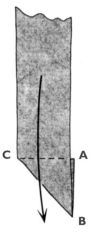

2   *Fold the length of the strip down along horizontal crease CA.*

3   *Now fold the strip to the left along diagonal crease DA. Be careful to keep all the layers lined up at the edges.*

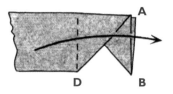

4   *Fold the strip to the right, making a vertical crease.*

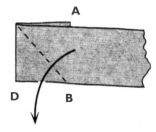

5 *Fold the strip down along a diagonal crease. Keep the layers lined up.*

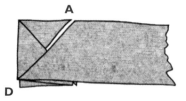

8 *Continue the sequence established above until the whole strip is folded up. Be extremely careful to keep all the layers lined up exactly.*

6 *Fold the strip back up making a horizontal crease . . .*

9 *Unfold the strip to see this crease pattern along the strip.*

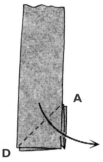

7 *. . . and then fold to the right along a diagonal crease.*

10 *Now mountain-fold the other diagonals on each square, all along the strip. Keep it neat, and be careful to make the creases the same way up as the existing diagonals.*

11   *Fold valley creases through the exact point where the diagonals intersect. Note that both diagonals are mountain creases, and all horizontals are valleys.*

13   *. . . and then the top right to the bottom-left corners. Keep it neat!*

12   *The creases made in Step 11 form squares along the strip. Mountain-fold diagonals on these squares just formed, connecting the top left to the bottom right-hand corners of each square . . .*

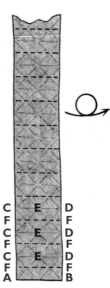

14   *Make valley folds midway between the existing valley creases. These new creases each pass through two mountain diagonal 'crosses'. This is the completed crease pattern. Check that when you look at the paper all the diagonal creases are mountains, all the horizontals are valleys, and all the creases join, connect, or intersect with accuracy. Identify AB, Cs, Ds, Es and Fs. Turn over.*

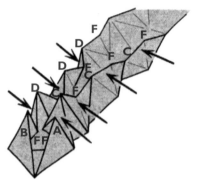

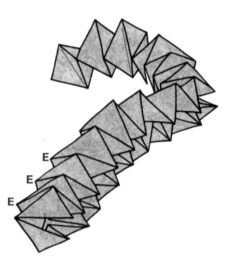

15 Hold the edges of the strip at the first DC pair along from BA. Push them together gently and E should collapse downwards. Push a few more DC pairs together moving along the strip. F should tuck in and down on top. Continue like this, pushing BA up, to concertina up all the Es and to reinforce the creases. Note that all creases form—nothing is wasted.

16 When concertinaed, the strip will look something like this. Repeat with as many strips of identical width as you wish to fold. Glue them into one enormously long strip. Alternatively, bend one end of the streamer round to meet the other and glue to form a circular decoration. If the creases need to be redefined, push the ends towards each other, squeezing the concertina flat together. The streamer can be stored easily in this position from one Christmas to the next.

BELL

Inflatable origami—blow-ups—are always fun to make, but because paper and water don't really mix, there are very few such models; the Waterbomb is perhaps the best known. When folding, leave a small hole at the bottom corner to blow into. Do not close it completely by folding *too* neatly! If the hole is too small, snip it open with scissors.

PAPER
Use a 6-8 in. (15-20 cm) square of light- or medium-weight paper or foil.

OTHER EQUIPMENT
To suspend the bell you will need a needle and thread.

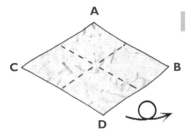

1 *Make horizontal and vertical valley folds across the paper. Turn over, so that the creases rise towards you.*

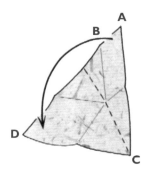

2 *Fold A over to D as shown. Unfold. Repeat this move, folding B over to C.*

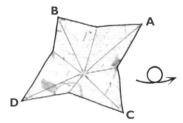

3 *The crease pattern should look like this. The paper is three-dimensional. Turn over so that the middle rises up. Push the horizontal and vertical mountain folds towards each other so that the central peak rises up, as shown. Four triangles are formed, meeting at E.*

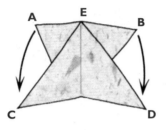

4 *Flatten the paper so that two triangles lie either side of the center.*

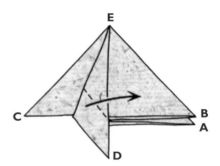

7 *Fold up D as shown so that it lies along edge CB.*

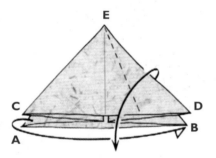

5 *Fold D inwards so that edge ED lies along the center crease. (It may help to mark ABCD in pencil.) Swing A on the left around the back to the right so that it lies behind B.*

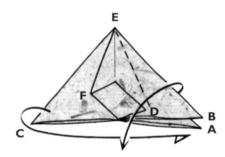

8 *The paper now looks like this. The folds in Steps 5-7 are now repeated with B, then A, and then C. As in Step 5, fold B inwards so that edge EB lies along the center crease, covering D. Swing C on the left around the back to lie behind A on the right.*

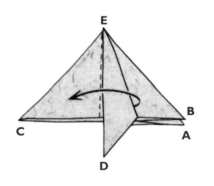

6 *Swing D over to the left.*

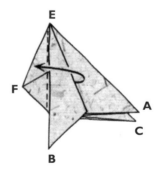

9 *Swing B over to the left to lie on top of F. Fold up B like D in Step 7.*

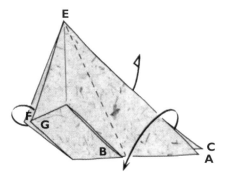

10 *As in Step 5, fold A inwards so that edge EA lies along the center crease, covering B. Swing F on the left around the back to lie hidden behind C on the right. Swing A over to the left to lie on top of G. Fold up A like D in Step 7.*

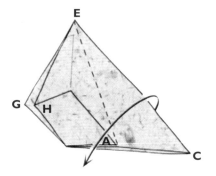

11 *As in Step 5, fold C inwards so that edge EC lies along the center crease, covering A.*

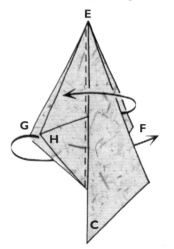

12 *Swing G on the left around the back and to the right to lie behind F. Swing C over to the left, to lie on top of H.*

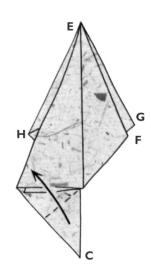

13 *Fold up corner C, as shown. Crease flat.*

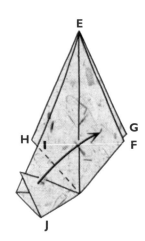

14 *Fold the flap up as shown . . .*

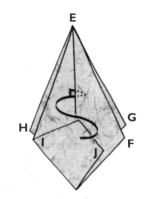

15 *. . . and slide J under the edge that runs down the center of the paper, pushing it deep into the pocket.*

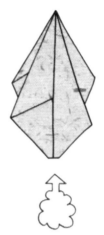

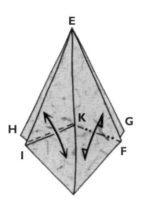

16 *The paper is now symmetrical. Carefully form valley creases between I and K, and H and K on the left, and mountain creases between F and K, and G and K on the right. Do not crease beyond the center.*

18 *At the bottom end, there should be a small hole. Blow into it and the bell should inflate! Inflating it is easier if the four flaps are spread apart and if the hole is clearly visible. The flexible creases just made will form a definite rim to the bell.*

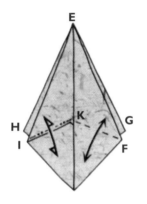

17 *Now make mountain creases on the left and valleys on the right, placing these creases on top of the previous ones. This will form creases that can bend backwards and forwards. Bend them to and fro several times so that they are very flexible.*

19 *The Bell is complete. To suspend, attach a loop to the top of the bell with needle and thread.*

ANGEL

This elegant, semi-abstract design is far removed from the literal style of representation seen in some origami models. Despite its basic design, it succeeds well in capturing the likeness of a subject with just a few folds—which in many ways is just as difficult as using many. The Angel can be used to decorate the front of a Christmas card, or attached to the top of the Christmas tree with a loop of adhesive tape.

PAPER

A rectangle of medium-weight paper or foil, proportioned 3:2, or a sheet of $8^{1}/_{2} \times 11$ in. (A4) or $5^{3}/_{4} \times 8^{1}/_{2}$ in. (A5) paper are all suitable for this piece.

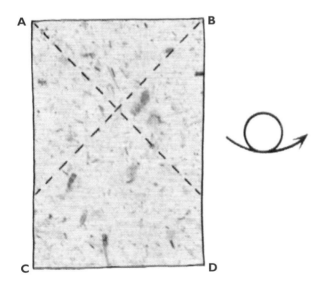

Fold A over to the right so that it lies on edge BD. Crease and unfold. Repeat, folding B over to the left to lie on edge AC. Crease, unfold, and turn over.

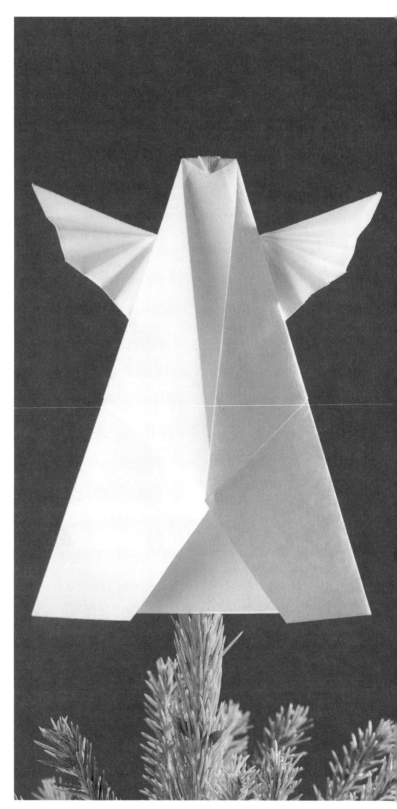

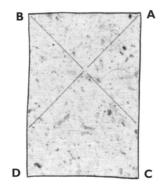

2 *The creases now rise towards you.*

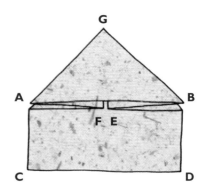

5 *... like this. Flatten the paper.*

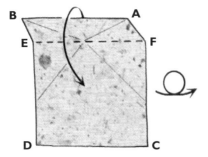

3 *Make a horizontal valley fold that passes through the centerpoint of the mountain 'cross'. Turn back over.*

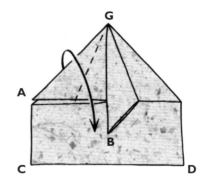

6 *Imagine a center crease from the top point (G) down the middle of the paper. Fold in A and B to lie along that imaginary crease. Keep it neat at G. B has already been folded.*

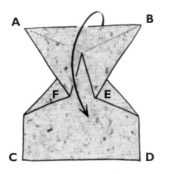

4 *Holding the sides of the paper at E and F, let A and B rise up as the sides are brought inwards ...*

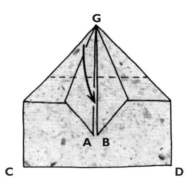

7 *Fold G down to AB. Crease firmly.*

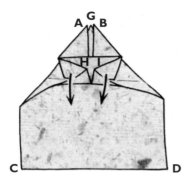

8   *Hold G, A and B, and swing them back up to where G used to be at the top. Keep a firm hold of them. The paper does not lie flat in the middle.*

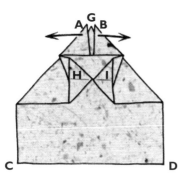

9   *Flatten the paper to form triangles H and I. Hold the paper with your left hand at H, and . . .*

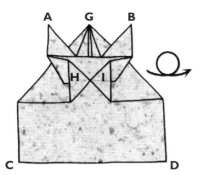

10   *. . . pull B and A away from G (see the next drawing to check the new position). Flatten and crease. Turn over.*

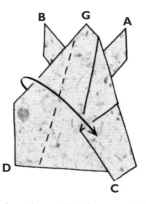

11   *Fold in the sides so that they overlap in the center (see next drawing). Note that they do not quite meet at G. C has already been folded.*

12   *Tuck D and C behind. Fold down G. Carefully pleat the wings.*

13   *The Angel is complete.*

STANDING HEART

A Valentine's Day design for the practical romantics among us, this free-standing heart is durable enough to last for months displayed on a table or shelf—maybe even until the Buttonhole (see page 130) arrives the following year . . .

PAPER

You will need a 6-8 in. (15-20 cm) square of light- or medium-weight paper that is white on one side and red on the other.

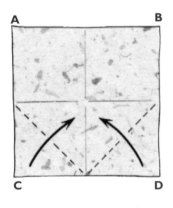

1 White side up, fold the square in half, horizontally and vertically. Unfold. Fold C and D to the center.

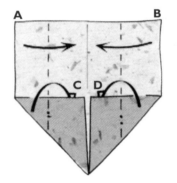

3 Refold along the Step 2 creases, but reverse-fold the colored triangles behind C and D . . .

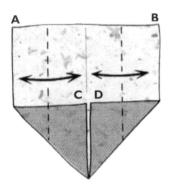

2 Fold A and B to the center crease. Unfold.

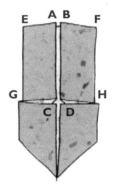

4 . . . like this. Turn over.

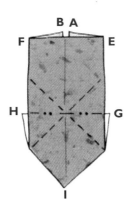

5 *Pre-crease as shown. Note that GH is a mountain crease.*

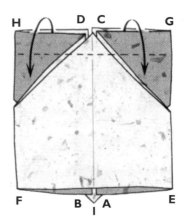

8 *Pull down edge HG as shown and squash flat the triangles at H and G . . .*

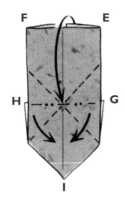

6 *Collapse so that edge FE drops to be level with corner I.*

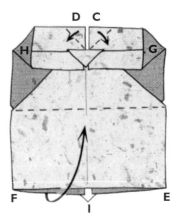

9 *. . . like this. Turn in D and C. Lift edge FE along a horizontal crease midway up the paper, separating FE from I and providing a back edge to support the heart when it is stood up. Turn over.*

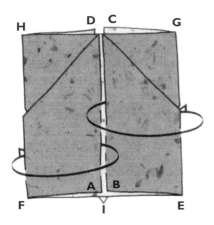

7 *Open the central slit and fold B and then A behind edge FE, so that the new top layer becomes white. To do this, unfold the paper almost back to Step 1, then re-crease and collapse back to Step 8.*

10 *The completed Standing Heart.*

SERVIETTE FOLDS

The use of paper as a means of table decoration is often forgotten. Most people take paper and its uses for granted and, although paper serviettes are used each day, it is seldom that one thinks of folding them decoratively or of using a little imagination to make simple place name cards or serviette rings. Using the ideas found in this chapter, it is easy to draw together the whole table setting. Make a theme for the whole setting by choosing a color, perhaps picked out from the dinner service or table cloth, or use a topic to suit the season. Once you have mastered the basics, the rest is up to your imagination alone!

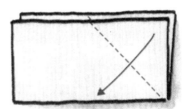

2 *Fold down the top right-hand corner.*

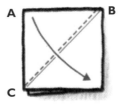

3 *Fold the bottom-right corner across to the left edge.*

SAIL SERVIETTE

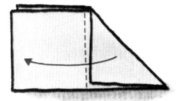

4 *Fold corner A downwards. Note B and C.*

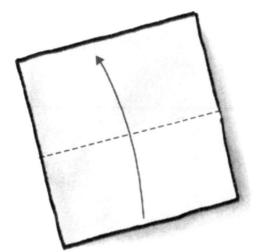

| *Fold the bottom edge up to the top.*

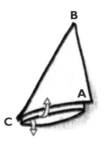

5 *Open corner C, flattening the crease BC.*

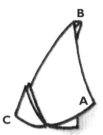

6 *Fold up the tip of corner C . . .*

7 *. . . to lock and complete the sail serviette.*

Below *This is a simple, attractive serviette, quick to make and easy to unfold.*

COCKADE NAPKIN

This is one of the most decorative and spectacular napkin folds, impressive enough to use on the most important occasions. It's sure to make a big impact on your dinner guests.

> **PAPER**
> Use a 4-ply paper napkin for the best results, although 3- and 2-ply are adequate too.

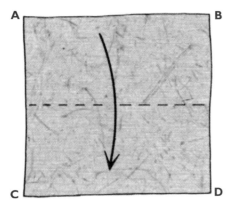

1   *If the napkin is already folded into quarters (as most are), skip forward to Step 3; otherwise, fold AB down to CD.*

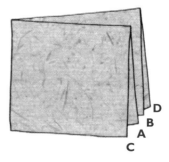

3   *Note CABD. Rotate to Step 4 position.*

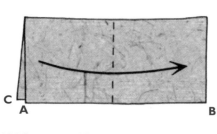

2   *Fold AC across to BD.*

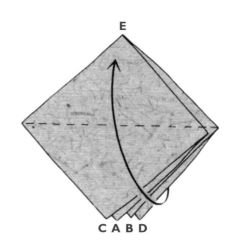

4   *Fold CABD up to E.*

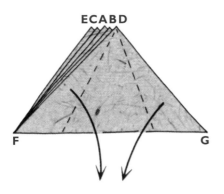

ECABD

F   G

5 *Fold the sloping edges of the triangle inwards so that FE and GE meet in the middle.*

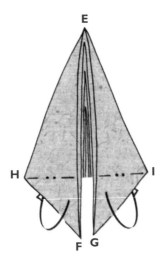

E

H   I

F G

6 *Fold F and G behind to form a straight edge between H and I.*

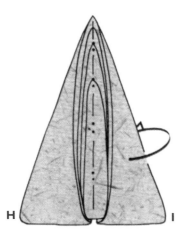

H   I

7 *Fold I behind, folding the shape in half down the middle.*

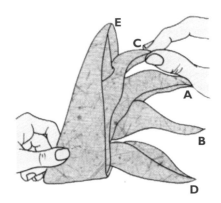

E

C

A

B

D

8 *Grip H and I firmly with one hand. With the other hand pull D out as far as possible from the nest of layers. Repeat with B (not pulling it as far as D) and likewise pull out A, and finally C.*

9 *The Cockade Napkin is complete.*

FLAME SERVIETTE

Above *This fold is more complex than the previous one, but makes a spectacular display. Fold two together of different colors for extra visual effect.*

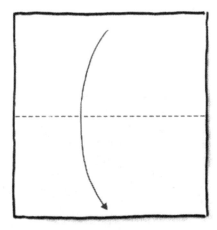

| 1 | Fold the top edge down to the bottom. |

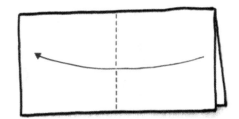

2 Fold the right-hand edge over to the left.

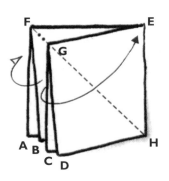

3 *Look carefully at the lettered corners. Fold A and B behind to touch E and fold C and D to the front to also touch E. Crease FH and GH . . .*

6 *. . . like this.*

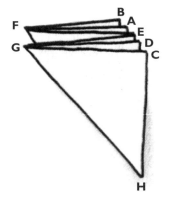

4 *. . . like this.*

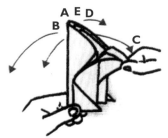

7 *Hold the serviette firmly at the bottom. There are five layers of corners at the top. Tug corner C as shown, pulling it as far out as possible. Do the same with corner D next to it, but not pulling it as far. Repeat on the other side, pulling B further than A.*

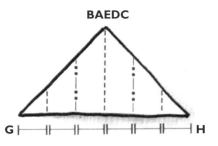

5 *Pleat the triangle into six equal divisions, to look . . .*

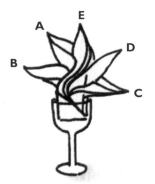

8 *The flame serviette is complete. To hold its shape, the design needs to be placed in a wine glass or tumbler.*

PLACE CARD

A finishing touch to a place setting is
to make a card that carries the name of the
guest who is to sit there. This is ideal for
more formal occasions. The same design
can also hold photographs, artwork, or give
exhibition information.

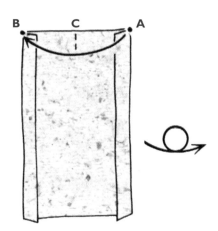

PAPER
Use a medium-weight paper of 8½ x 11 in. (A4) size
for the frame, and thin card for the insert.

OTHER EQUIPMENT
Scissors or craft knife and metal ruler; writing pen.

---

2 Bring top corners A and B together and pinch to locate
the middle of the top edge (C). Do not make a long
crease. Unfold and turn over.

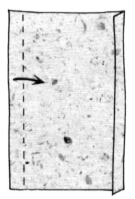

1 Fold in about 1 cm (½ in.) along the longer edges. The
right-hand side is shown already folded.

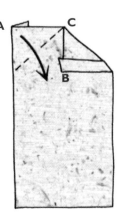

3 Fold A and B into the middle, using the pinch at C to
find the point on the top edge where the creases
meet. B is shown already folded.

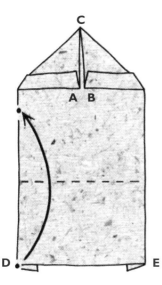

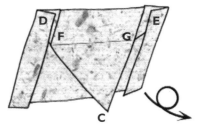

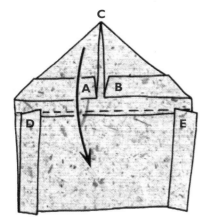

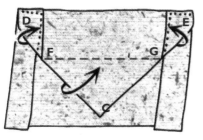

4 *Fold up D and E to lie just below the base of the triangle. The exact placement is unimportant.*

7 *This is the back of the place-card holder, with C forming a stand. Turn over.*

5 *Fold down C and crease along a line just above DE.*

8 *Measure the proportions of the holder. Cut a piece of paper or card fractionally smaller. Write the person's name on it and tuck the short edges into the pockets at the sides of the place-card holder.*

6 *Flip loose corners D and E to the front, trapping the corners of the large C triangle behind them. Make a valley crease between F and G, lifting corner C.*

9 *The Place Card is complete.*

NAPKIN RING

Instead of folding paper napkins, roll up linen napkins and present them at the side of each place setting inside the napkin ring described here. The effect achieved is less flamboyant, but just as impressive.

To personalize each ring, stencil a monogram, initial, or image, such as a flower, on to the central shield.

PAPER
Use a 2:1 rectangle of light- or medium-weight paper, approximately 8 x 4 in. (20 x 10 cm).

OTHER EQUIPMENT
To decorate the napkin ring you will need a purchased or homemade stencil; brush and paints, or coloring pencils, felt-tip pens, etc.

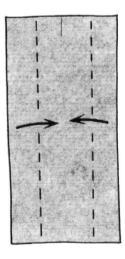

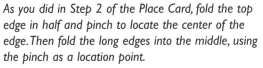

As you did in Step 2 of the Place Card, fold the top edge in half and pinch to locate the center of the edge. Then fold the long edges into the middle, using the pinch as a location point.

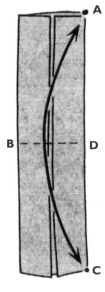

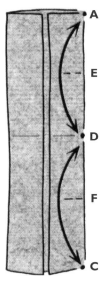

2 Fold A down to C to make crease BD. Unfold.

3 Fold A to D making only a short crease at the right-hand edge (E), and unfold. Repeat, folding C to D, to make F.

96

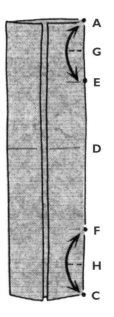

4   *Fold A to E, making a short crease at the right-hand edge (G). Repeat, folding C to F, to make H.*

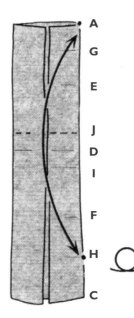

6   *Fold A down to H. Crease right across to make J, and unfold. Turn over.*

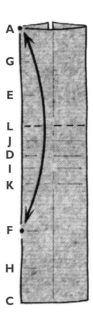

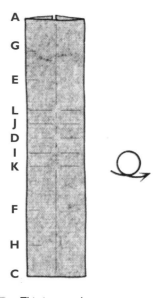

8   *Fold A down to F. Crease right across to make L, and unfold.*

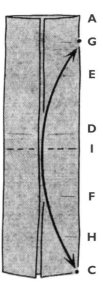

5   *Fold C up to G. Crease right across to make I, and unfold.*

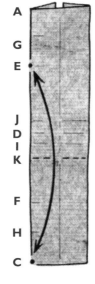

7   *This is the crease pattern at present. Fold C up to E. Crease right across to make K, and unfold.*

9   *This is now the crease pattern. Turn over.*

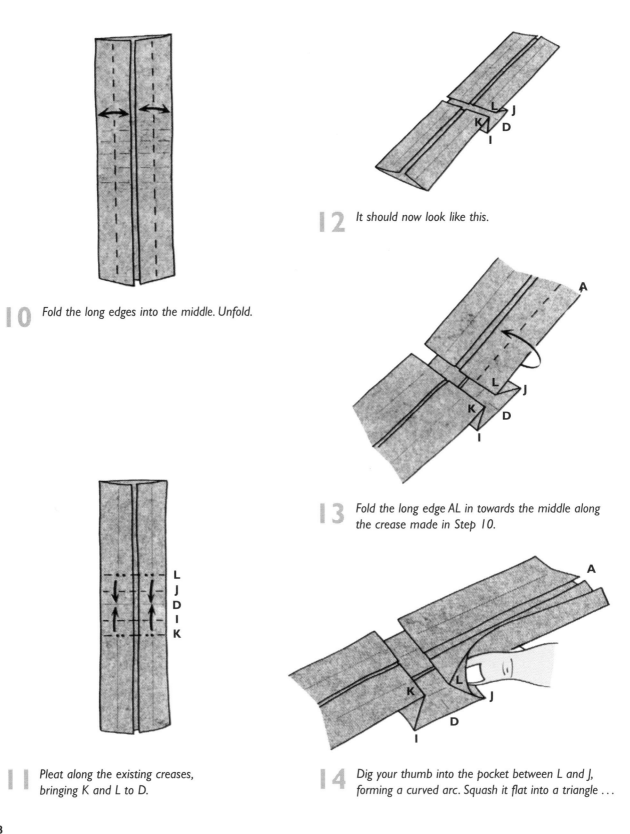

10 *Fold the long edges into the middle. Unfold.*

11 *Pleat along the existing creases, bringing K and L to D.*

12 *It should now look like this.*

13 *Fold the long edge AL in towards the middle along the crease made in Step 10.*

14 *Dig your thumb into the pocket between L and J, forming a curved arc. Squash it flat into a triangle . . .*

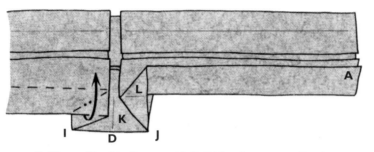

15 *... like this. Repeat with K, folding it across, pulling it into an arc, digging a thumb in the pocket under K, and squashing it to make a triangle. The points of the triangles should meet.*

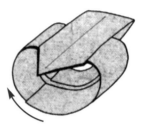

18 *Feed one end of the strap into the other to fasten the ring.*

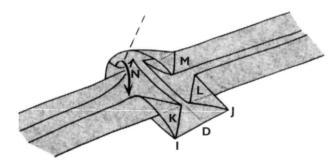

16 *Now fold in the long edges on the opposite side of the strip, but instead of digging your thumb in the pockets as you did under K and L, swing M and N right across, opening up another pocket. Squash this flat forming a triangle. The points of the triangles point away from each other, the long sides meeting.*

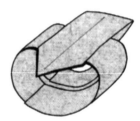

19 *The Napkin Ring is complete.*

17 *It should look like this. When turned over, there should be a simple shield shape on the reverse.*

ANIMALS AND FLOWERS

What qualities make the basis of a particular design so memorable? Eastern symbolism aside, perhaps it is because something about that design is unique. What's more, the designs all have a clever or entertaining finish to make the folding worthwhile. Origami is very much a performing art.

The best contemporary designs reveal qualities typical of oriental arts and crafts—elegance, stylization, and, in designs of living creatures, more regard for character than for form.

The wide range of beautiful papers often mean that more attention is given to the *look* of a design than to its sequence of folds, so that the artistry lies more in the relationships between the paper, the subject, and the manipulative finesse of the folder.

BIRD

Whereas some origami designs can be naturalistic, other designs, such as this one, are really symbols. Here is a bird—not a duck, a swan, or anything more specific—just a bird: it has a head, wings, and a tail, so it *must* be one, even though it doesn't look like any particular species. So, you may be asking yourself, is the design a remarkable distillation of form, or merely an example of inadequate technique? Surely the former. Use a 6-8 in. (15-20 cm) square of paper.

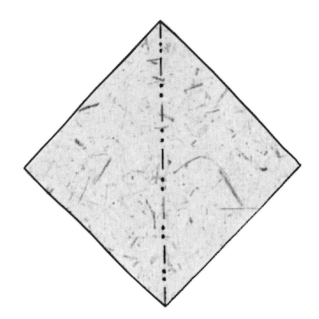

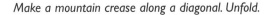

1 *Make a mountain crease along a diagonal. Unfold.*

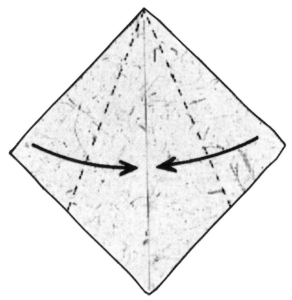

2 *Fold two edges to the center crease. Be careful to make a neat corner at the top.*

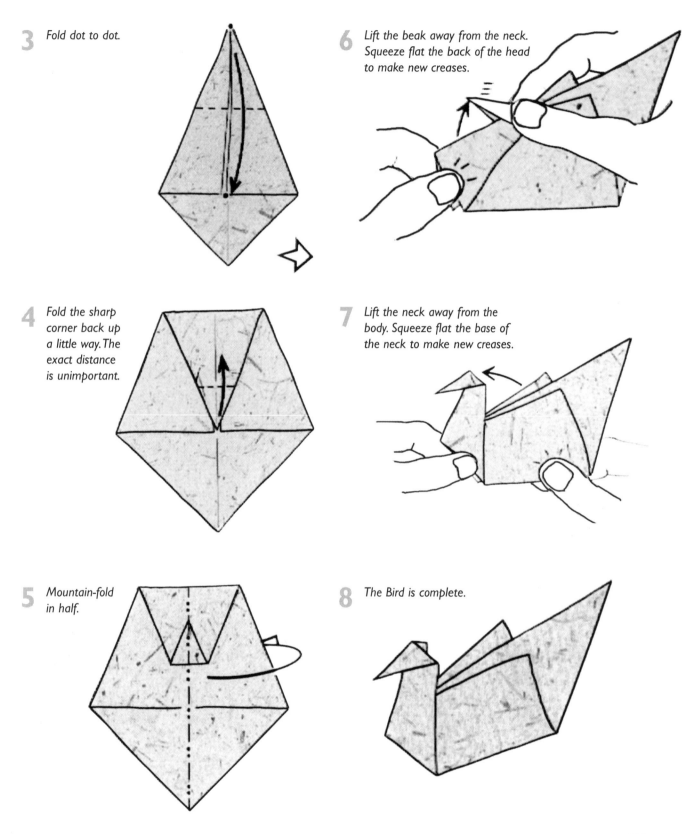

3 Fold dot to dot.

4 Fold the sharp corner back up a little way. The exact distance is unimportant.

5 Mountain-fold in half.

6 Lift the beak away from the neck. Squeeze flat the back of the head to make new creases.

7 Lift the neck away from the body. Squeeze flat the base of the neck to make new creases.

8 The Bird is complete.

WATERLILY

This is the full version of a spectacular napkin fold sometimes seen in restaurants. Note the remarkable manner in which the uninteresting shape made up to Step 6 is gradually opened up and transformed into the beautiful completed design—it is almost like magic. Use a paper napkin. Ordinary paper will rip at Step 7.

Fold the corners to the center.

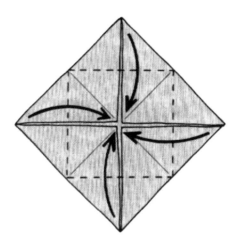

2 *Again, fold the corners to the center.*

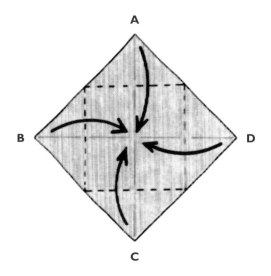

5 *Yet again, fold the corners to the center.*

3 *Once again, fold the corners to the center.*

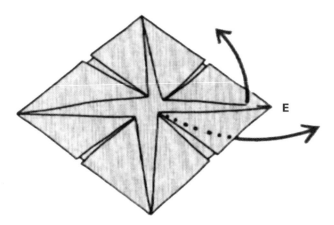

6 *Note E. Hold all the layers flat and pull out corner A mentioned in Step 4.*

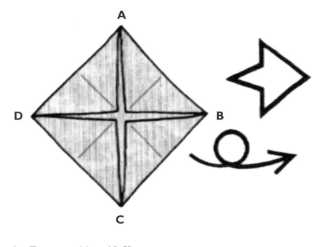

4 *Turn over. Note ABCD.*

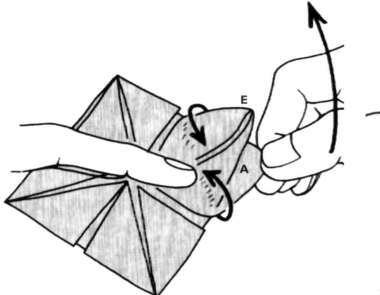

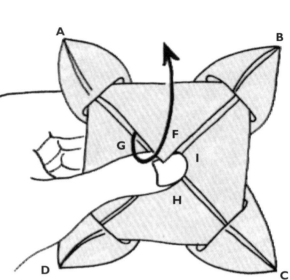

7 *Hold as shown. Pull A forcibly upwards, so that it unpeels around E . . .*

9 *Turn over. Note FGHI. Lift F . . .*

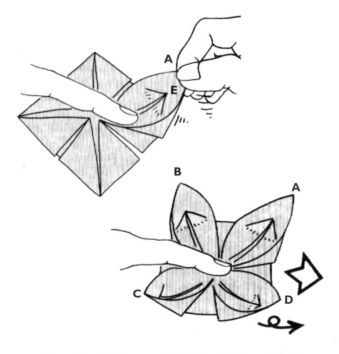

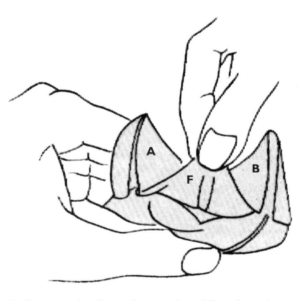

8 *. . . like this. Repeat with B C and D, keeping hold of the center.*

10 *. . . and pull it up between A and B, as far as it will go. Repeat with G, H and I, still keeping hold of the center.*

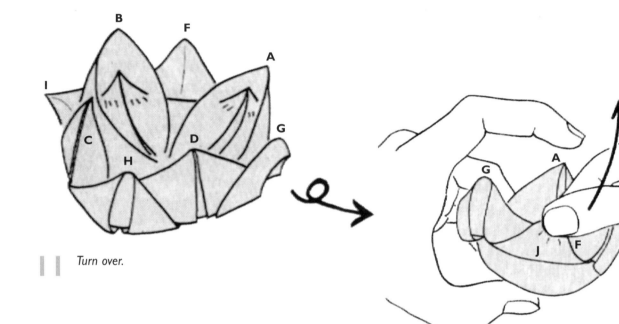

11 *Turn over.*

13 *... and pull it up in front of A. Repeat with K, L and M.*

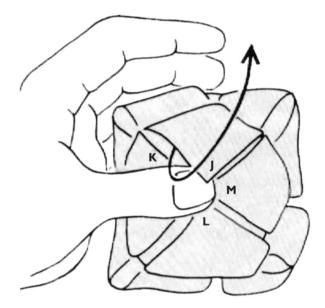

12 *Note JKLM. Lift J ...*

14 *The Waterlily is complete.*

YOSHIZAWA'S BUTTERFLY

Here are the instructions for Yoshizawa's best-known butterfly, drawn by the creator for use in the book and reproduced without alterations or additions. This butterfly is the logo of the International Origami Center, which Yoshizawa founded to help spread friendship and peace through origami. The design is so well-known that it has almost become traditional.

Yoshizawa does not give the written, step-by-step instructions as we have done in other designs, but by now the reader should be familiar enough with the diagrams and symbols to be able to follow his instructions.

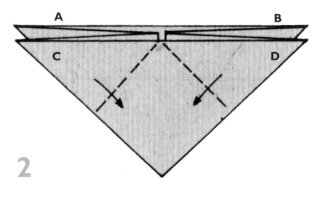

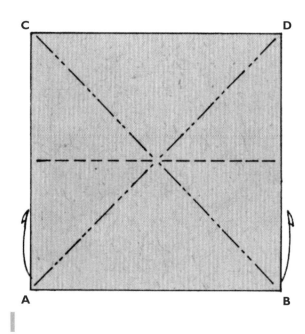

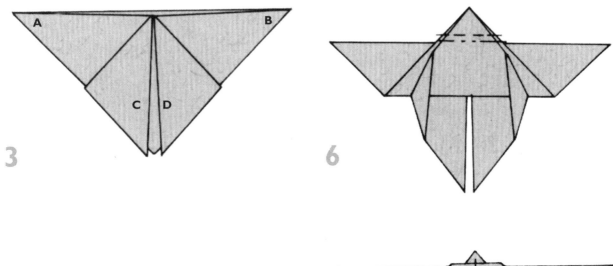

3

6

4

7

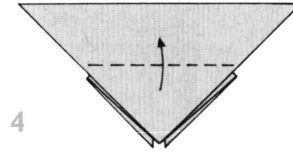

5

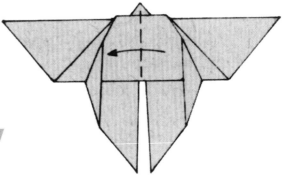

8

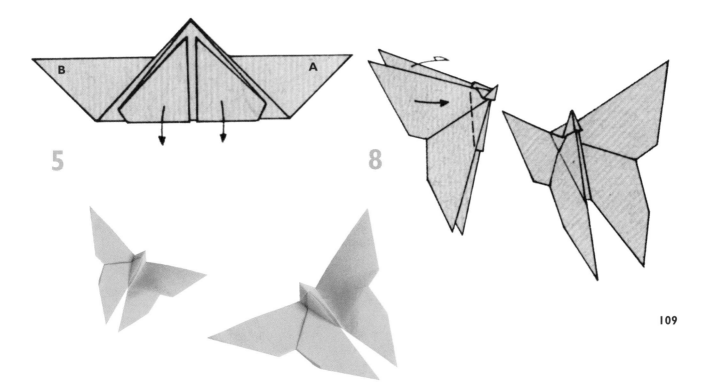

TULIP AND STEM

Here is the first two-piece design in the book and one of the simplest and most appealing of all origami flowers. Its creator, Kunihiko Kasahara (Japan), has written over 100 origami books—including some in English—that feature his own prolific output. To make the Tulip and Stem, make the Tulip square half the size of the Stem square, so that (for example) if the Tulip is made from a 4 in. (10 cm) square, the Stem is made from an 8 in. (20 cm) square. The Tulip begins with Step 6 of the Flapping Bird (see page 113) turned upside down and the Stem begins with Step 3 of the Bird (see page 102).

BLOOM

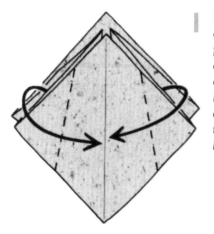

1 *With the open corner at the top, fold the front corners to the center crease. Note that the creases taper towards the top. Repeat behind.*

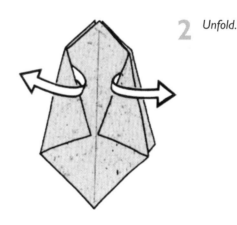

2 *Unfold.*

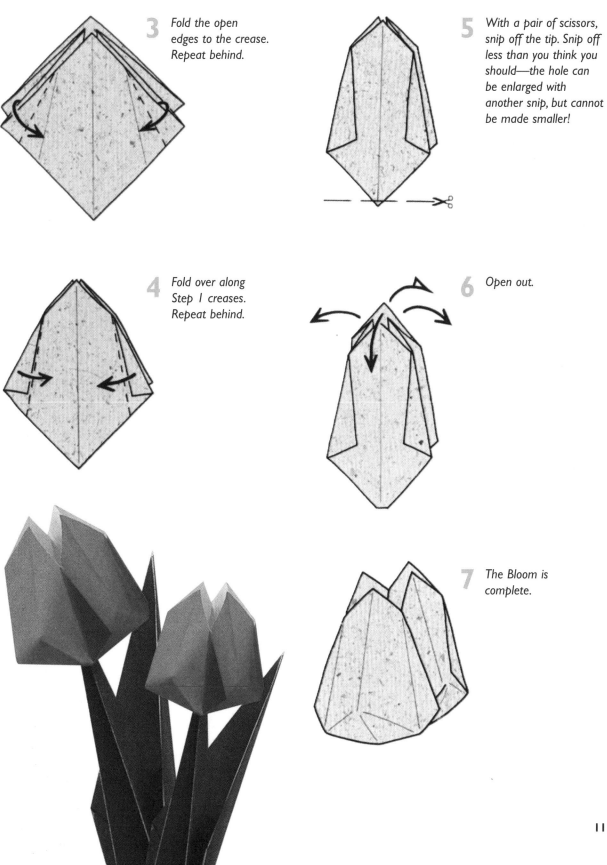

3 Fold the open edges to the crease. Repeat behind.

4 Fold over along Step 1 creases. Repeat behind.

5 With a pair of scissors, snip off the tip. Snip off less than you think you should—the hole can be enlarged with another snip, but cannot be made smaller!

6 Open out.

7 The Bloom is complete.

STEM

1 *Fold the short edges to the center crease.*

2 *Narrow the bottom corner. Keep it neat.*

3 *Fold in half, dot to dot.*

4 *Pull the sharp point out to the dotted position. Squeeze the paper flat at the bottom to let the sharp point retain its new position.*

5 *The Stem is complete. Insert the sharp spike into the base of the Bloom.*

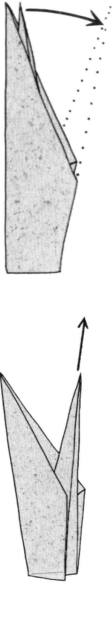

FLAPPING BIRD

Here is perhaps the greatest of all "action models." The bird shape is itself satisfying, but the wide, graceful arc made by the wings when flapped is dramatic and appealing. If you want to carry a design in your wallet or handbag to entertain people with and show them what origami is capable of, this must surely be the one. Use a 6-10 in. (15-25 cm) square of paper.

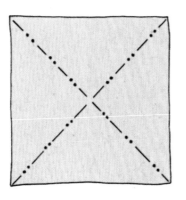

1   *Mountain-fold both diagonals. Unfold.*

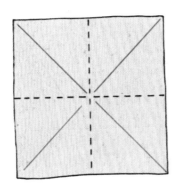

2   *Valley-fold horizontally and vertically. Unfold.*

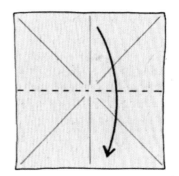

3   *Fold the top edge down to the bottom along the existing crease.*

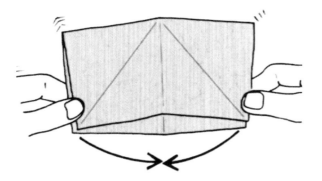

4   *Hold as shown. Swing your hands together . . .*

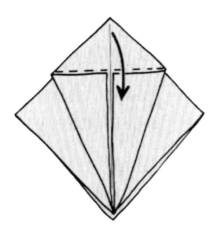

7   *. . . like this. Fold down the top triangle.*

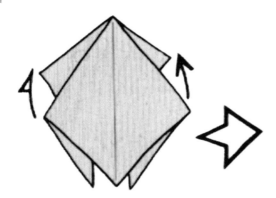

5   *. . . to create this 3D star shape. If the pattern of mountains and valleys is incorrect it will not form, so check Steps 1-2.*

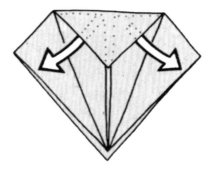

8   *Pull out the side triangles.*

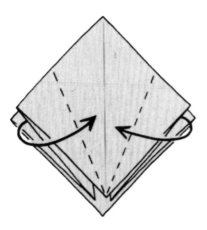

6   *With the closed (neat) corner at the top, fold in the lower front edges to the center crease . . .*

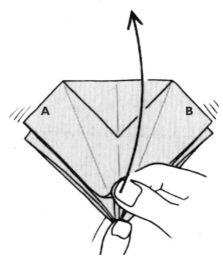

9   *Take hold of just the top layer. Lift it upwards . . .*

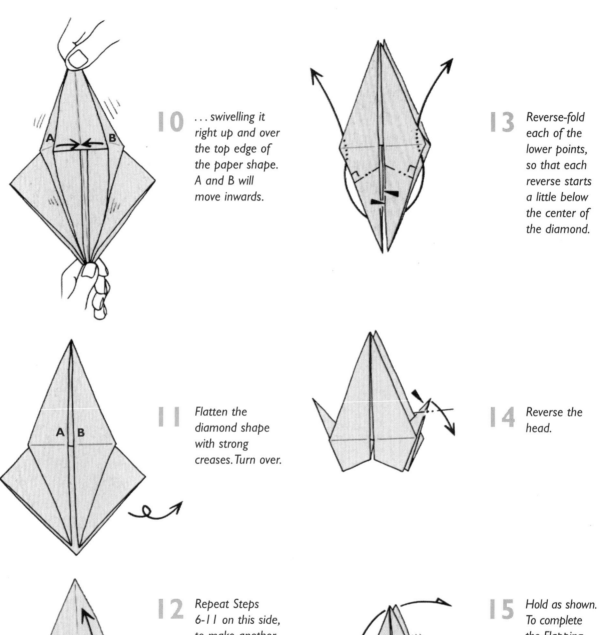

10 *. . . swivelling it right up and over the top edge of the paper shape. A and B will move inwards.*

13 *Reverse-fold each of the lower points, so that each reverse starts a little below the center of the diamond.*

11 *Flatten the diamond shape with strong creases. Turn over.*

14 *Reverse the head.*

12 *Repeat Steps 6-11 on this side, to make another diamond shape to match the first. Note the loose triangle hidden between them.*

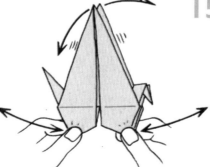

15 *Hold as shown. To complete the Flapping Bird, move your hands gently apart and together, apart and together, and the wings will flap!*

CAT

This is a design by Mrs Toshie Takahama. The cat is regarded by many creative folders to be a very difficult subject to capture in paper, because its shape is very simple and curved. But many origami experts would agree that Mrs Takahama's Cat is the most successful version yet achieved, being well proportioned, full of character, instantly recognizable, and pleasing to fold. The design benefits from being made from a textured paper such as Ingres (Strathmore), or another appropriate paper. Begin with Step 3 of the Bird (see page 102), using a 6-8 in. (15-20 cm) square of paper as in that design.

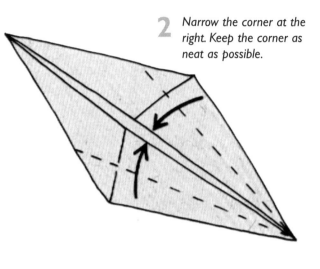

2 *Narrow the corner at the right. Keep the corner as neat as possible.*

3 *Fold in half. Note A and B.*

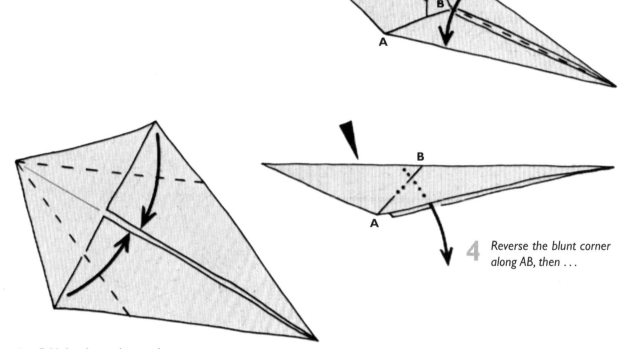

1 *Fold the short edges to the center.*

4 *Reverse the blunt corner along AB, then . . .*

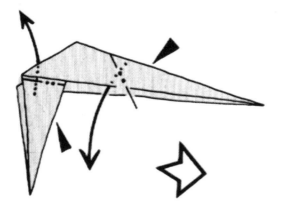

5 *... reverse it back up level with open edge. Reverse the sharp corner to the position shown in Step 6.*

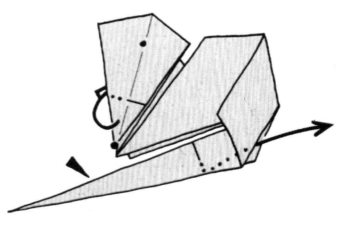

8 *Tuck the point inside the face, folding dot to dot. Reverse the tail.*

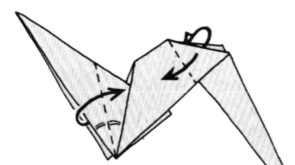

6 *Valley the front layer at the left across to the right, so that the point stands upright. Turn the sharp point inside out.*

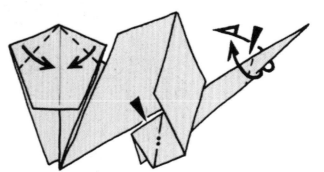

9 *Fold the ears forward. Reverse the hind legs. Outside-reverse the tail.*

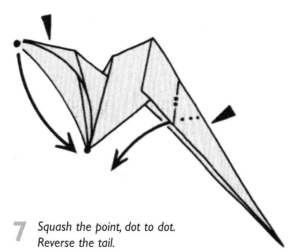

7 *Squash the point, dot to dot. Reverse the tail.*

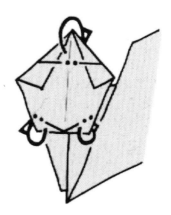

10 *Shape the nose. Fold the top of the head behind.*

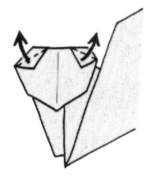

11 *Fold up the ears.*

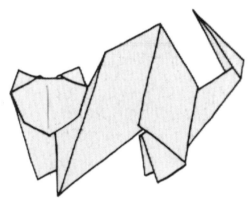

12 *The Cat is complete.*

ROOSTER

This design by Florence Temko of the United States is a superb example of how a few carefully placed inside and outside reverse folds can create a design with style and character from the very familiar origami shape shown in Step 6 (sometimes called a Fish Base). The design when folded *looks* folded, which, curiously, not all origami does. A design that has clearly been folded without the need to cut or fold pieces together is somehow more satisfying. Use a 6-8 in. (15-20 cm) square of medium-weight paper. Crease and unfold both diagonals.

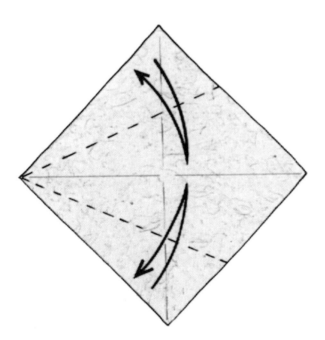

1 Fold the bottom left and top left edges to the center crease. Unfold.

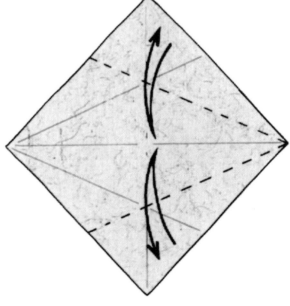

2 Repeat on the right.

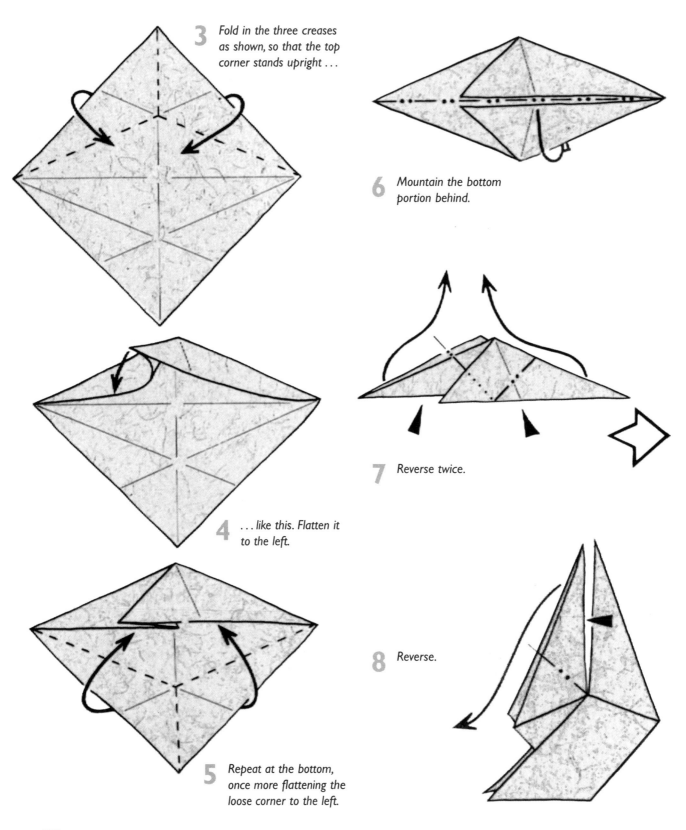

3 *Fold in the three creases as shown, so that the top corner stands upright . . .*

4 *. . . like this. Flatten it to the left.*

5 *Repeat at the bottom, once more flattening the loose corner to the left.*

6 *Mountain the bottom portion behind.*

7 *Reverse twice.*

8 *Reverse.*

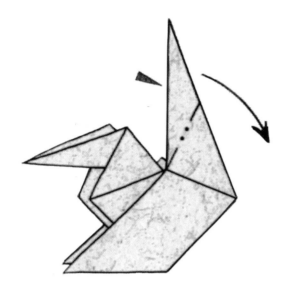

9 *Reverse. Note the angle.*

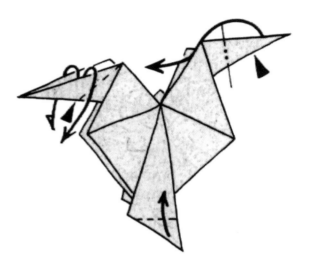

11 *At the left, outside-reverse. At the right, reverse. Valley the feet. Repeat behind. The valley creases on the feet should be at such an angle that the Rooster can balance.*

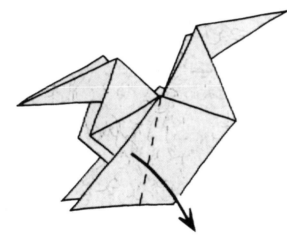

10 *Valley, repeat behind.*

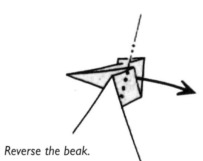

12 *Reverse the beak.*

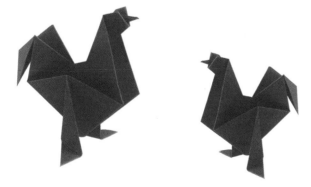

13 *The Rooster is complete.*

DAFFODIL

Technically, this design by Ted Norminton of England is the most advanced in this chapter and should only be attempted by experienced folders; however, even if you are unable to achieve this straight away, it is great practice to try to make such a complex design. Compare it with the simpler Tulip and Stem on page 110— the two extremes of style show how beauty can be achieved by very different means. Note the method in Steps 1-6 for folding an accurate hexagon. Persevere with the difficult "sink" at Step 11—practice will make it easier. Use a medium-weight yellow square for the bloom and a green square of the same size for the stem. A 10 in. (25 cm) square will create a life-size bloom.

BLOOM

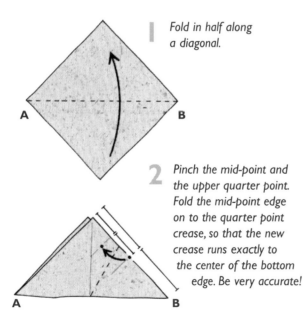

1 Fold in half along a diagonal.

2 *Pinch the mid-point and the upper quarter point. Fold the mid-point edge on to the quarter point crease, so that the new crease runs exactly to the center of the bottom edge. Be very accurate!*

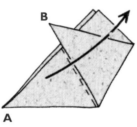

3 *Fold the left corner across.*

4 *Cut off the upper portion of paper, as shown.*

5 *Open out . . .*

6 ...to reveal a perfect hexagon! Crease mountains and valleys as shown, collapsing them to make Step 7.

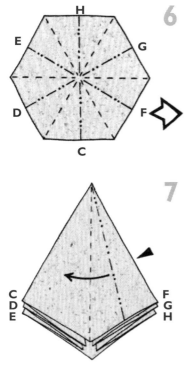

7 If the bottom edge runs straight across, turn the whole shape inside-out to make the shape seen here. Lift F and squash ...

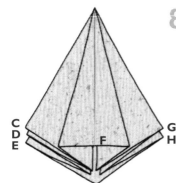

8 ...like this. Repeat with C D E G and H. When squashing, try to keep the same number of layers left and right.

9 Lift point F along the marked creases (petal fold).

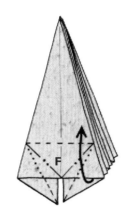

10 Unfold the Step 9 creases. Repeat five more times.

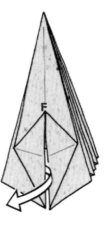

11 Invert or sink the top corner down into the body of the paper, at the level shown. Open out the hexagon to do so, then collapse it back into shape when the rim of the sink has been creased into a continuous mountain crease and the center inverted. This is an arduous procedure, even for experts, so persevere.

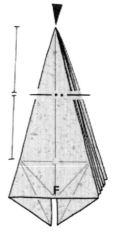

12 Tuck F up inside the front layer, reversing some of the Step 9 creases. Repeat five more times around the layers.

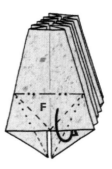

13 Fold one layer across to the left, to reveal ...

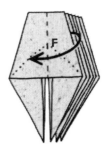

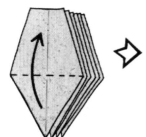

14 *...a clean face. Fold up the bottom triangle. Repeat five more times around the layers.*

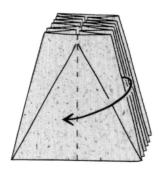

15 *Fold one layer across ...*

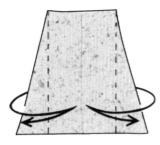

16 *...to reveal a clean face. Note that for clarity, only the front layer will now be drawn. Crease and unfold as shown.*

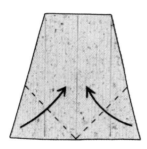

17 *Fold the corners up to the center crease.*

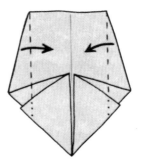

18 *Re-fold the Step 16 creases, so that the bottom portion of each crease disappears into the lower triangle.*

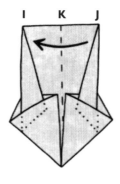

19 *Fold the layer across. Repeat Steps 15-19 five more times. Note I J and K.*

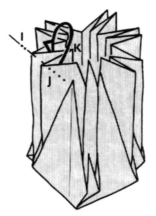

20 *Note I J and K again. Fold K behind, so that I and J are brought together and locked. Repeat five more times within the Bloom.*

21 *Pull down each of the six petals and reverse the rim of the Bloom to shape it.*

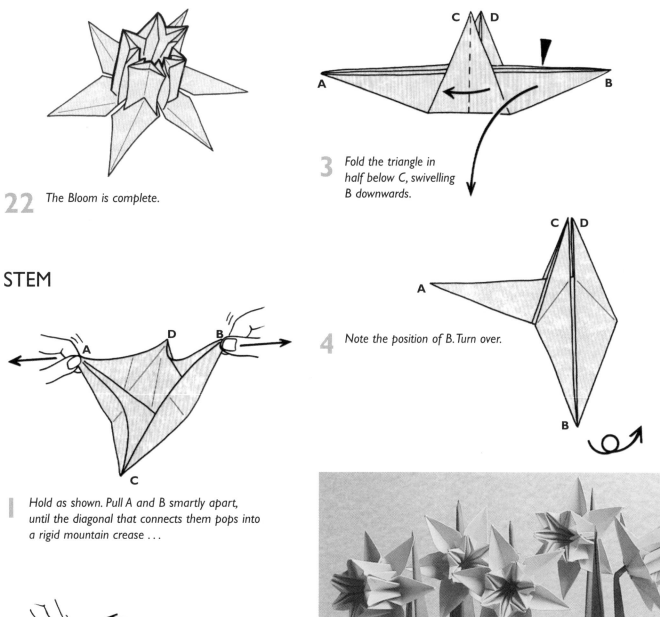

22 *The Bloom is complete.*

STEM

3 *Fold the triangle in half below C, swivelling B downwards.*

4 *Note the position of B. Turn over.*

1 *Hold as shown. Pull A and B smartly apart, until the diagonal that connects them pops into a rigid mountain crease . . .*

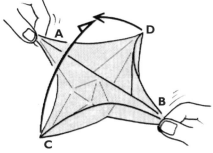

2 *. . . like this. Flatten bringing C and D together.*

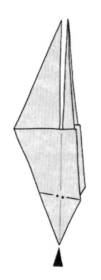

5 Repeat Step 3, swivelling A down to B

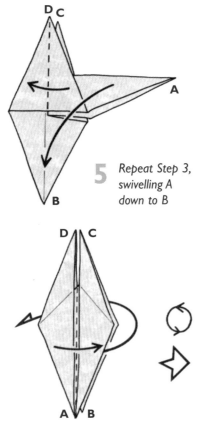

6 Fold a layer across at the front. Repeat behind but on the opposite side. Rotate the paper upside-down.

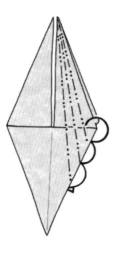

7 Narrow the front layer at the right. Repeat behind.

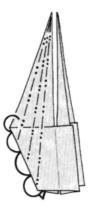

8 Push in or sink the bottom corner. Note that the crease tilts upward at the left. Repeat behind.

9 Narrow the flap on the left. Repeat behind.

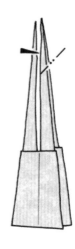

10 Reverse.

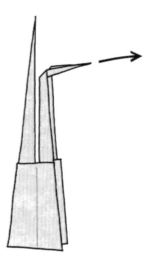

11 The Stem is complete. Insert the spike into the back of the Bloom.

FOX

The stylization typical of Japanese designs is shown to good effect in this design by Mitsue Okuda. What's more, although the front and back are folded differently (the tail is to one side), the design looks good from all angles. The head is a particularly interesting feature of the design, being so remarkably simple. It just goes to show that some of the most effective aspects of origami are also some of the simplest. Use a rectangle of thin or medium-weight paper, twice as long as it is wide, for instance 4-8 in. (10-20 cm).

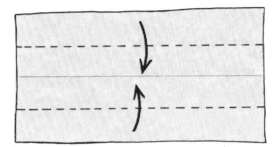

1 *Fold the long edges to the center crease.*

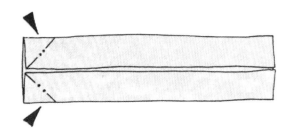

2 *Reverse twice at the left.*

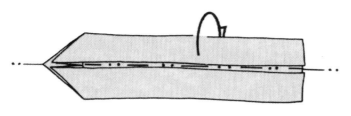

3 *Mountain-fold in half.*

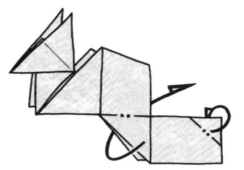

7 *Mountain the tail. Fold the left ear around the back.*

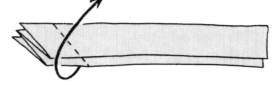

4 *Valley-fold.*

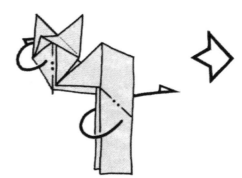

8 *Narrow the tip of the tail. Mountain-fold the tail behind.*

5 *Outside-reverse.*

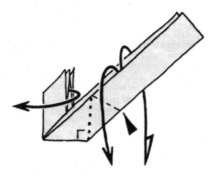

6 *Pull two layers across to the left to allow the center point (the nose) to rise. Outside-reverse on the right, as shown.*

9 *Narrow the tail. Pull the ears forward.*

10 *The Fox is complete.*

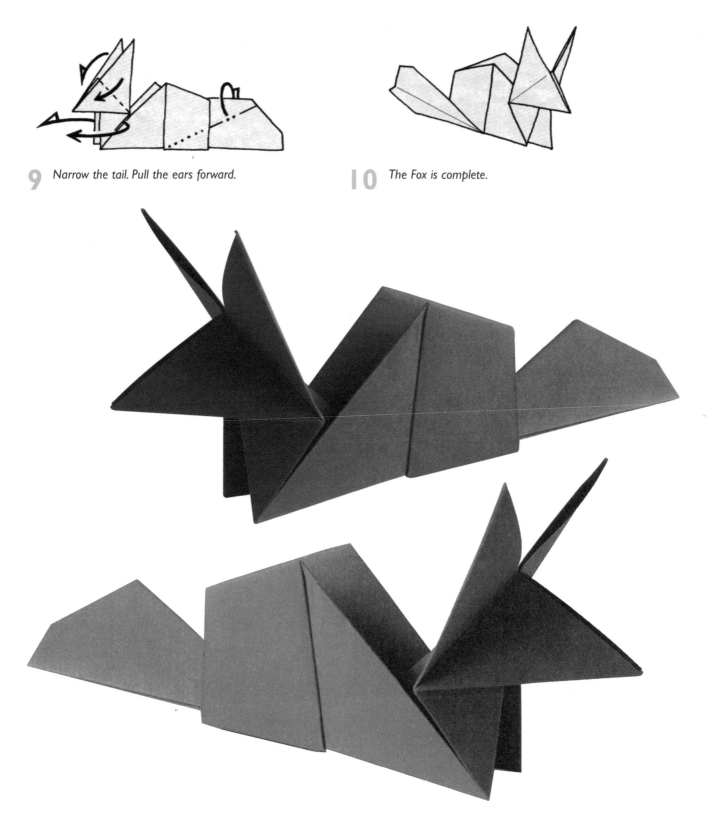

BUTTONHOLE

This is a beautiful origami design that will make a much admired gift, particularly if the papers that you use are chosen with care. The flower is the Iris from the Floral Centerpiece (see page 133).

PAPER

The **leaf** and the **flower** are each made from a 4 in. (10 cm) square of lightweight paper (such as origami paper). These dimensions will make quite a small buttonhole, so fold with care.

The **stem** is made from a square of lightweight paper, half the size of that used for the flower or leaf, and trimmed to a 3:1 rectangle.

Flower

See Floral Centerpiece (page 133) and follow the instructions for the Iris to complete the flower design.

LEAF

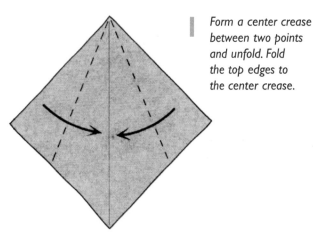

1 Form a center crease between two points and unfold. Fold the top edges to the center crease.

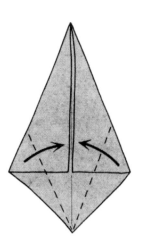

2 Fold the bottom edges to the center crease.

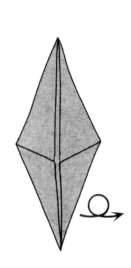

3 Turn over.

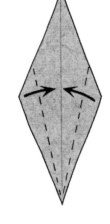

4 Fold the bottom edges to the center crease.

5 *Mountain-fold the right half behind the left half.*

8 *The completed leaf.*

STEM

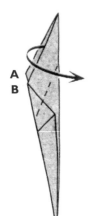

6 *Fold the front layer B across to the right. A and B will separate.*

1 *Roll up the paper for the stem as tightly as possible.*

2 *At the loose end, roll over the tip to lock the tube.*

3 *The stem is complete.*

ASSEMBLY

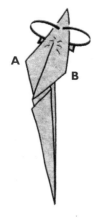

7 *Invert the leaf from a concave shape to a convex one.*

1 *With your tongue, wet the bottom of the flower to soften the paper. Push the stem through the wet paper, so that the rolled end catches deep inside the bloom preventing the stem from falling right through.*

2 Tuck the stem into the pocket in the leaf.

3 The completed Buttonhole. A better shape may be achieved if a mountain fold is made where shown.

FLORAL CENTERPIECE

Of all the projects in this chapter, this is the one that will require the most time and the most equipment, and will also take the most artistry to design and arrange. That said, it is also the project that will be the most admired, so all the hard work you put into this will be worth it. It makes a stunning centerpiece to any room or dining table for any occasion. Choose your papers with great care, coordinating the colors, tones, and textures.

PAPER

For the **iris**, use light- or medium-weight paper approximately 6-8 in. (15-20 cm) square.

For the **leaves**, use medium-weight paper 8-10 in. (20-25 cm) square—the paper should be a little larger than that used for the iris.

For the **vase**, use heavyweight paper 10-14 in. (25-35 cm) square—the paper should be 1½ times the size of that used for the iris. For a particularly sturdy vase, use thick artist's paper—Ingres or watercolor paper—and employ the 'wet folding' process explained in the section on Papers (see Introduction).

OTHER EQUIPMENT

Pencil; scissors; florist's wires (3 or 4 for each stem); gutta tape (green binding tape, available from florist's shops); adhesive tape; glue; and tapioca balls or rice grains.

IRIS

1   Crease the two diagonals, both valleys. Turn over.

2   The creases now rise towards you. Fold the four corners into the middle. Unfold.

3   Valley-fold in half vertically and unfold. Valley-fold in half horizontally.

4   Push the four corners together into the middle so that the valley folds on the diagonals collapse inwards . . .

133

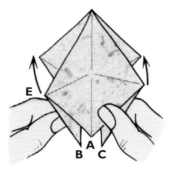

5 *... and four triangular flaps are formed in a star shape. Flatten the paper so that there are two flaps either side of the center ...*

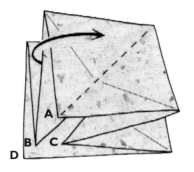

6 *... like this. Lift E so that it stands vertically.*

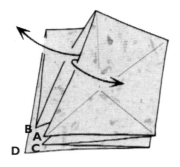

7 *Press the folded edge to open the pocket inside E. Hold ABCD neatly together.*

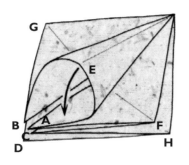

8 *Continue to press on E, until it squashes flat. Crease it firmly.*

9 *Turn over.*

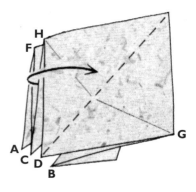

10 *Lift up H ...*

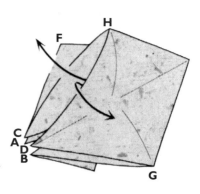

11 *... and press down on the fold to open its pocket, as in Step 8, to squash H flat. Keep the points ABCD together.*

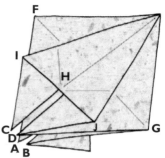

12 *It should now look like this. Fold I over to touch J. Then lift F so that it stands upright. Press down on the fold to squash it flat. Turn over and repeat with G.*

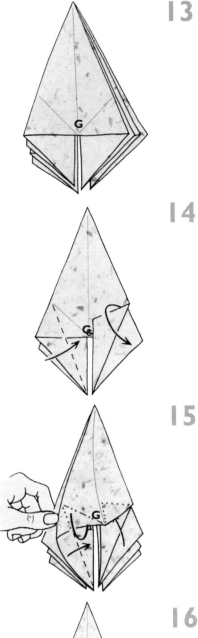

13 *All four flaps are now squashed and the paper is symmetrical.*

14 *Fold in the side points of the top layer at the lower, broader end to lie along the central crease, covering G. The right-hand side is shown already folded. Unfold.*

15 *With one hand, lift up G. With the other, re-form the creases made in the last step. Push these folds under G, using the old mountain creases made in Step 2, until the paper lies flat, as shown on the right of the diagram.*

16 *Turn over.*

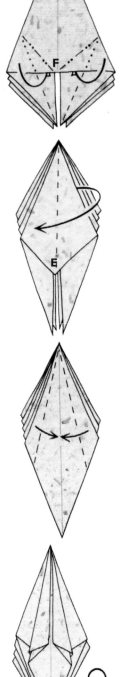

17 *Repeat Steps 14-16 on either side of F. There should now be four layers either side of the center. Fold two layers on the right over to the left and turn over, so there are two layers on the left and six on the right. Fold two on the right over to the left . . . so that there are four layers on either side with H on top. Repeat Steps 14—16 with H. Turn over and repeat with E.*

18 *The paper is now completely symmetrical with four layers on each side. Fold one layer from the right over to the left.*

19 *This will expose a blank face. Fold in the top edges of the upper layer so they lie along the middle. Keep it neat!*

20 *This is the result. Turn over.*

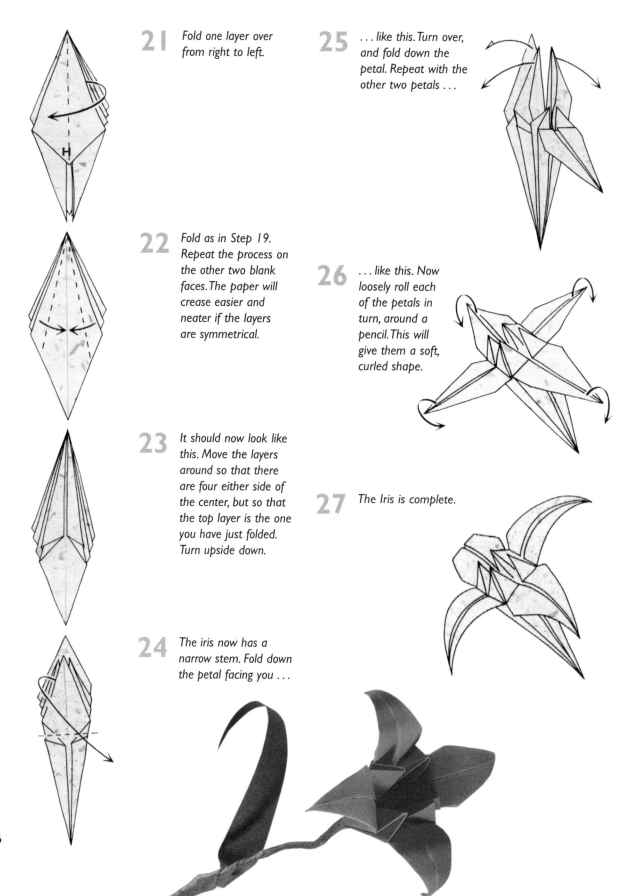

21 Fold one layer over from right to left.

22 Fold as in Step 19. Repeat the process on the other two blank faces. The paper will crease easier and neater if the layers are symmetrical.

23 It should now look like this. Move the layers around so that there are four either side of the center, but so that the top layer is the one you have just folded. Turn upside down.

24 The iris now has a narrow stem. Fold down the petal facing you . . .

25 . . . like this. Turn over, and fold down the petal. Repeat with the other two petals . . .

26 . . . like this. Now loosely roll each of the petals in turn, around a pencil. This will give them a soft, curled shape.

27 The Iris is complete.

LEAVES AND STEM

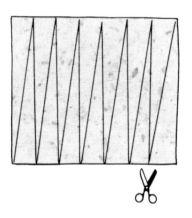

1 Cut the square into long tapering strips, as shown. One square will make 12 or more leaves.

2 Fold the paper in half at the square end by about 1 in. (2½ cm). Curl the tip of the leaf.

3 With a pair of scissors, cut out a small V shape in the middle of the crease, not too near the end.

WIRING UP

1 Overlap two florist's wires and twist together. Overlap another wire and join it by twisting. For longer stems, simply twist in more wires. Poke one end of the wire through the cut in the leaf, position the leaf a little way down the wire, and then twist the square end of the leaf tight around the wire, at such an angle that the leaf points upwards, not horizontally. Secure the end of the twisted leaf with a piece of adhesive tape.

2 Push the end of the wire through the bottom of the iris by moistening the paper with your tongue. Once through, bend over the top of the wire, and then drop the end back into the flower until it catches tight near the base of the stem. Wind green gutta tape on to the wire, starting at the bottom. At the top, wind the tape round the base of the iris, pulling it tight to secure the iris to the wire. Wind the tape to the bottom of the stem.

VASE

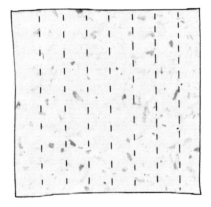

1 Divide the square into eighths, making sure that all creases are valleys.

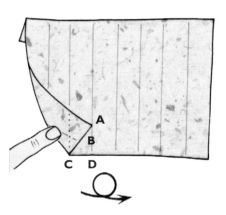

3 Fold A across to touch the third crease (D) and make a sloping crease between the first and second creases (B and C) that will exactly touch C. Make sure this crease does not extend beyond the first and second creases.

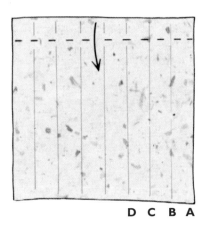

D C B A

2 Fold down the top edge by about 1 in. (2½ cm). Turn over.

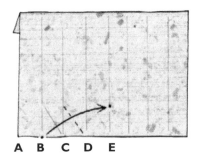

A B C D E

4 Unfold, moving A back to its original position. The crease should be like this, to the left of C. Repeat Step 3, but this time folding B over to the fourth crease (E), and make a crease between C and D.

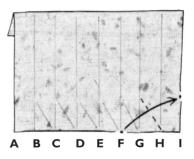

A B C D E F G H I

5 Keep repeating this move by folding C to crease 5 (F), then D to crease 6 (G), E to crease 7 (H), and F to the right-hand edge (I). The creases should look like this.

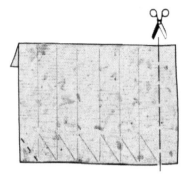

6 *Fold a crease that runs into B, from the left-hand edge, parallel to the crease that runs into C. Cut off the right-hand $^1/8$th of paper. Turn over.*

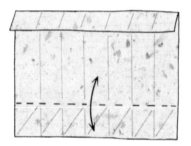

7 *Make a horizontal valley crease that connects the tops of all the sloping creases. Unfold.*

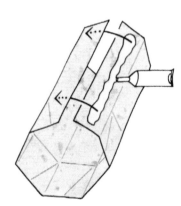

8 *Fold the bottom edge up to the horizontal crease just made. Then cut along this crease, discarding the bottom piece.*

9 *Reinforce the vertical creases to form a tube. Glue the right-hand panel, then bring over the left-hand edge, and tuck the right-hand panel under the flap at the top to help lock it in place. The vase now has six sides.*

10 *Push the end of the vase in so the sloping creases all overlap each other, collapsing into the center.*

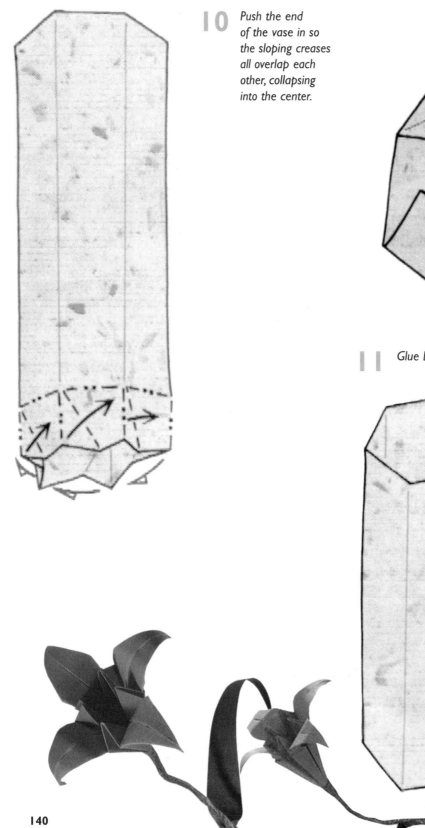

11 *Glue beneath the triangles to lock them in place.*

12 *The completed Vase. Before arranging the flowers, weight the vase with tapioca balls or rice. This also helps the iris stems to stand straight, instead of falling to the vase's edge.*

EASTER BUNNY

There are many origami bunnies for you to try, but here is one with a difference: it is one of the few made from two pieces, and the only one in which both sections of the design are blow-ups.

PAPER
Use two squares of lightweight paper, the head square about two-thirds the size of the body square, for each bunny.

OTHER EQUIPMENT
Paper glue.

BODY

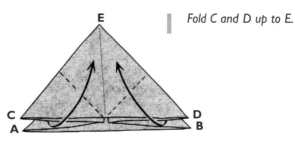

1 Fold C and D up to E.

2 Fold A and B behind to E.

3 Fold F across to the right so that it goes a little beyond the center crease. Repeat behind with G.

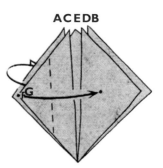

4 Fold down corner C. Repeat behind with A.

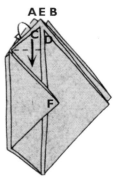

5 Valley-fold the small triangle as shown, and tuck it between the two layers of paper that run down to F. Repeat behind with A.

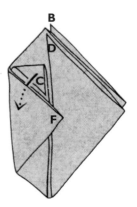

6 Fold H across to the left, tucking it underneath F. Repeat behind with I.

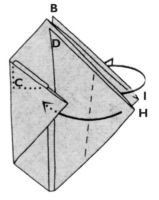

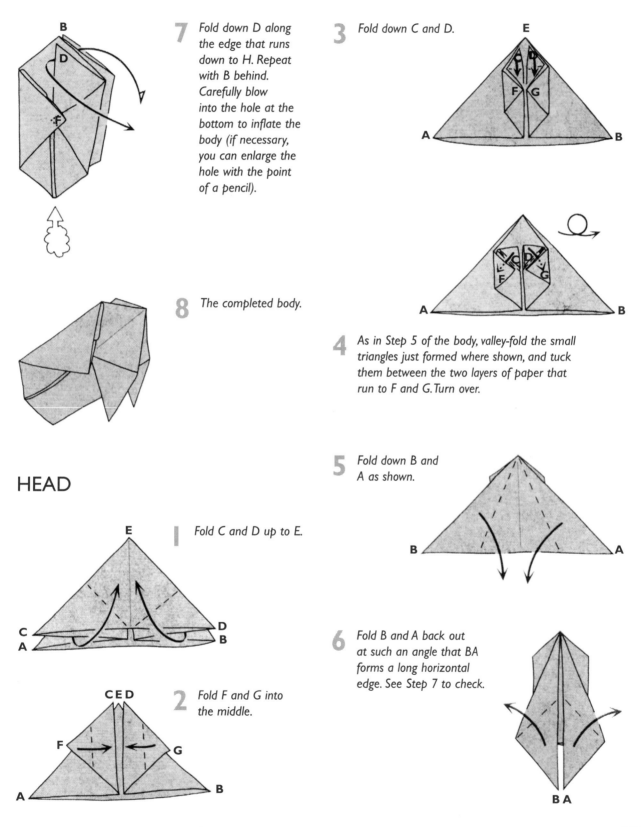

7 Fold down D along the edge that runs down to H. Repeat with B behind. Carefully blow into the hole at the bottom to inflate the body (if necessary, you can enlarge the hole with the point of a pencil).

8 The completed body.

HEAD

1 Fold C and D up to E.

2 Fold F and G into the middle.

3 Fold down C and D.

4 As in Step 5 of the body, valley-fold the small triangles just formed where shown, and tuck them between the two layers of paper that run to F and G. Turn over.

5 Fold down B and A as shown.

6 Fold B and A back out at such an angle that BA forms a long horizontal edge. See Step 7 to check.

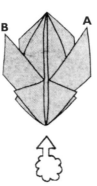

7 *Fold up B and A as shown, so that the bottom edge lies along the middle crease. These are the bunny's ears.*

8 *It should look like this. As with the body, carefully blow into the hole at the bottom to inflate the head.*

9 *The completed head. If needed, use a little paper glue to attach the head to the top of the body.*

10 *The Easter Bunny fully assembled.*

BARKING DOG

This fun and innovative design is sure to give you great satisfaction. Paul Jackson, the designer of this unique piece, discovered the action at Step 5 quite by accident, whilst playing with the paper and looking for ways to resolve the shape into an acceptable design. From there, the head and tail just folded themselves. Use a 6-8 in. (15-20 cm) square of thin or medium-weight paper, differently colored on the two sides. Start at Step 3 of the Bird on page 103.

1 *Mountain-fold in half.*

2 *Reverse-fold, to the position shown in Step 3.*

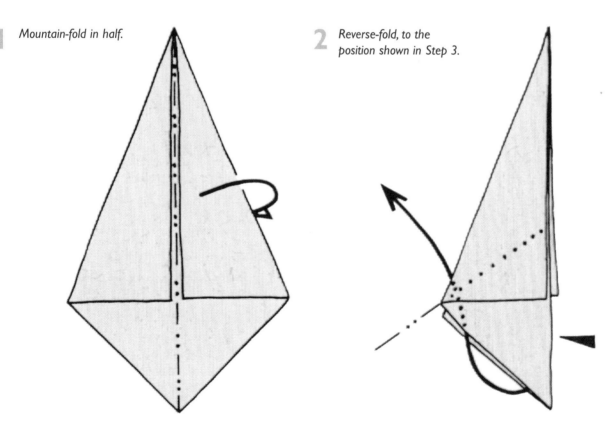

3 *Outside-reverse fold, to the position shown in Step 4. Note A.*

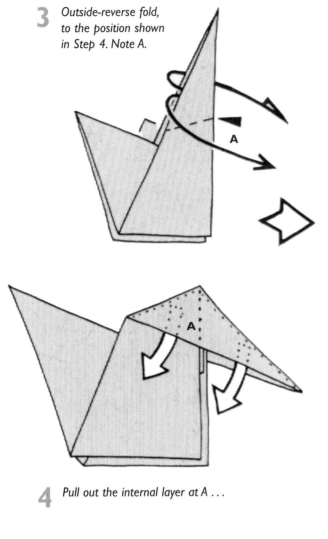

6 *The Barking Dog is complete. In this pose it begs.*

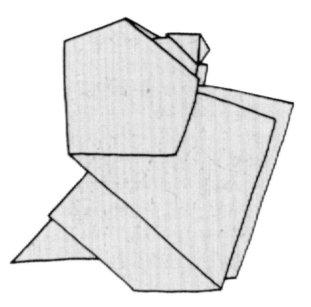

4 *Pull out the internal layer at A . . .*

5 *. . . like this. Repeat behind. Make three reverse folds on the head (the exact placement is unimportant). Pleat the tail.*

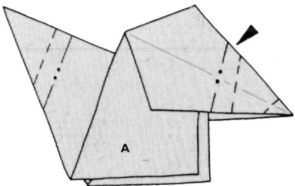

7 *To make it bark, hold as shown and move your left hand to the left and back. The head will move up and down, as though barking!*

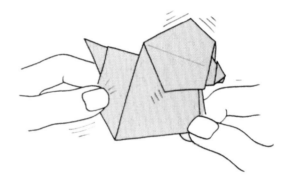

CHICK

Having completed this design, you will see how, in origami terms, a chick could be said to be a blob with a beak. Once this is understood, it becomes a relatively easy challenge for a paper folder to design a chick. Have a go yourself.

Make a clutch of chicks and some Easter Bunnies to make a centerpiece for the dining table, or use one or two to decorate the top of an Easter cake.

PAPER
You will need a lightweight yellow paper, 4 in. (10 cm) square for each chick.

OTHER EQUIPMENT
Pencil.

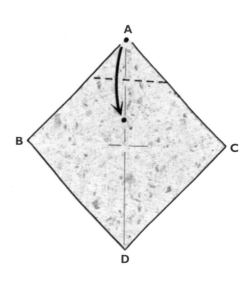

1 *Fold B to C, crease and unfold. Then fold A to D and pinch in the middle to mark to centerpoint of the square. Unfold. Fold down A to a point a little above the center of the square.*

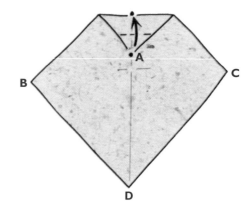

2 *Fold A back up to the crease just made.*

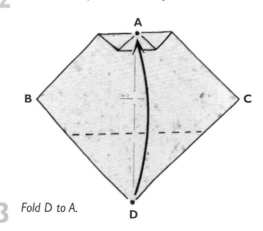

3 *Fold D to A.*

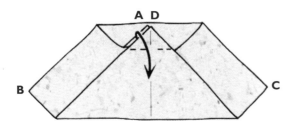

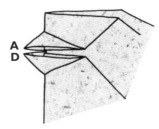

4 *Fold D back down along the line of the crease made in Step 2.*

8 *The paper is now the same both front and back.*

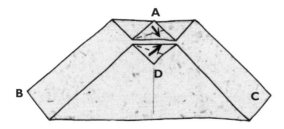

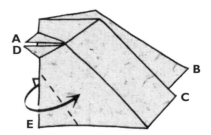

5 *Fold in the left-hand sloping edges of the two triangles so that A and D lie along the creases made in Steps 2 and 4.*

9 *Fold the bottom corner E backwards and forwards along a diagonal line to make a flexible crease, as shown.*

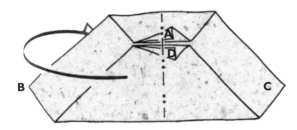

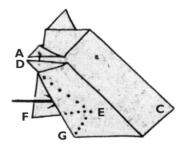

6 *Fold in half, taking B round the back to lie behind C. Do not flatten A and D—let them spring forward.*

10 *Moving B and C slightly apart, press E inwards between F and G, forming a reverse fold along the creases made in Step 9.*

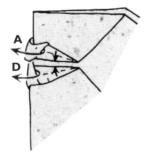

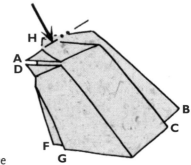

7 *Pull A and D to the left to make sloping creases like those made in Step 5.*

11 *Push in H to form a reverse fold, which blunts the chick's head.*

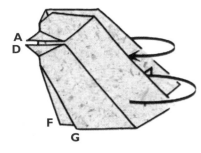

12 *Curl the tail-end of the chick by rolling the ends around a pencil to give it a rounded shape and to finish it off.*

13 *The completed Chick.*

PRACTICAL AND FUN

4

One of the best things about origami is that the items you can
create can have either a practical or decorative purpose—
sometimes both! The projects that follow show origami and its
diverse, creative best.

SUN HAT

No party is complete without a party hat; but on this model the visor gives good protection from the sun, so it has a practical use both in and out of doors.

> **PAPER**
> A sheet of medium-weight paper, proportioned 5:8.
> For a child's head, use a sheet 10 x 16 in. (25 x 40 cm).

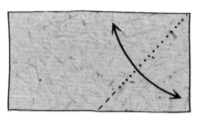

1   *Bring the bottom right-hand corner up to the top edge, in such a way that if a crease was made it would start at the top-right corner. However, do not make a crease; instead, make a short pinch at the bottom edge.*

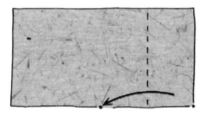

2   *Fold the bottom corner to the pinch.*

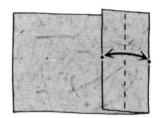

3   *Fold the flap in half. Unfold.*

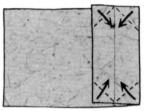

4   *Turn in the corners to the center crease in the flap.*

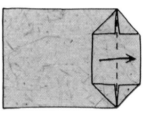

5   *Fold the flap in half, left to right, creating a pocket.*

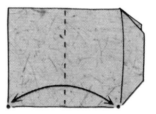

6   *Fold the bottom-left corner to the edge of the pocket. Unfold.*

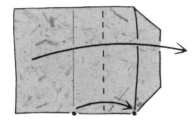

7 Fold the Step 6 crease to the edge of the pocket.

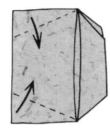

10 Turn in the corners a little. Note the gash between A and B.

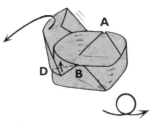

13 . . . like this. Swivel the visor out and to the left, and crease DB (repeat at back) to hold the visor in place. If the angle of the visor is too high or too low, re-crease Step 11 in another position. Turn over.

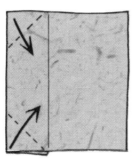

8 Turn in the corners to the Step 6 crease.

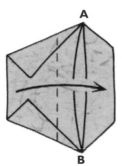

11 Fold the loose flap across to the right.

14 The Sun Hat is complete.

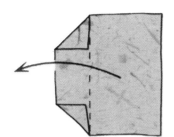

9 Fold the loose flap back to the left.

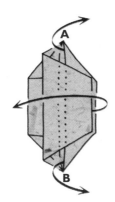

12 Lift up the top flap and open out the gash between A and B, creating a box form . . .

DISH

The Dish is unique in origami: it is the only known circular design. What's more, the final shape is very attractive and the opening-out moves in Steps 11-12 are particularly satisfying. Use a 6-8 in. (15-20 cm) square of paper. If you wish to add an interesting decorative effect to this design, use a paper differently colored on its two sides.

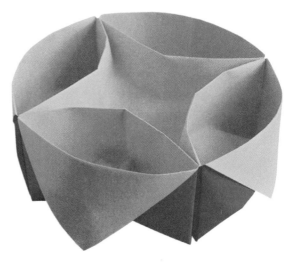

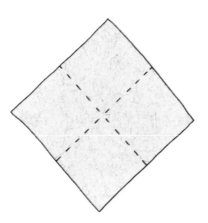

1   *Valley-fold in half horizontally and vertically, to make four squares. Unfold each crease.*

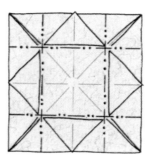

3   *Fold the corners to the center.*

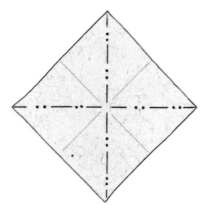

2   *Mountain-fold each diagonal. Unfold.*

4   *Fold the corners back out to the edge.*

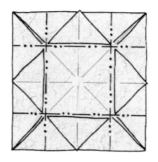

5 *Crease and unfold four mountain folds as shown. (It is probably easier to make valley folds by turning the paper over.)*

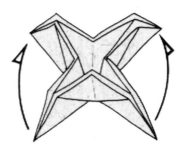

8 *...like this. Note the X shape of the paper. Flatten the X shape with two points to either side.*

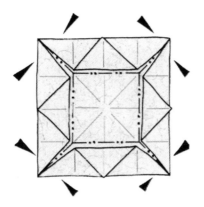

6 *Make short mountain diagonals. Pinch the edges near the corners ...*

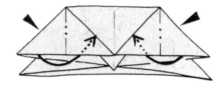

9 *Reverse-fold the front corners inside.*

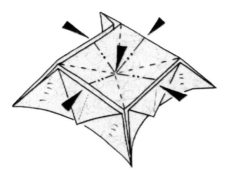

7 *... to raise a table shape in the center and make the paper 3D. Push down on the center point whilst pushing the edges of the "table" towards the center ...*

10 *Repeat behind.*

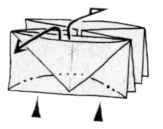

11 *Push the bottom edge upwards with a curved crease, so that the top edges of the pocket separate in a curved shape.*

13 *The Dish is complete. Neaten the interior edges to make an attractive star-shaped central pocket.*

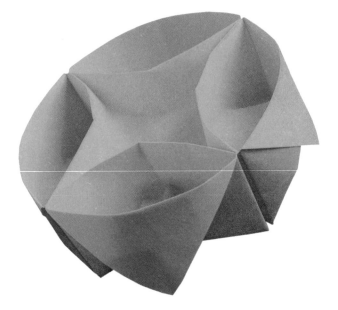

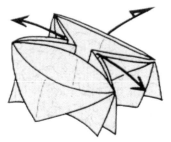

12 *This is the result. Repeat on the other three sides.*

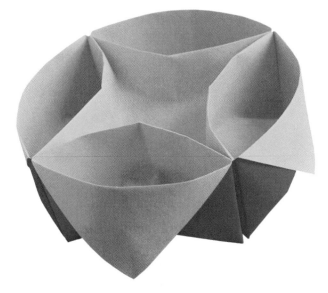

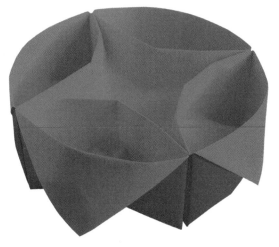

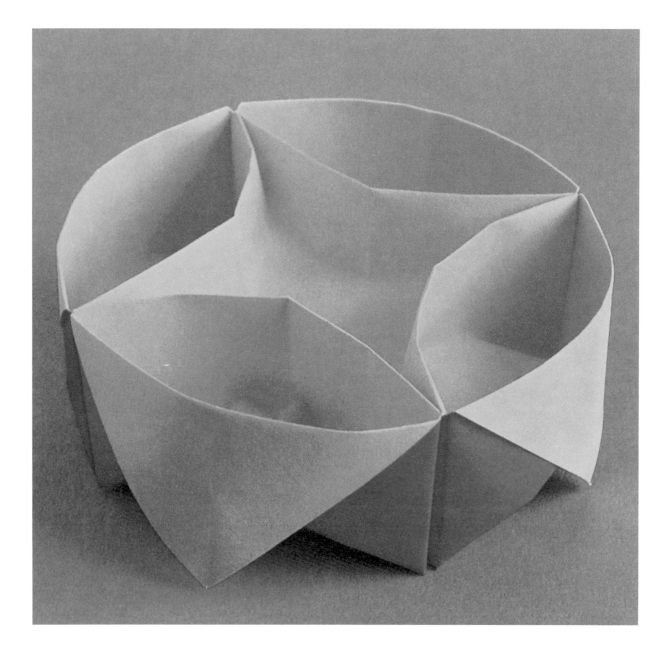

MASK

The biggest problem that faces you when designing an origami mask is in creating holes for the eyes without having to resort to scissors. One clever solution is to use a strip of paper for folding, as in this case. Using this strip-folding technique, a whole range of diverse mask designs can be created. Try some of your own and decorate them to suit different occasions.

PAPER
Use a strip of lightweight paper, proportioned 6:1; 24 x 4 in. (60 x 10 cm) for adults and 18 x 3 in. (45 x 7.5 cm) for children, are good average sizes.

OTHER EQUIPMENT
adhesive tape; length of elastic cord.

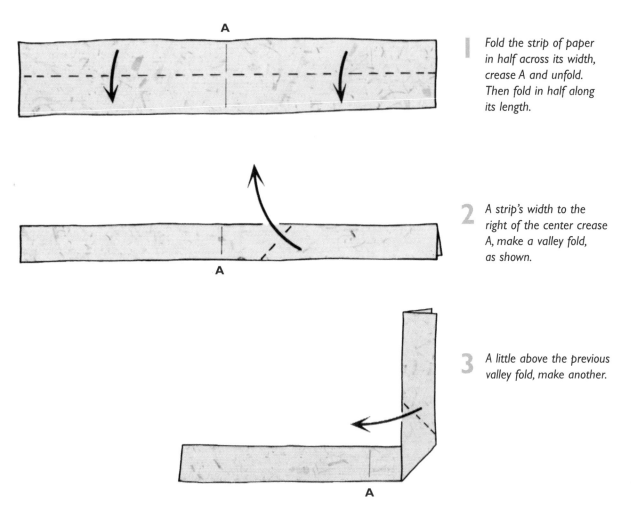

1 *Fold the strip of paper in half across its width, crease A and unfold. Then fold in half along its length.*

2 *A strip's width to the right of the center crease A, make a valley fold, as shown.*

3 *A little above the previous valley fold, make another.*

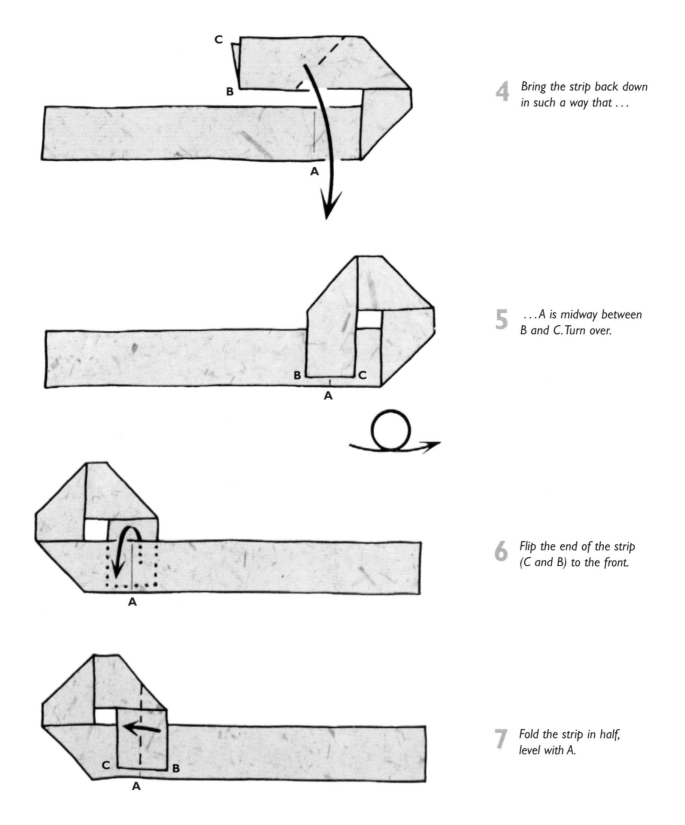

4 *Bring the strip back down in such a way that . . .*

5 *. . . A is midway between B and C. Turn over.*

6 *Flip the end of the strip (C and B) to the front.*

7 *Fold the strip in half, level with A.*

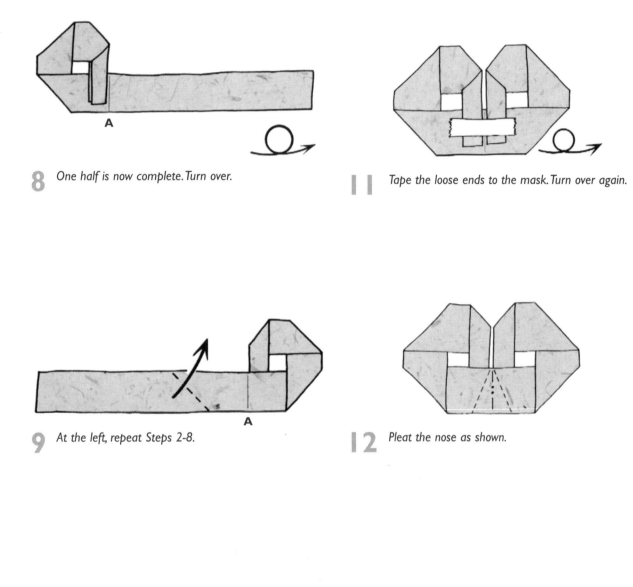

8 *One half is now complete. Turn over.*

9 *At the left, repeat Steps 2-8.*

10 *Turn over.*

11 *Tape the loose ends to the mask. Turn over again.*

12 *Pleat the nose as shown.*

13 *Fold down the top edges, creating eyebrows.*

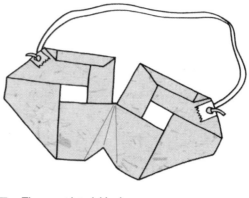

14 *Add sticky tape as shown. To create enough strength to hold the elastic without tearing, tape a few layers over each other. Pierce the tape and feed the elastic through. Tie the ends to the mask, leaving enough elastic between the knots to hold the mask to your head.*

15 *The completed Mask.*

CUBE

The creator of the Cube, Shuzo Fujimoto (Japan) has conducted a great deal of research into the geometry of folding, including important discoveries about how to fold accurate polygons (pentagons, hexagons, and so on) from a square; how to divide an edge into accurate thirds, fifths, etc., without "guesstimating;" and how to fold a one-piece solid such as a tetrahedron or anicosahedron. If all this sounds rather dry (it isn't!), just enjoy folding his Cube. In particular, enjoy Step 5—surely one of the "best moves" in all origami. Use a 6-8 in. (15-20 cm) square of thin or medium-weight paper.

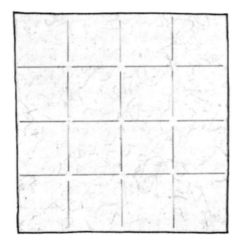

1   *Carefully divide the paper into quarters, horizontally and vertically, to create 16 squares.*

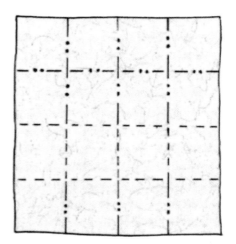

2   *Re-crease the creases to look like the pattern of mountains and valleys shown here.*

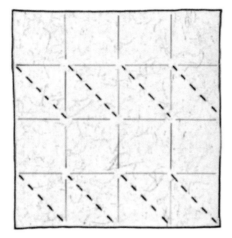

3 *Add eight short diagonals. Be precise.*

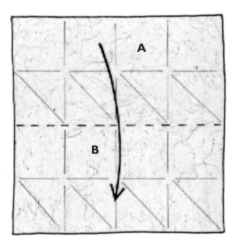

4 *Fold in half. Note squares A and B.*

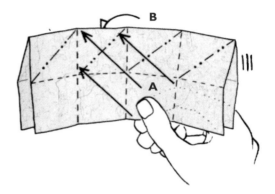

5 *Hold as shown. Note square A at the front and B behind. Slide A up and to the left, so it exactly covers B. The paper will then curl into a cube form. All the marked creases must form cleanly and simultaneously.*

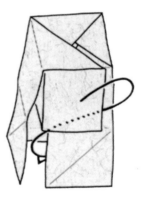

6 *Tuck the front square inside to lock the top.*

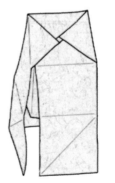

7 *Turn over.*

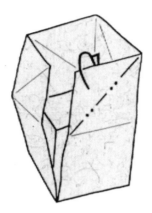

8 *Fold in the corner.*

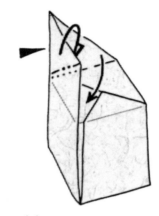

11 *. . . and the next.*

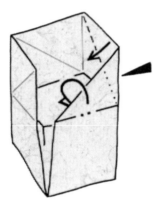

9 *Push in the next corner to form part of the lid.*

12 *Tuck the triangle inside the cube to lock the top.*

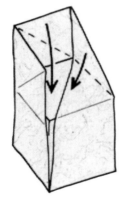

10 *Push in the next corner . . .*

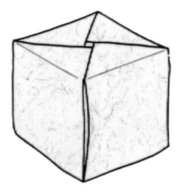

13 *The Cube is complete.*

WITCH ON A BROOMSTICK

Although simple in its final appearance, this model is tricky to fold. The secret is to make the early folds very accurate so that it collapses into shape without difficulty.

The Witch on a Broomstick is ideal for suspending from the ceiling. Make a whole coven to accompany a Man in the Moon (see p.175) and a haunting of Ghosts (see p.195) for a suitably eerie Hallowe'en celebration.

PAPER
Use a 6-8 in. (15-20 cm) square of lightweight paper, white or colored on one side and black on the reverse.

OTHER EQUIPMENT
To suspend the model you will need a needle and thread.

SPECIAL NOTE
Reverse folds (see Steps 7 and 8) are explained in detail in the section on Folding Techniques (see Introduction).

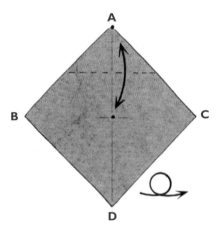

1 *Black side up, fold B to C, crease and unfold. Then fold A to D and pinch in the middle to find the center point of the square—unfold. Fold A to the center mark. Unfold. Turn over.*

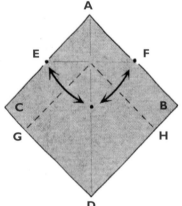

2 *White or colored side up, fold E to the center mark, creasing only from G to crease EF. Unfold. Repeat with F, creasing from H to crease EF. Unfold.*

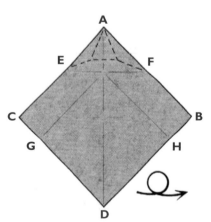

3 *Make five short, separate creases on triangle AFE. Turn over.*

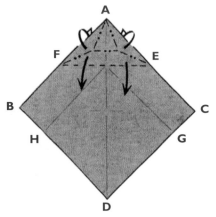

4 *Fold down crease FE, neatly collapsing all of the Step 5 creases . . .*

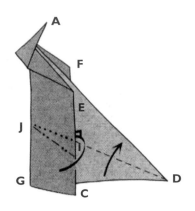

7 *Refold the Step 6 crease, but reversing the short crease JI to a mountain, pushing G up behind E. This is a reverse fold. Repeat behind.*

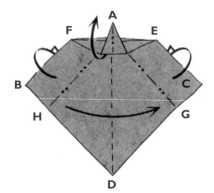

5 *. . . like this. Collapse the paper in half by lifting the triangle below A, folding edges BF and CE behind and swinging H across to G. Look at Step 6.*

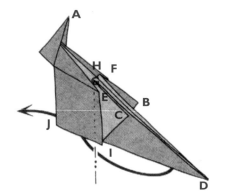

8 *Reverse-fold D, so the crease begins at G and is behind the C flap. Edge GD reverses to touch corner J . . .*

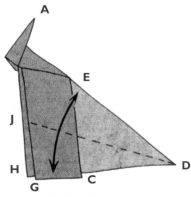

6 *Fold edge GD to edge ED. Unfold. Repeat behind.*

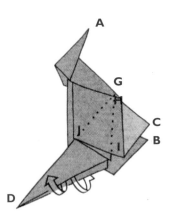

9 *. . . like this. Turn the layers on triangle D inside-out, so the triangle (broomstick) turns from black to white (or colored). For this open out the paper back to Step 5.*

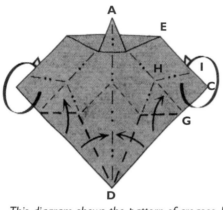

10 *This diagram shows the pattern of creases. Refold the creases shown by a heavy dash from mountain to valley creases—all other creases remain the same. Collapse back to result in Step 11.*

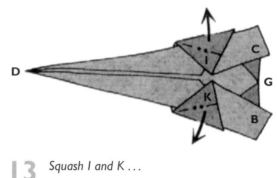

13 *Squash I and K . . .*

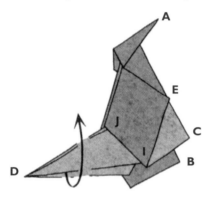

11 *Open out triangle D and view from below.*

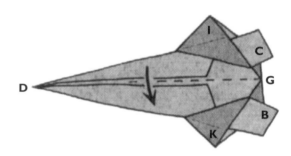

14 *. . . like this. Fold in half to resemble Step 10.*

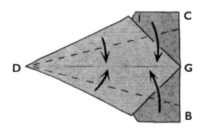

12 *Narrow triangle D, folding into the crease DG, taking B and C in with the white edge.*

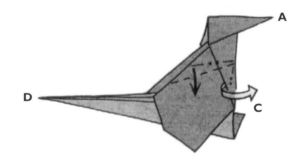

15 *Crimp across the body to form the arms, allowing the extra layer at the witch's spine to swivel backwards to create a hunched back.*

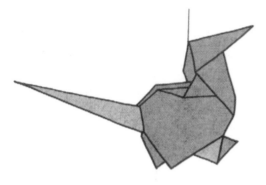

16 *The completed Witch on a Broomstick. To suspend, attach a loop to the witch's hat (experiment to find the best position to balance the model) with a needle and thread.*

STRETCH WALL

The basic grid made in Step 6 can, with the addition of diagonal creases, be collapsed into any number of geometric patterns, some very complex. This design by Yoshihide Momotani of Japan is one of the most astonishing, being elastic—that is, it can expand and collapse. Also, whereas the front is a horizontal pattern of bricks, the reverse shows the same pattern, but vertically! The design is not difficult to follow, but it is time-consuming, so patience is needed when making this. Fold the grid very carefully and the later folds will fall into place. The final "unpicking" of the edges in Steps 18-20 is a very pretty and dramatic conclusion. Use a sheet of thin or medium-weight paper at least 8 in. (20 cm) square.

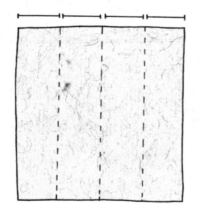

1   *Crease accurate quarters, all valleys.*

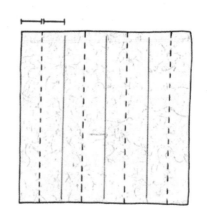

2   *Crease accurate eighths, all valleys.*

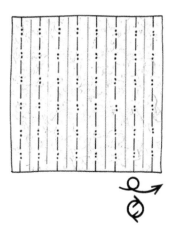

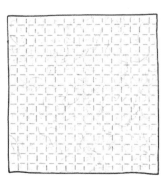

6 ... to make this grid.

3 *Place mountains midway between the valleys. Turn over and rotate the paper.*

4 *Check that the top crease is a valley (if it isn't, turn the paper over so that it is).*

7 *Make pleats where shown ...*

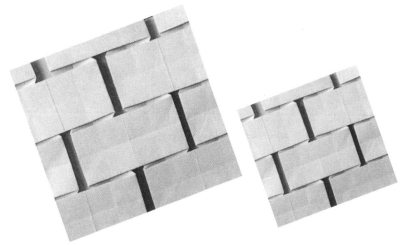

5 *Repeat Steps 1-3, creasing valleys as quarters and eighths, then mountains in between ...*

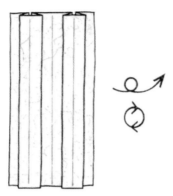

8   *... like this. Turn the paper over and rotate.*

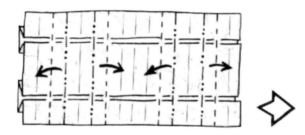

9   *Pleat again.*

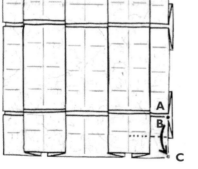

10   *The pleats are complete. Note A B and C. Fold dot to dot, so the lower pleat swivels downwards . . .*

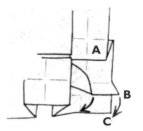

11   *... like this. Note the diagonal crease that has to be made beneath the vertical pleat to accommodate the swivel.*

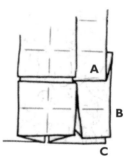

12   *The swivel and hidden diagonal creases are complete.*

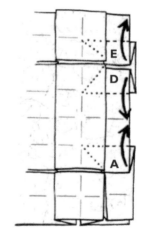

13   *Repeat the swivel with A D and E.*

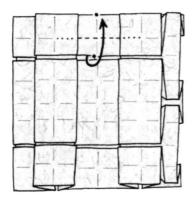

14 *Repeat down the center, swivelling the pleat upwards to lie level with the top edge.*

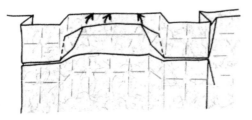

15 *As before, diagonal creases need to be made beneath the vertical pleats, this time one at each end of the swivel.*

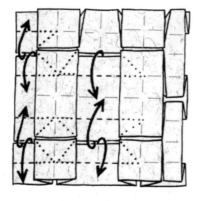

16 *The swivel is done. Repeat three more times down the center, and four times down the left-hand edge.*

17 *The swivels are complete. Turn over.*

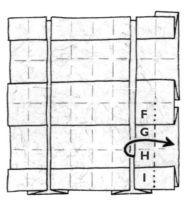

18 *Note FG and HI. Fold edge GH across to the right, so that G separates from F and H separates from I . . .*

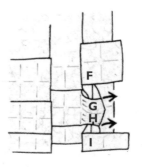

19 *. . . like this. Pull out the paper beneath F and I, so that edge GH can flatten to the right . . .*

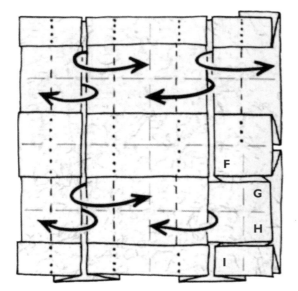

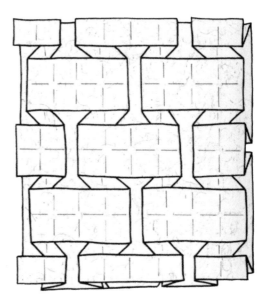

20 . . . like this. Repeat, unbuttoning more edges to reveal a regular brick pattern.

21 The Stretch Wall is complete. Hold opposite edges and pull apart to open the bricks.

MAN IN THE MOON

This design looks very attractive on a greetings card or as a hanging decoration, suspended on a length of thread. Watch out, though—you must make the reverse folds very carefully or the proportions of the face will distort.

PAPER
Use a 6-10 in. (15-25 cm) square of light- or medium-weight paper.

OTHER EQUIPMENT
To suspend the model you will need a needle and thread.

SPECIAL NOTE
Reverse folds (see Steps 6, 7, and 11) are explained in detail in the section on Folding Techniques (see Introduction).

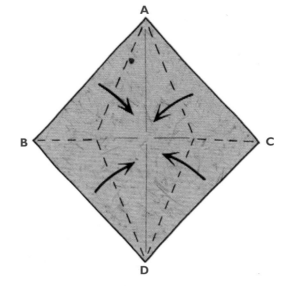

 Crease BC as a valley and AD as a mountain. Unfold both.

2 *Fold edges AB and AC to crease AD, creasing down from A only as far as crease BC. Repeat on the bottom half, folding DB and DC to crease AD and creasing from D up as far as BC. Crease from this intersection to B and C, collapsing the paper . . .*

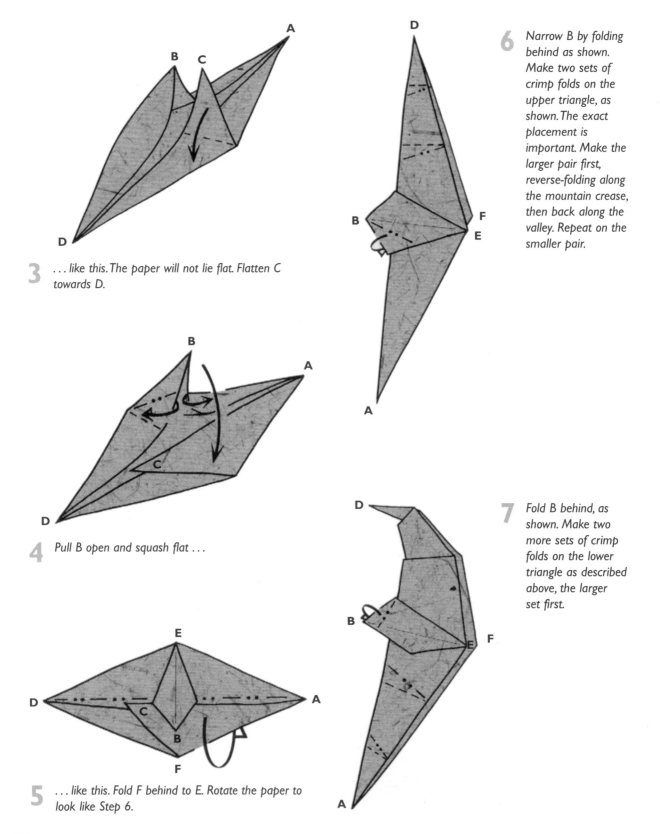

3 ... like this. The paper will not lie flat. Flatten C towards D.

4 Pull B open and squash flat ...

5 ... like this. Fold F behind to E. Rotate the paper to look like Step 6.

6 *Narrow B by folding behind as shown. Make two sets of crimp folds on the upper triangle, as shown. The exact placement is important. Make the larger pair first, reverse-folding along the mountain crease, then back along the valley. Repeat on the smaller pair.*

7 *Fold B behind, as shown. Make two more sets of crimp folds on the lower triangle as described above, the larger set first.*

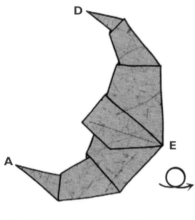

8 *The crimps are complete. Turn over.*

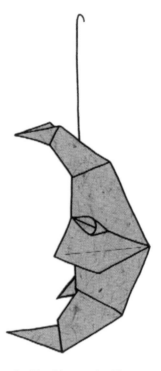

11 *Pull out corner G with a reverse fold, so that G becomes visible above edge HI.*

14 *The Man in the Moon is complete. To suspend the model, attach a loop to the top with needle and thread.*

9 *Pleat C as shown, so that it creates . . .*

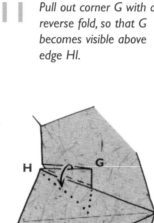

12 *Pull down the top layer of edge HG, partly squashing G open to form an eye . . .*

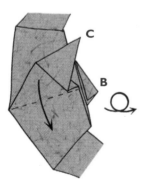

10 *. . . this shape. Fold C downwards. Turn over.*

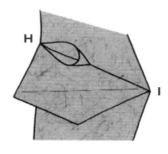

13 *. . . like this.*

INCENSE BURNER

The Reverend Philip Shen (Hong Kong) specializes in creating geometric designs that collapse into shape from a carefully laid-out pattern of pre-creases. The Incense Burner is one of his finest designs, particularly because the final shape is conjured from a very familiar pattern of pre-creases—the kite shape in Step 2 is known to all paper-folders, yet simply to repeat it on each corner and add the central star shape is enough to create a beautiful design. It just goes to show that the simplest designs are often the most elegant. Use a 6-10 in. (15-25 cm) square of medium-weight paper.

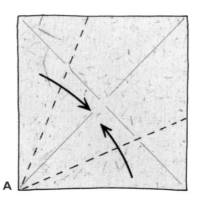

1 *Fold the two edges meeting at A to the center crease.*

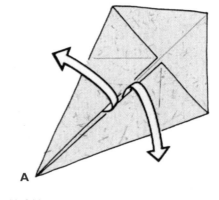

2 *Unfold.*

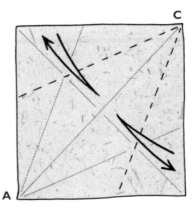

3 *Repeat with the other two edges meeting at C.*

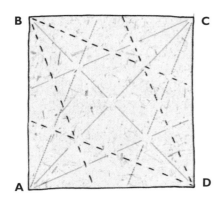

4 Repeat with the two edges meeting at B, then those meeting at D.

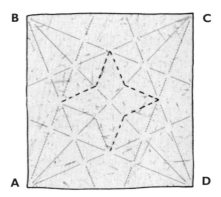

7 Repeat with B C and D, making 6 more short creases.

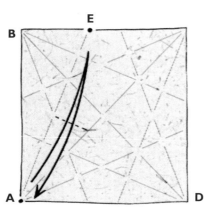

5 Fold A to E, E being at the end of the upper crease made in Step 1. Crease only where shown.

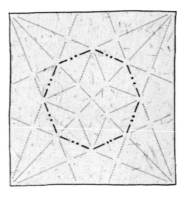

8 Re-crease the octagon with mountain creases.

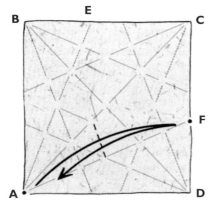

6 Repeat, folding A to F, F being at the end of the lower crease made in Step 1.

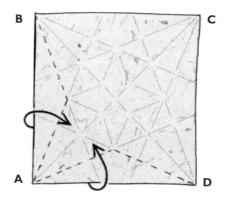

9 Fold in the creases as shown.

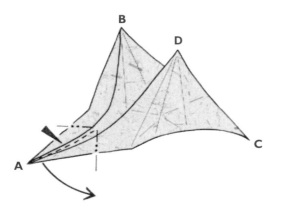

10 *Reverse A along existing creases . . .*

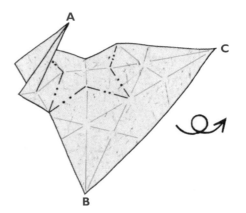

12 *Strengthen the inner star shape with mountain creases. Turn back over and repeat Steps 9-11 with B C and D, forming three more legs.*

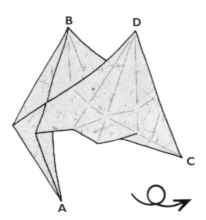

11 *. . . like this. Turn over.*

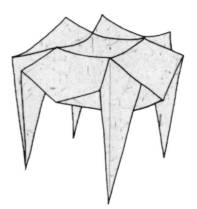

13 *The Incense Burner is complete.*

EGG BASKET

This basket has clean lines and is very strongly locked together. It is ideal for displaying eggs at Easter, but can be used all year-round as a presentation or storage bowl for all kinds of things. Made with strong paper, it lasts a surprisingly long time.

PAPER

Use heavyweight paper, 10-15 in. (25-38 cm) square. For a very sturdy basket, use thick artist's paper—Ingres or watercolor paper—and employ the "wet folding" process explained in the section on Papers (see Introduction).

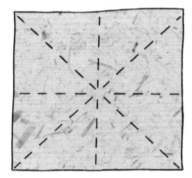

1 *Crease as shown—horizontally, vertically and diagonally, making sure that all creases are valleys.*

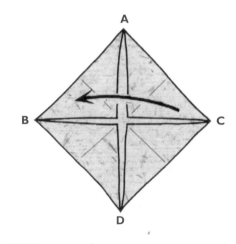

2 *Fold the corners into the middle.*

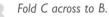

3 *Fold C across to B.*

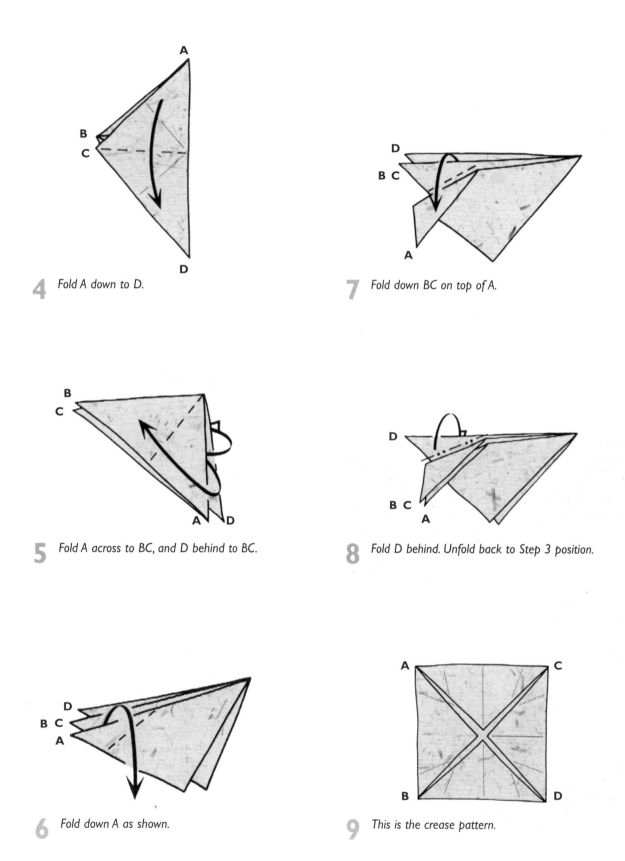

4 Fold A down to D.

7 Fold down BC on top of A.

5 Fold A across to BC, and D behind to BC.

8 Fold D behind. Unfold back to Step 3 position.

6 Fold down A as shown.

9 This is the crease pattern.

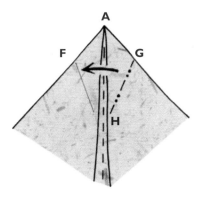

10 *The crease that runs to corner A should be a valley and the short crease from G to H, a mountain. If not, crease them . . .*

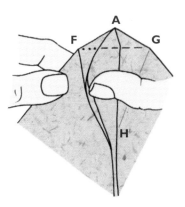

13 *Open up the paper on the left as shown, along the valley crease between F and H. Corner A will lift towards you.*

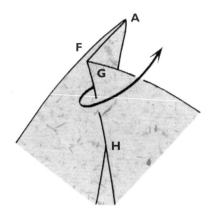

11 *. . . folding G across to F. Unfold.*

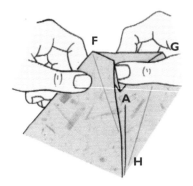

14 *Continue to open up the paper, letting A rise until it collapses down between the layers on the left, in an asymmetric way.*

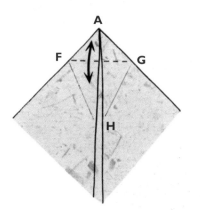

12 *Crease and unfold a valley fold between F and G.*

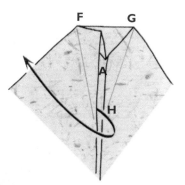

15 *Lift up the whole of the single layer of paper left of center, but letting A remain collapsed down.*

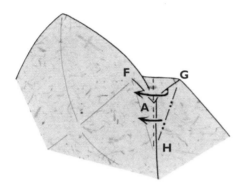

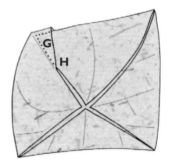

16 *As in Step 10, re-crease along AH and GH, bringing G across to F, on top of A.*

18 *This neatly locks the paper into a tight, slightly rounded corner. Repeat Steps 10-18 on the other three corners.*

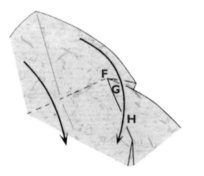

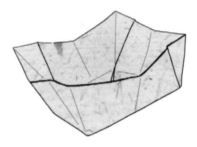

17 *Lower the single layer on the left back to its position in Step 15, but folding it down in front of G—trapping G between the layers.*

19 *The completed Egg Basket.*

SAMPAN

This design has a remarkable climax when, at Steps 10-12, the entire shape is turned inside-out to suddenly reveal the completed Sampan. A few other origami designs contain inversions to part of their structure, but none to this extent. A simpler variation is to regard Step 5 as a flat, uncreased square, then to proceed as diagrammed, but omitting Step 13 to create a boat without a canopy. Use a 6-8 in. (15-20 cm) square of paper with different colors on the two sides. Begin by creasing both diagonals, then folding a pair of opposite corners to the middle.

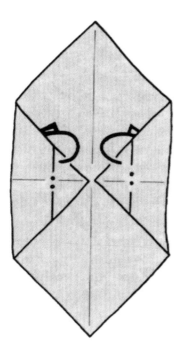

1 *Tuck the corners inside.*

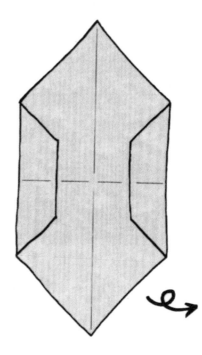

2 *Turn over.*

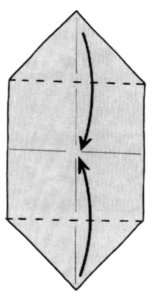

3 *Fold the remaining corners to the center.*

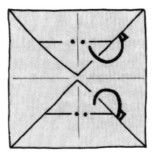

4 *Similarly, tuck these corners inside.*

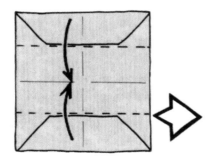

5 *Fold the top and bottom edges to the center.*

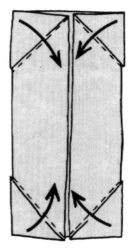

6 *Turn in the triangles.*

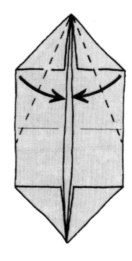

7 *Narrow one end, then . . .*

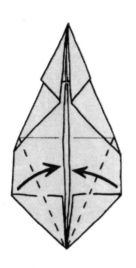

8 *. . . narrow the other.*

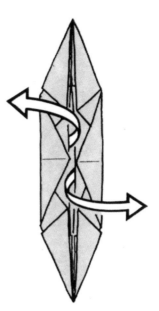

10 *Pull the side layers right apart to expose a clean base . . .*

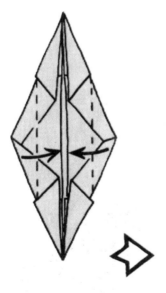

9 *Fold the side corners to the center.*

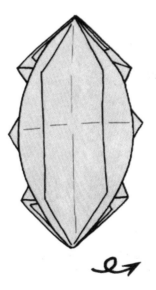

11 *. . . like this. Keep the layers pressed together. Turn over.*

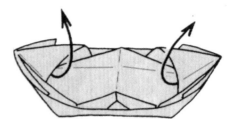

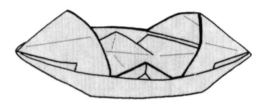

13   *. . . like this. Lift up the canopies.*

12   *The arrowed corners point towards you. Push them down with considerable force, so that they invert backwards and the Sampan turns inside-out . . .*

14   *The Sampan is complete.*

FACE

Many liberties can be taken with the shape of a face before it becomes unrecognizable, which is why origami faces are a particularly interesting subject for creative paper folders. Not all the features need be present in order to convey the idea of a face. This design by Steven Casey (Australia), for example, does not have a mouth. Other designs may only have a nose, or just the hair, or may be extraordinarily detailed, even sculpted-looking. The shapes for this face are strong and harmonious, and the sequence is clean and flowing. Use a 6-8 in. (15-20 cm) square of paper with different colors on the two sides.

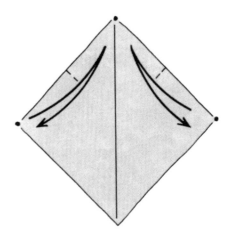

1 Fold the top corner to the left and right corners in turn, pinching the midpoints of the top edges.

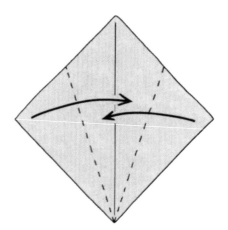

2 Make creases that connect each midpoint with the bottom corner, folding the left and right corners across the middle.

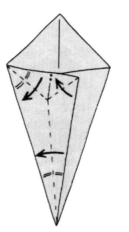

3 Make creases to bisect each of the three angles on the triangular flap, so that the flap collapses to look like Step 4. Repeat on the right.

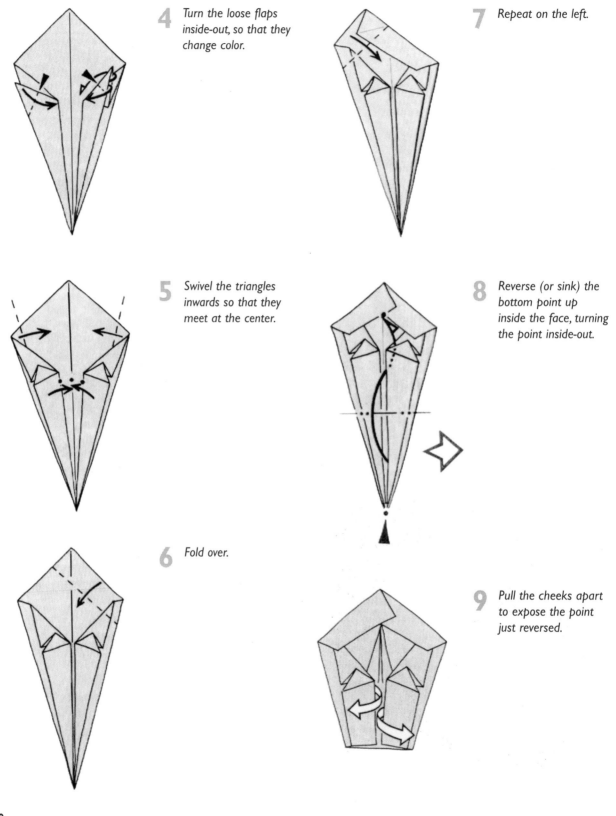

4 Turn the loose flaps inside-out, so that they change color.

7 Repeat on the left.

5 Swivel the triangles inwards so that they meet at the center.

8 Reverse (or sink) the bottom point up inside the face, turning the point inside-out.

6 Fold over.

9 Pull the cheeks apart to expose the point just reversed.

10 *Form three creases as shown, to make the point stand upright . . .*

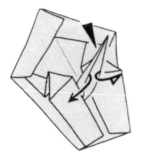

11 *. . . like this. Squash it flat.*

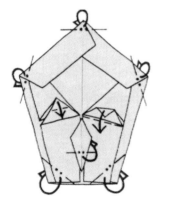

12 *On the left, fold down the loose point of the eye to look like the eye drawn on the other side of the face; then fold it downwards. Blunt the nose. Round off the chin and hair.*

13 *The Face is complete.*

ROSETTE

Another design by the author. The idea is a development from a known fan lock, but here done twice between Steps 7-10, once either side of the center. The result is Step 11, which was then found to "snap" open obligingly to hold a satisfying circular shape under tension. For storage it can be collapsed flat back to Step 10! Use an rectangle of medium-weight paper, twice as long as it is wide—for instance 4 x 8 in. (10 x 20 cm).

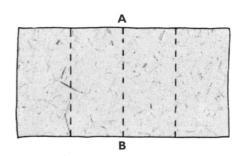

1 *Valley-fold into quarters. Note A and B.*

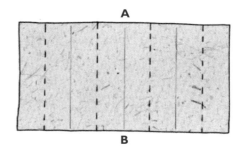

2 *Valley-fold into eighths.*

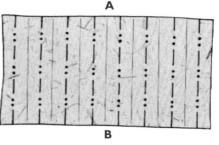

3 *Place mountains between the valleys, so that . . .*

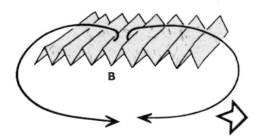

4 ... the folds concertina together. Unfold the central crease AB.

7 Fold in half. Note CD.

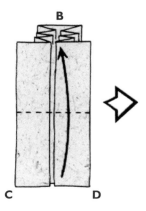

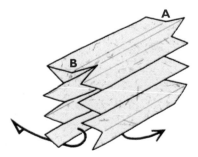

5 Unfold the first crease at each end of the pleats ...

8 Allow the pleats to cascade open between A and B, but hold the central layers flat at C and D. At the right, turn in the corners with valley folds; and at the left, with mountain folds.

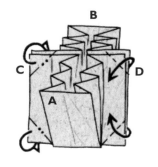

9 At the right, valley the projecting pleat into the line of pleats. At the left, do the same, but with a mountain fold.

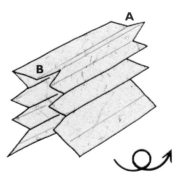

6 ... like this. Squash the pleats flat. Turn over.

10 Spread AB apart.

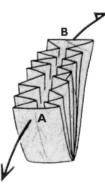

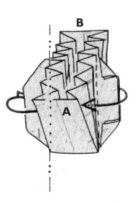

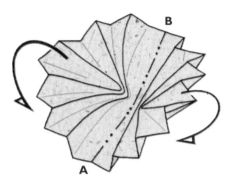

11 *Make a straight mountain fold connecting AEB. This will "snap" the rosette into its final shape. Be forceful!*

12 *The Rosette is complete.*

GHOST

Several Ghosts, of varying sizes, could be suspended on a thread to decorate the home for Hallowe'en, or smaller ones can be used to decorate invitation cards to a "Trick or Treat" party. The drawn eyes are a cheat, perhaps, but there's no doubt that they are a suitably ghoulish effect.

PAPER
Use a square of lightweight white paper; start with a sheet 6-8 in. (15-20 cm) square.

OTHER EQUIPMENT
Marker pen; to suspend the ghost, you will need a needle and thread.

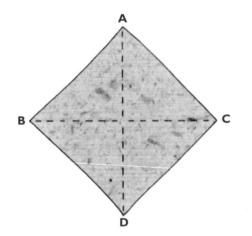

1 *Crease and unfold both diagonals as valleys.*

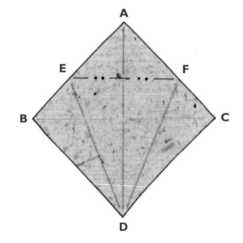
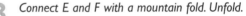

3 *Connect E and F with a mountain fold. Unfold.*

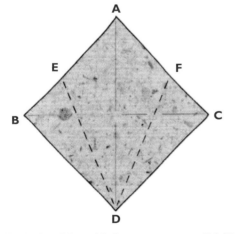

2 *Fold edges DB and DC to center crease DA. Unfold.*

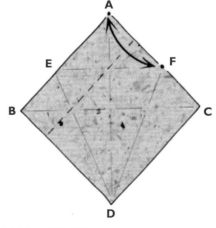

4 *Fold A to F. Unfold.*

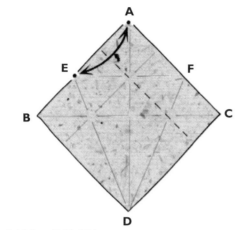

5 *Fold A to E. Unfold.*

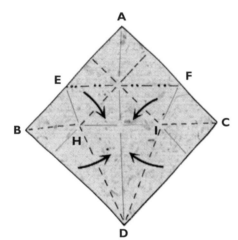

6 *Carefully collapse along the marked creases. Bring E and F into the center. Let A swing down to touch E. Pull B and C downwards. Look at Step 7.*

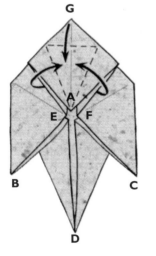

7 *Fold in the diagonal edges above EF to the center crease, then fold down the top corner G on top.*

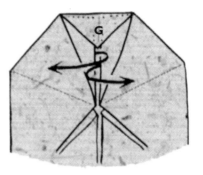

8 *Unfold the side triangles, leaving the top corner folded down.*

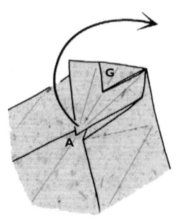

9 *Pick up the single-layer corner A, and swivel it up and over the top edge of the paper . . .*

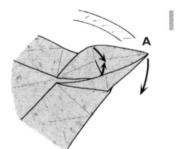

10 *. . . like this. The paper becomes 3-dimensional. Flatten corner A, allowing the sides to collapse inward towards the center crease.*

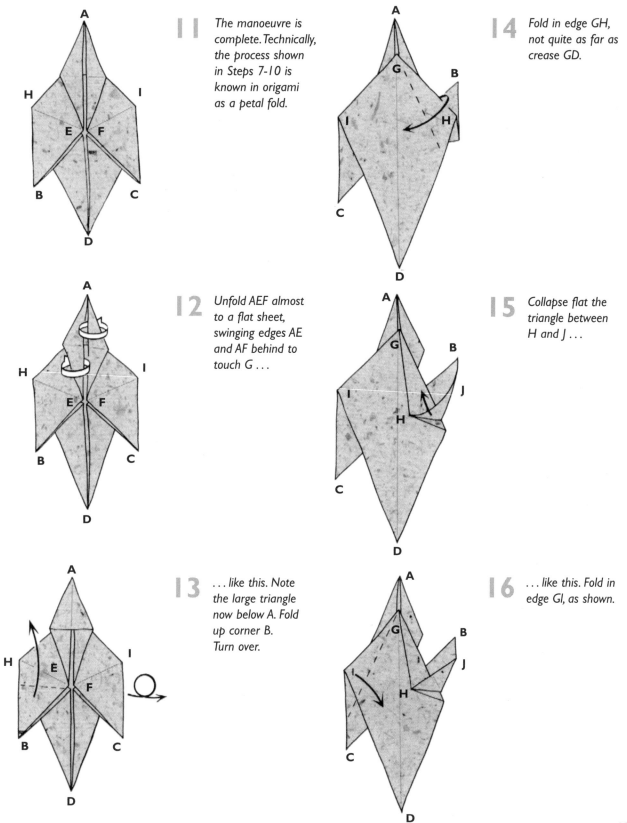

11 The manoeuvre is complete. Technically, the process shown in Steps 7-10 is known in origami as a petal fold.

12 Unfold AEF almost to a flat sheet, swinging edges AE and AF behind to touch G . . .

13 . . . like this. Note the large triangle now below A. Fold up corner B. Turn over.

14 Fold in edge GH, not quite as far as crease GD.

15 Collapse flat the triangle between H and J . . .

16 . . . like this. Fold in edge GI, as shown.

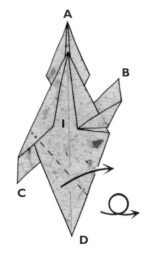

17 *Fold out D to the right. Turn over.*

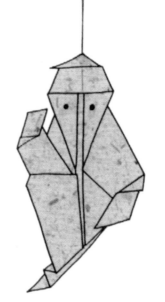

20 *The completed Ghost. Draw in the eyes, as shown, with a marker pen, and suspend using a needle and thread to attach a loop to the ghost's head.*

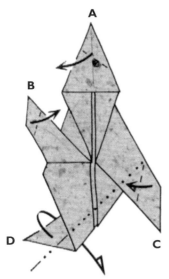

18 *Fold A out to the left. Fold in B and C. Pleat D downwards.*

19 *Narrow A. Pleat D back upwards.*

BOW TIE

Simple to make and fun to wear, the Bow Tie is an ideal way of breaking the ice at parties for all age groups! You can decorate the Bow Tie with some self-adhesive colored shapes—dots or squares, for example—for a truly individual effect.

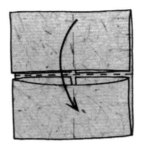

3 *Fold in half across the middle.*

PAPER
Use a good-quality 4-ply paper napkin, or fold two 2-ply napkins together. A single 2-ply napkin will make a floppy bow tie.

OTHER EQUIPMENT
Elastic band, approximate diameter 1½ in. (3½ cm); cord elastic, 12 in. (30 cm) in length. To decorate the bow tie use self-adhesive colored shapes.

4 *The folding is now complete.*

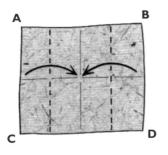

1 *Fold the napkin in half, horizontally and vertically. Unfold. Fold AC and BD to the central vertical crease.*

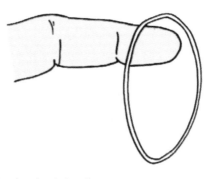

5 *Take the elastic band . . .*

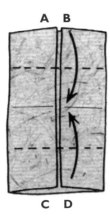

2 *Fold AB and CD to the central horizontal crease.*

6 *. . . and wrap it around a finger three times.*

200

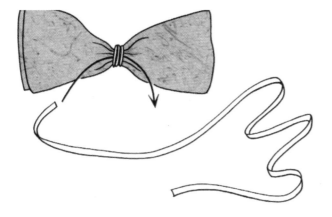

7 *Slip the band on to the bow tie, so that the paper bunches neatly in the middle. Take the length of cord elastic and thread it between the elastic band and the bow tie.*

8 *Tie the ends of the cord elastic together, decorate the front of the bow with self-adhesive colored shapes, if wished, and the Bow Tie is ready to wear.*

JUNK

The sequence of folds to make the Junk (a Chinese sailing boat) is regarded by many experts as the most beautiful in all origami, particularly the transformations in Step 2, Steps 5-7, Steps 13-15, and Steps 19-20. Note how the sequence progresses effortlessly from one step to the next—like notes in a melody or steps in a ballet, topped by the final, extraordinary opening-out climax. Use a 6-8 in. (15-20 cm) square of paper with different colors on the two sides. Begin with Step 1 of the Sampan (see p.185).

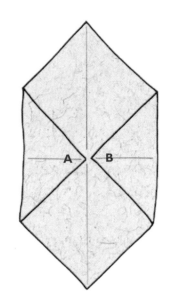

1 *Note A and B. Turn over.*

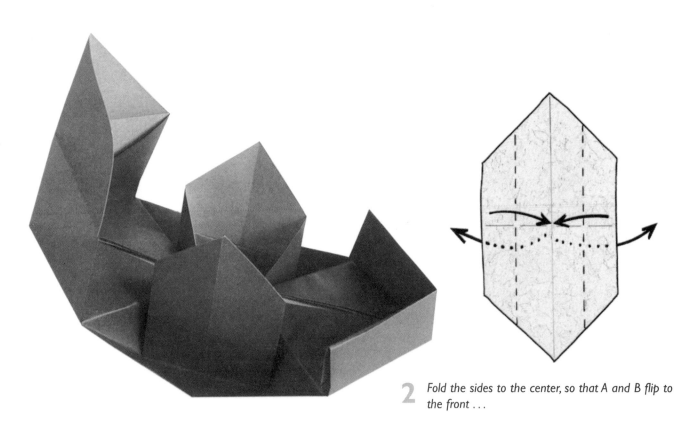

2 *Fold the sides to the center, so that A and B flip to the front . . .*

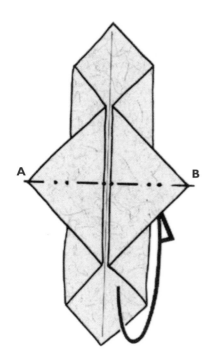

3 *. . . like this. Mountain-fold the lower portion behind.*

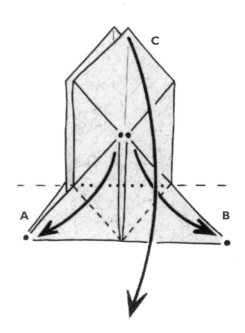

5 *Fold dot to dot, left and right. This will open the slit down the center and swivel C downward by a considerable distance.*

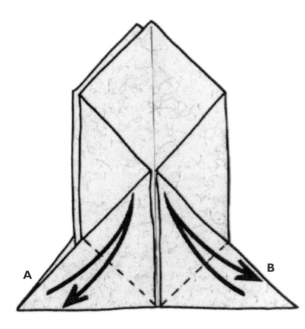

4 *Pre-crease as shown, through all layers.*

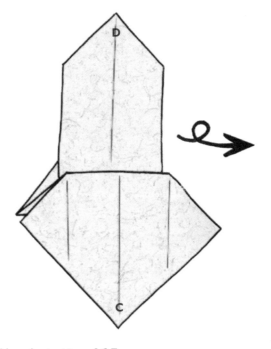

6 *Note the position of C. Turn over.*

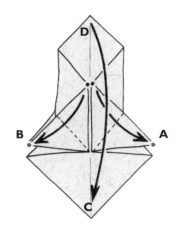

7 *Repeat 4-6 with D.*

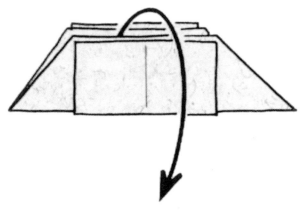

10 *Pull down the front two layers.*

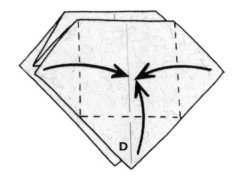

8 *Fold the corners to the center. Repeat behind.*

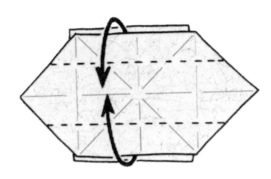

11 *Narrow the top layer.*

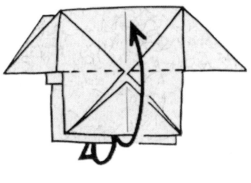

9 *Fold the lower edge up to the top. Repeat behind.*

12 *Turn over.*

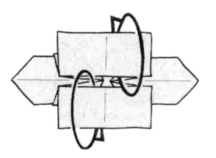

13 *Swivel the top flaps around to the back ...*

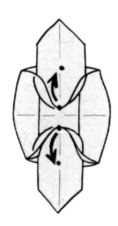

14 *... like this. The paper is now 3D, so flatten it by folding dot to dot.*

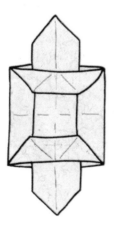

15 *The result is this picture frame, or an intriguing belt-and-buckle illusion. Turn over.*

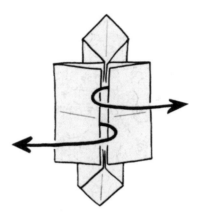

16 *Fold out the side flaps.*

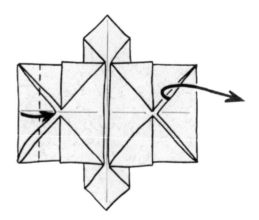

17 *On the left, fold in the edge. On the right, unfold the triangle.*

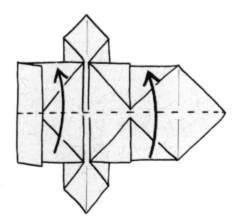

18 *Fold in half, as seen above.*

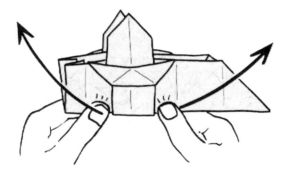

19 *Hold tightly, as shown above. Pull the paper outwards, then upwards—so that the inner layers inside the "belt" are unrolled into view.*

20 *The Junk is complete. Strengthen all the creases.*

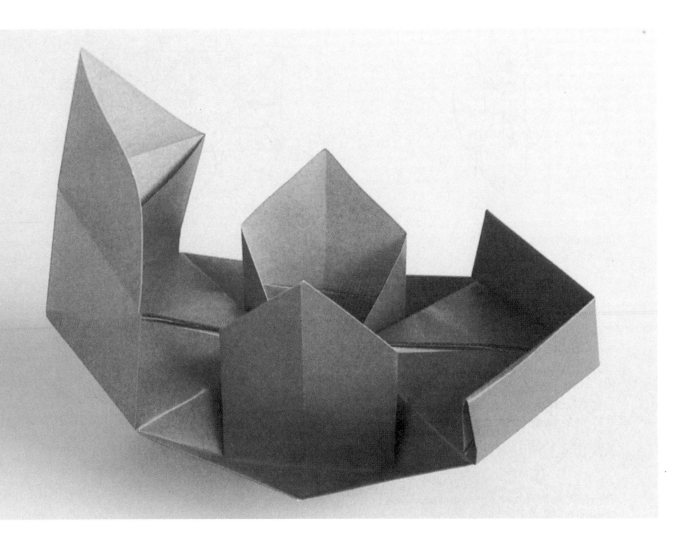

POP-UP DOUBLE CUBE

The late and much-missed Eric Kenneway
(England) specialized in creating designs that
were marvelous to fold, but which when
complete, did not always look too spectacular.
For him, the joy of origami was in the folding,
not the looking; the process rather than the
outcome. His Pop-up Double Cube is perhaps
an extreme example of his thesis—it has a
fine sequence with intriguing moves at Steps
4-6, Step 11 and the climactic opening at
Step 16, but the result looks quite ordinary.
But don't let this deter you from trying it—of
its kind, it is a masterpiece. Use a 6-8 in.
(15-20 cm) square of medium-weight paper.

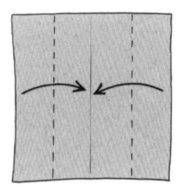

1   *Valley the edges to the center crease.*

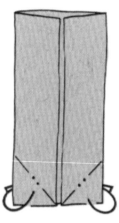

2   *Mountain the bottom corners behind.*

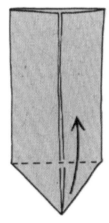

3   *Fold up the triangle.*

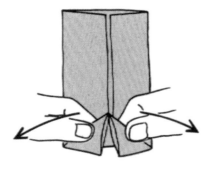

4   *Moisten your fingers for a good grip and hold as shown. Pull the outer layers, sliding them out to the sides . . .*

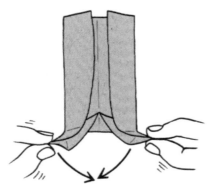

5   *. . . like this. Flatten the paper by bringing the corners together.*

6   *The move is complete. Repeat Steps 2-6 at the top.*

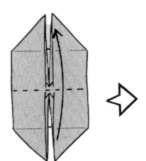

7   *Fold in half.*

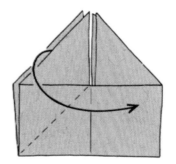

8   *Fold across to the right.*

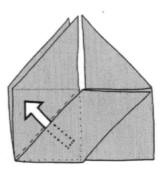

9   *Pull out the hidden corner.*

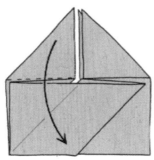

10   *Fold down the triangle.*

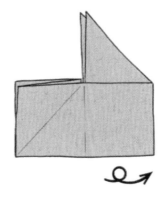

13   *The left side is complete. Turn over.*

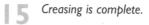

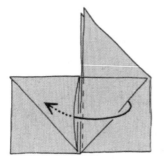

11   *Tuck the loose triangle right into the pocket. Keep it neat.*

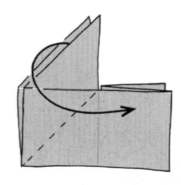

14   *Repeat Steps 7-13 on this side.*

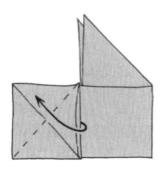

12   *Fold the loose corner up and to the left.*

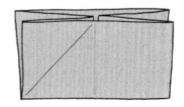

15   *Creasing is complete.*

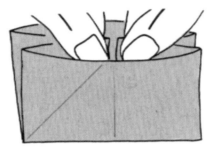

16 *Hold as shown and pull the central flaps upwards and outwards . . .*

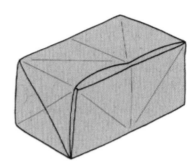

17 *. . . like this, to form the completed Pop-up Double Cube.*

ARCHITECTURAL MODULE

This is not strictly a "modular" design, because there could be several different modules here locking together. The system is very much like a set of children's building blocks, which can be put together in many ways. Make as many as you can, then experiment with them to see what you can make—the photo shows just a few of the possibilities. The system is by Didier Boursin (France). Medium-weight paper with squares of 4 in. (10 cm) will work well for this interesting geometric design.

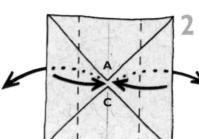

2 Fold the edges to the center crease, allowing corners B and D to flip to the front.

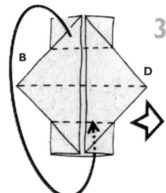

3 Crease three valleys as shown. Tuck the top edge deep inside the pocket at the bottom, locking the module into a triangular shape.

BAR MODULE: END LOCK

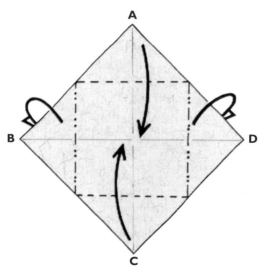

1 Valley corners A and C to the center. Mountain corners B and D behind to the center.

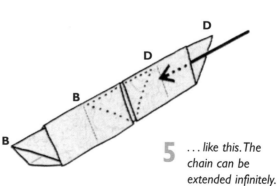

4 The completed module. The protruding triangles can lock into other modules . . .

5 . . . like this. The chain can be extended infinitely.

BAR MODULE: SIDE LOCK

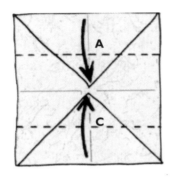

1   *Begin with Step 2 above. Fold the top and bottom edges to the center crease.*

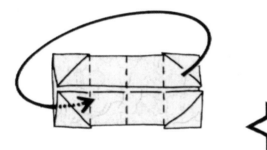

2   *Crease three valleys. Tuck the right-hand edge deep inside the pocket at the left edge, locking the module into a triangular shape. Allow corners B and D to flip out.*

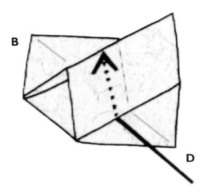

3   *The completed module. The protruding triangles can tuck into other modules . . .*

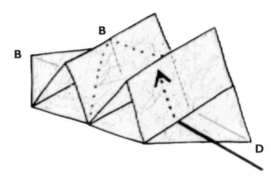

4   *. . . like this. The chain can be extended infinitely.*

BAR MODULE: END AND SIDE LOCKS

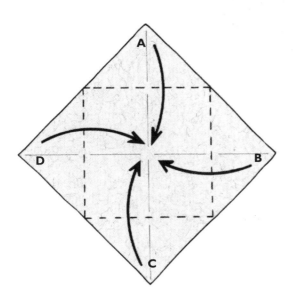

1 *Fold the four corners to the middle.*

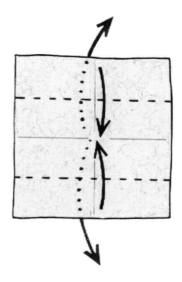

3 *Fold the top and bottom edges to the center crease, allowing corners A and C to flip out.*

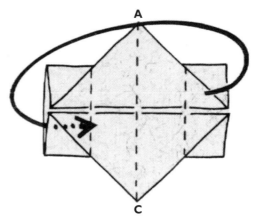

4 *Crease three valleys. Tuck the right edge deep into the pocket to lock the module into a triangular shape.*

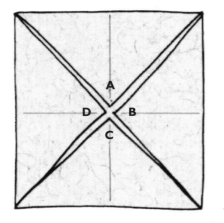

2 *Turn over.*

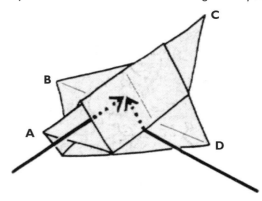

5 *The module is complete. Other modules can interlock at either end or either side, or both.*

FOUR-WAY JUNCTION

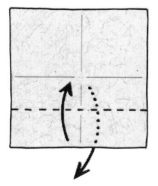

1 Begin with Step 3 of the End and Side Locks module above. Fold the bottom edge to the center crease, allowing C to flip to the front.

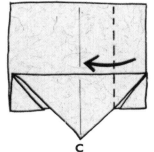

2 Fold the right edge to the center, allowing D to flip to the front.

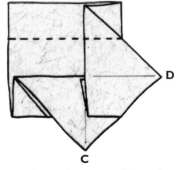

3 Fold the top edge to the center, allowing A to flip to the front.

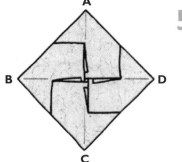

4 Fold the left edge to the center, allowing B to flip to the front. Reverse the bottom section of the crease, so that . . .

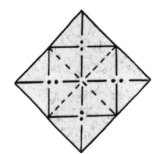

5 . . . the paper is completely symmetrical around the center point. Turn over.

6 Crease and unfold mountains and valleys as shown, allowing the center to rise towards you.

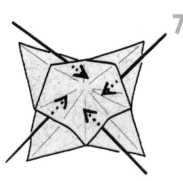

7 The completed module. Each protruding module can interlock with an End Lock module or Corner Junction (shown next).

CORNER JUNCTION

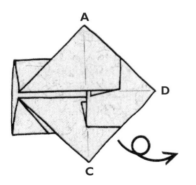

1 Begin with Step 4 of the Four-way Junction module. Turn over.

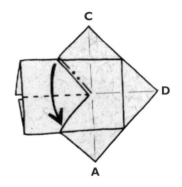

2 Form valley and mountain creases as shown, to make the shape 3D. The center should rise towards you.

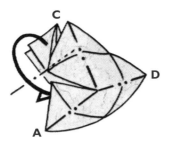

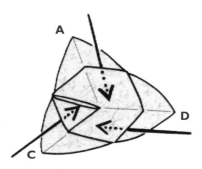

3 *Fold the loose square inside the pyramid. Strengthen the creases that run from the apex to corners A C and D.*

4 *The completed module. Each protruding triangle can interlock with an End Lock module or a Four-way Junction.*

ETERNALLY OPENING ORIGAMI

This design is Step 13 of the Flapping Bird (see p.113) turned upside-down. This fun piece is nothing more than the classic Bird Base, familiar to all experienced folders. What makes it remarkable is that no one until Takuji Sugimura of Japan realized that it could perform the addictive dance described here. The lesson, of course, is never to disregard the familiar—in case it holds a wonderful secret. Use 6-8 in. (15-20 cm) square of paper.

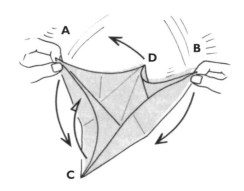

2 *. . . like this. Begin to bring A and B back together below C and D . . .*

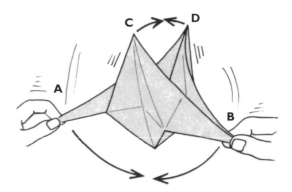

3 *. . . like this. Continue until A and B are together at the bottom.*

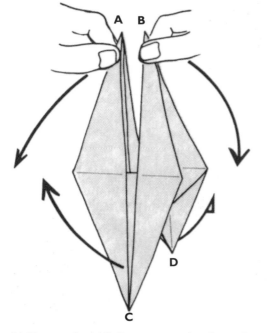

1 *Hold points A and B. Separate your hands, moving them outwards and downwards, allowing C and D to rise . . .*

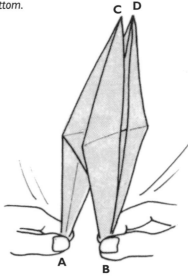

4 *The movement is complete. Strengthen the creases.*

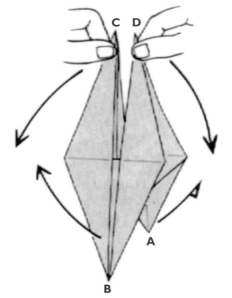

5 *Transfer your hands to C and D and repeat Steps 1-4.*

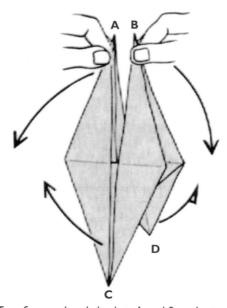

6 *Transfer your hands back to A and B, and repeat and repeat and repeat! Be careful at Step 2 not to pull A and B too far apart, or the paper will "snap" and lock to look like Step 2 of the Daffodil stem on pages 125-126.*

GIFT ENVELOPE

This envelope should not be mailed, but it is an attractive and creative way to present a card delivered by hand. Give it a go the next time you have to give a card to somebody.

PAPER
Use lightweight paper, preferably textured, patterned, or hand-decorated.

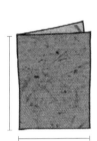

1 Measure the greeting card.

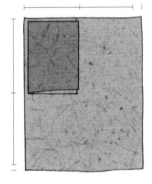

2 Put the card into a corner of the envelope paper. Measure twice the height and twice the width of the card on the paper, then add a little extra. Trim the paper to these dimensions.

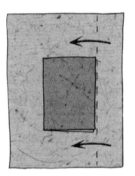

3 Place the card approximately in the center of the paper, square to the edges. Fold in the right-hand edge.

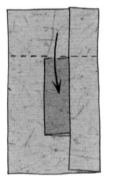

4 Fold down the top edge.

5 Fold in the left edge, as shown.

6 Fold and unfold the bottom edge, as shown.

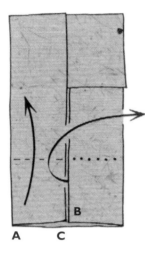

7 *Valley-fold A up the left-hand edge. Open B . . .*

VARIATION

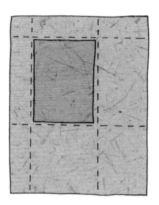

1 *The card can be placed anywhere on the paper at Step 3, even right up into a corner, as shown.*

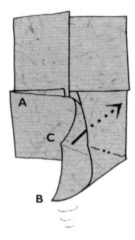

8 *. . . and push C deep inside, making a mountain fold across the bottom.*

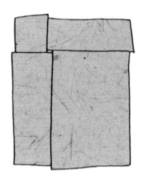

2 *Follow the steps as before to achieve this off-center look.*

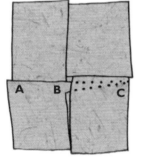

9 *The completed Gift Envelope.*

RIGHT Gift envelopes in an array of sizes, shapes, and colors add a special touch to hand-delivered greetings cards for all occasions.

GIFT BOXES

All the lids in these examples are locked using the same twist technique, but a change in the angle of twist can create surprisingly diverse results. Both lids and boxes must be constructed with great accuracy so that all the edges are parallel, the angles are equal, and the creases are placed with care.

PAPER
Use heavyweight paper or thin card for the boxes and their lids. If you wish to use the "wet folding" process explained in the section on Papers (see Introduction), select heavyweight Ingres or watercolor paper.

OTHER EQUIPMENT
Paper glue; protractor; ruler; pencil.

Above *The completed eight-side gift box (RIGHT). To make six-sided and five-sided boxes (LEFT and CENTER) with flat lids, see instructions overleaf.*

LID

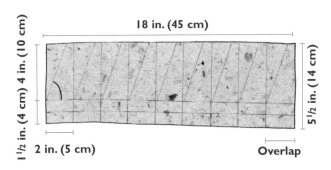

18 in. (45 cm)

1½ in. (4 cm) 4 in. (10 cm)

5½ in. (14 cm)

2 in. (5 cm)   **Overlap**

1 *Carefully measure the outside dimensions of the lid (18 x 5½ in./45 x 14 cm) and cut out the lid as shown. Draw in the positions of the nine panels and pleats and the bottom lip, using the measurements shown. The critical angle of 70° should be accurately made for each pleat.*

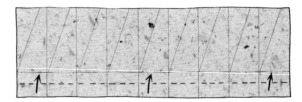

2 *Fold up along the bottom crease.*

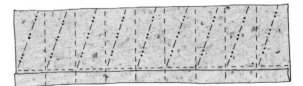

3 *Crease mountains and valleys as shown.*

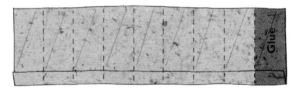

Glue

4 *Reinforce the vertical creases. Apply glue to the right-end panel, and then join it to the back of the left-end panel. This will create an eight-sided sleeve.*

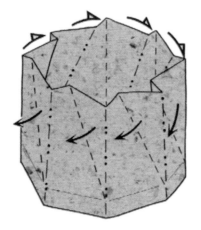

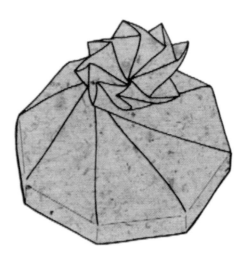

5 *Carefully pleat mountains and valleys as shown. For Step 6 to form, all creases must form at the same time and interlock equally around the middle. It may take a little time to wriggle all the pleats into place, but it will help if the bottom edge is kept as close to a perfect octagon as possible. If it goes out of shape, the locking will become more difficult.*

6 *The lid is complete.*

BOX

15½ in. (39 cm)

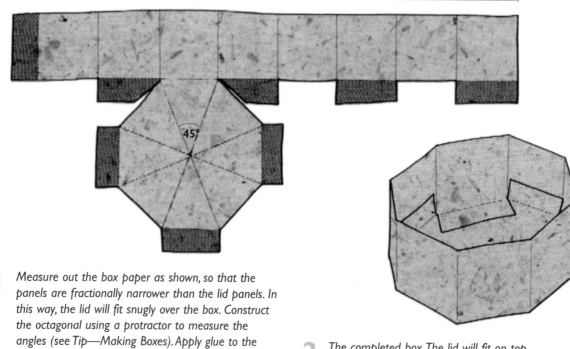

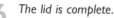

45°

I *Measure out the box paper as shown, so that the panels are fractionally narrower than the lid panels. In this way, the lid will fit snugly over the box. Construct the octagonal using a protractor to measure the angles (see Tip—Making Boxes). Apply glue to the tabs and fold the box into shape.*

2 *The completed box. The lid will fit on top.*

FLAT LIDS
Eight-sided

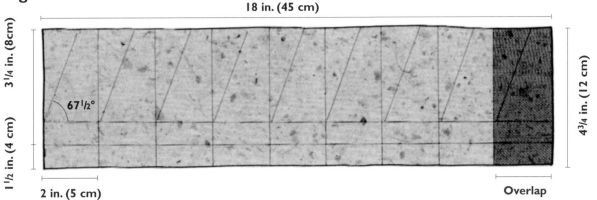

18 in. (45 cm)

3¼ in. (8cm)

1½ in. (4 cm)

4¾ in. (12 cm)

67½°

2 in. (5 cm)

Overlap

1 The lid on the first drawing had a 70° angle. This caused the locking point to rise above the level of the lid, creating a pyramid effect. If you reduce the angle to 67½°, the lock will be level with the top of the lid and so the lid will be flat. In all other respects, make the lid as before.

Six-sided

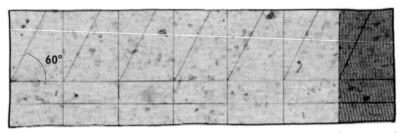

60°

Overlap

2 A 60° angle with seven panels (one to overlap) will create a flat six-sided lid. The box piece must also, of course, be six-sided, with an hexagonal base.

Five-sided

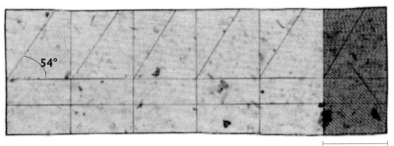

54°

Overlap

3 Similarly, a 54° angle with six panels will create a flat five-sided lid.

TIP—MAKING BOXES
To accurately construct the regular-sided base of a box with the required number of sides, follow this method. Divide the number of sides into 360°. Draw a dot on the paper or card used to make the box and with a protractor, measure off around it the equal angles found in the previous sentence. Connect these points to the center dot with ruled lines, to create a 'spoke' effect. With the point of a pair of compasses on the center dot, draw a circle of the required size (slightly smaller than the circumference of the matching lid). Draw lines between the points where the circle crosses the spokes to complete an accurate, regular-sided shape.

WRAPPING AND GREETING CARDS

INTRODUCTION

There seem to be more and more occasions for exchanging gifts and cards—Christmas, birthdays, Valentine's Day, Mother's Day . . . the list goes on. In the pages that follow, you will find ideas and techniques for creating different looks for presents and cards. Whether you need to wrap a gift for a dedicated gardener (cover the wrapping paper with dried leaves and berries), or make a card to celebrate a wedding, there is an idea here.

Handmade cards are not only much more personal than shop-bought ones, they are often also little works of art in their own right, and may even be framed as an original picture. Many craft workers and artists produce their own greetings cards because they can be a unique form of expression.

Making greetings cards enables you to achieve excellent results in a short space of time and with very few materials. Many of the projects require nothing more than a few paints, some colored card, a crayon or pen, and your imagination. You can use sponges or your fingers instead of paintbrushes, and allow your designs to evolve as you explore the different techniques.

The emphasis is on using natural and recycled materials. You can find an amazing range of materials and inspiration all around you—in the yard, on the beach, or among the everyday things you might otherwise decide to discard.

Keep a collection of gift-wrapping accessories, from old buttons to odds and ends of ribbon. On a walk along a beach or in a forest, keep an eye out for interesting objects, such as shells, driftwood, pine cones, and berries. Keep old cards and wrapping papers—you can cut out motifs from them.

Most of the projects and techniques can be enjoyed by the whole family. If you run out of ideas, simply look through the pages that follow and you are sure to come up with something original.

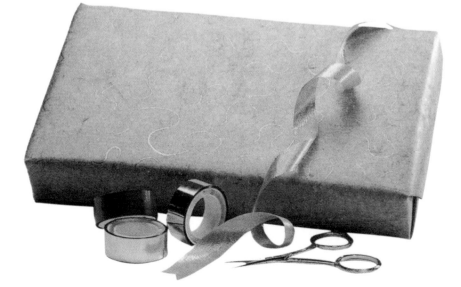

PAPER AND CARD

Collect a range of colors, weights, and textures in papers and cards. Sugar paper, Ingres paper, and cartridge paper are all useful. Watercolor paper is a very useful material to have because it will not break down when it is damp. This kind of paper also often has a slight texture, which can be exploited in your designs.

Try to reuse paper—tissue paper, brown paper, or even old gift-wrapping paper. Spattering paint on to crumpled tissue paper, for example, is an easy way to create original wrapping paper.

You can obtain pre-cut card blanks. These are supplied and scored in a variety of sizes, colors, and types. Many of them have pre-cut windows in ovals, hearts, squares, and rectangles. The cards are available in art and craft shops, and by mail order. You can also cut out your own cards from a medium-weight card, which gives you flexibility with both size and color. Choose a card that is heavy enough to stand upright—but is not so thick that it will not fold neatly.

BASIC GUIDELINES

These are apparently simple rules, but can make a dramatic difference to your results.

- **Always use a knife with a sharp blade and, if you want a straight line, use a ruler and a good, smooth-cutting surface. If you want a right angle, use a set-square.**
- **Make sure window mounts are square to your backing mount and always mount images square to their background, unless you are aiming for an asymmetrical effect.**
- **Prefer a craft knife to scissors, when you can.**
- **It is crucial to use a good-quality card mount of sufficient weight to support the image.**
- **Ensure the score mark is parallel to the mount edges, or the card will not fold well.**
- **Never let glue be seen on your pictures.**

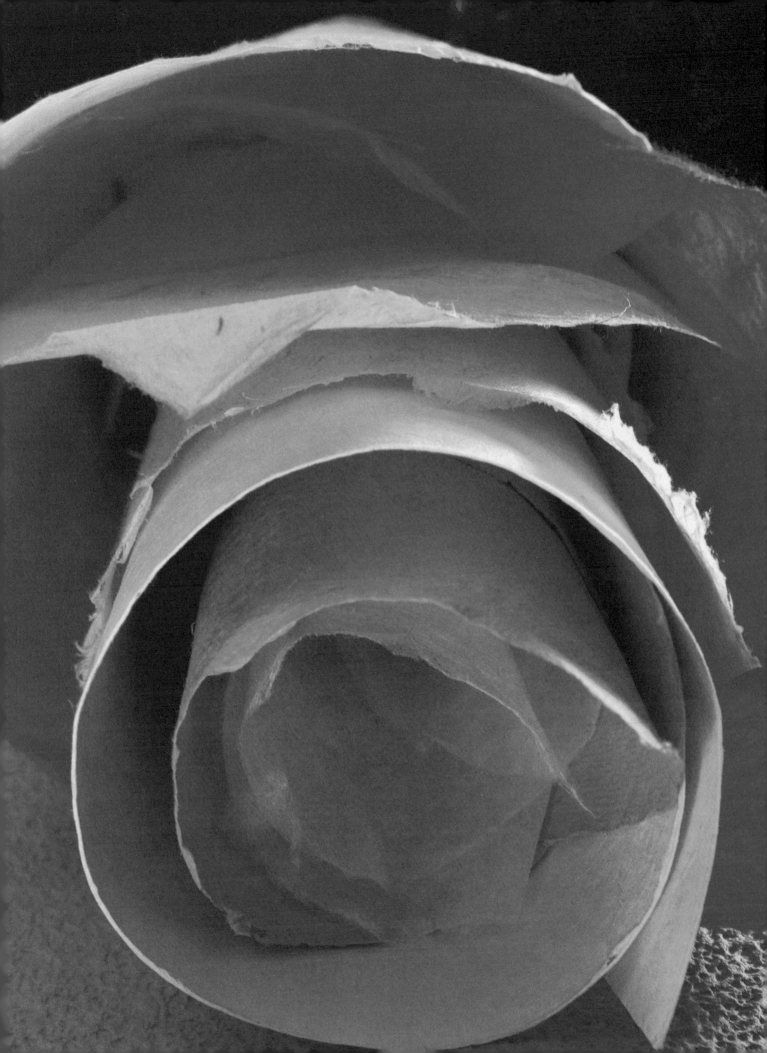

EQUIPMENT

You will need several paintbrushes, which come in a wide range of qualities and sizes. Sable brushes can be very expensive, but they can last for years. Synthetic brushes, or ones with a mixture of real hair and synthetic materials, are suitable for most work. You should aim to have at least one very fine brush, one medium-sized one, and one broad, flat brush in your collection, as these will enable you to achieve different effects.

Synthetic household sponges, torn or cut into pieces, can be used to apply paints. Use a separate sponge for each color, and discard after use.

Stencil brushes are available in a range of sizes and types. They have short, thick handles, and the brushes themselves are cut off flat.

Sometimes you will want to use a roller to spread ink evenly over a printing surface. After use, ensure that you wash immediately in warm water. If you have used an oil-based ink, clean the roller with mineral (white) spirit.

Some of the projects use rubberstamps. Look for a pattern or motif that can be used in several ways: some toy stores sell stamps representing characters from children's books, TV shows and movies. Designs range from simple, individual letters to intricate patterns. The stamps are used with ink pads, in a wide range of colors. Pigment inks, which are thick and rather creamy, are slow-drying but ideal for deep colors. Embossing inks are lightly tinted or colorless. Embossing powders are available in metallic, transparent, and colored finishes. The powder is a heat-sensitive compound that solidifies when exposed to extreme temperatures. The easiest way of applying heat is by means of a hand-held paint stripper, but you can use an iron or even a hot light bulb. Do not let the heat source come into contact with the embossing powder and do not over-heat the powder—or it will look rather dull and unexciting.

BASIC TECHNIQUES

The difference between a professional-looking handmade card and one that just looks home-made is simply the application of a few simple rules. Practicing these techniques will be worthwhile.

Making a Mount

You can buy readymade cards, with or without windows, but it is very straightforward to make your own.

Cutting and scoring a card mount

1   Use a medium-weight card or a thick paper. You can deckle-edge the paper (see opposite). Cut the card with a craft knife and straight-edge to the height you desire and double the width. Use a set square and ruler to ensure the corners are square.

2   Mark the center line of the card on the outside of the mount with a pencil and lightly score this line with a craft knife. Take care to mark only the top layer of the card with the knife. After completing your card, fold it along the score mark.

Cutting a window mount

1   Using a set square, mark the shape of your window on the card mount with a pencil. Measure with a ruler from the edge of the card mount to see the window is centered correctly.

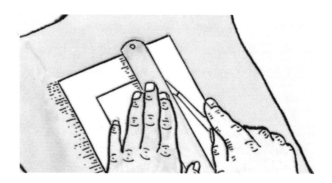

2   Carefully cut out the window using a craft knife and ruler. Be careful not to extend the cuts beyond the corners of the mount.

Tracing and transferring an image

Use tracing or thin layout paper to trace the lines of the picture. Turn the tracing over and scribble all over the back of the image. Turn the tracing the right way up and lay the picture on the mount. Go over the lines of the drawing again with a pencil to transfer on to your mount.

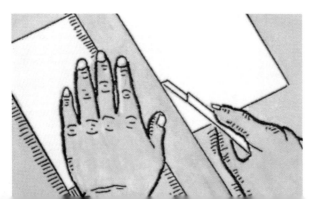

Masking an image

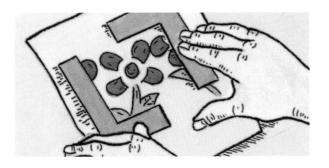

Cut two L-shaped pieces of card, using a set square to ensure that the corners are accurate. Use these to choose the area of a larger print or picture. By laying them on the picture surface and moving them, you can frame any size and shape of the picture. Mark the area chosen with a pencil mark at the corners and use a ruler and craft knife to cut the shape—add on a border to fit under a frame, if necessary.

Tearing a deckle edge

The torn edge seen on watercolor and handmade paper is very attractive, and is often preferable to a perfectly straight edge cut with a craft knife. Mark your line with a pencil mark at both margins. Fold the paper

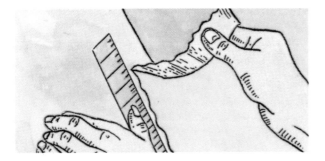

over sharply along this line. Use a ruler or kitchen knife pulled through the fold to tear the paper. Do this a little at a time while holding the paper firmly.

Antiquing paper

Brush dilute instant coffee over a photocopy of a print. Use a large brush or a sponge and test for color on a piece of paper, as it will dry a darker shade. Don't worry about water marks and color patches, as this will give a better effect. When dry, cut or tear out the pieces. If tearing, tear the picture area toward you and away from the background: this gives a stained edge. The effect achieved by this can be very convincing.

Mounting a print

Check that the print is square to the card mount by measuring from the edges. Mark the corners with pencil, so you can quickly register the glued print.

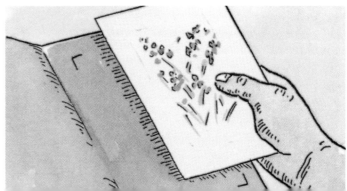

5
GIFT WRAPPING

The art of wrapping and the art of giving could be said to be one and the same. A beautifully wrapped box shows that you have chosen and wrapped a gift with care.

The ideas in this chapter offer a basic introduction to the art of wrapping. The secret is to choose your wrapping papers with care, then to fold them neatly. Accessories such as ribbons, bows, and gift tags are important decorative features, but will not disguise a badly wrapped box.

Almost any paper can be used to wrap a gift. Conventional, patterned gift-wrap papers are good, but consider using more unusual ones such as tissue paper, Ingres (Strathmore) paper, and others from artists' supply stores. In particular, consider using decorated papers. A hand-decorated wrapping paper will give your gift that special personal touch.

THE PERFECT WRAP

This technique is the best way to wrap a box so that it looks neat and well-folded. The method will work for a box or parcel of any shape.

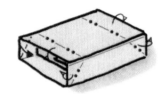

4 *Push in the sheet as shown. Be careful to keep it neat.*

1 Place the gift box on the wrapping paper. Trim the long edges of the sheet so that the overlap at the sides is the same as the height of the box. Fold over a hem of 1 in. (2.5 cm) along one short edge.

5 *Fold in side triangles to lie flat against the box, forming a tapered point at the bottom.*

2 Fix a strip of double-sided adhesive tape to the hem, almost the length of the box. Peel off the backing, then stick the hem to the top of the box 2 in. (5 cm) beyond the nearside edge.

6 *Fix a small piece of double-sided adhesive tape to the tapered point at the bottom and fold up.*

3 Trim the other short side of the wrapping paper to length, so that when a 1 in. (2.5 cm) hem is folded over and a strip of double-sided adhesive tape put on, the edge will fold up and stick to the box, level with the furthest edge.

7 *The box is complete. Reinforce all the creases as the finishing touch.*

PLEATED WRAPS

Here are three simple ways to pleat a sheet of wrapping paper to hold a name tag, a sheet of complementary wrapping paper, or a decorative form. As ever, be careful to fold as neatly as possible, perhaps practicing on scrap paper first. Try all three and see which you like best.

1a *For each, first make your item to be inserted between the pleats, preferably from thick paper or card. It can be any size – but the larger it is, the farther apart the pleats will be. Place the card in the middle of the wrapping paper.*

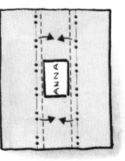

1c *Continue to wrap as described in "The Perfect Wrap" above. This will create a wrapped gift with pleats running down the length of the box.*

1b *Carefully construct two pleats across the top and bottom of the inserted card – so that the top pleat folds downwards and the bottom one folds upwards, trapping it between the pleats. The depth of the pleats should be at least ¾ in. (2 cm).*

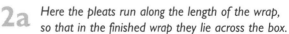

2a *Here the pleats run along the length of the wrap, so that in the finished wrap they lie across the box.*

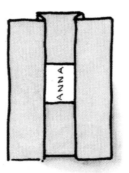

2b *Construct the pleats and fold over the card as before.*

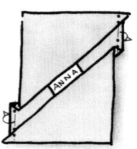

3b *Fold the excess paper behind (or cut it off), to restore the rectangular shape of the sheet.*

2c *Complete the wrap.*

3c *Wrap as before to create a band of pleats set at an angle to the sides of the box.*

TIPS
Try experimenting with other patterns of pleats to create practical or decorative features on a gift-wrapped box: horizontal pleats crossing vertical pleats; pleats across a corner; lines of parallel pleats; and so on. The effects can be surprisingly creative.

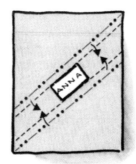

3a *An unusual variation. Lay the card at an angle in the middle of the wrapping paper and form the pleats as before.*

PENCIL PACKAGING

A large colored paper pencil is a novel way to wrap a gift. Fill the pencil with novelty items, stationery, or sweets. If the pencil is large enough, use it for a T-shirt, scarf, or pair of gloves. Fill the end of the pencil with crumpled tissue paper and make a pencil gift tag in a contrasting color. This interesting packaging idea is sure to be appreciated by the recipient of the gift.

TOOLS AND MATERIALS

- **Medium-weight paper: white, yellow, blue**
- **Tracing paper**
- **Ruler**
- **Scalpel**
- **Double-sided adhesive tape, or clear, all-purpose adhesive**

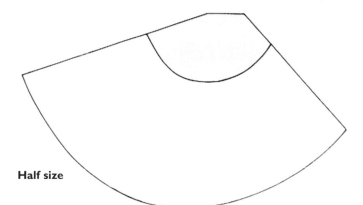

Half size

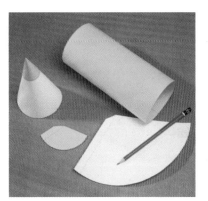

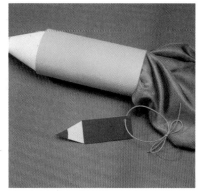

1   *Cut out a rectangle of yellow paper measuring 11 x 10 in. (28 x 25 cm) Use the template (Above RIGHT) to cut out the point of the pencil from pieces of yellow and white paper.*

2   *Form the rectangle into a tube and stick the long sides together. Form the yellow and white points into cones, making sure that they fit inside the end of the tube. Stick the yellow cone over the white cone.*

3   *Make a contrasting pencil tag and thread through some plastic thread. Push the top of the pencil into the tube and hold it in place with adhesive tape.*

PYRAMID BOX

This beautiful little box can be used either as a practical box or as a decoration. The size is variable. Start by drawing a line and draw a semicircle on this line. Place the compass point, with the same radius, at one end of the semicircle and mark the center and the point it crosses on the curve. Once you have done this, repeat from the other end. With the same radius setting, draw another semicircle so that it joins the first. Put the compass point on the join and mark the point it crosses on the curve. Join all the marks together, and you will see that four equilateral triangles emerge. Add one glue flap to the base of the first triangle, two tucking flaps with slits, and two tabs to correspond with the slits (see diagram). Cut out the basic shape and score all the other lines. Stick the glue flap and place the gift inside and close the box tightly with the tabs—it is quite tricky to tuck in the tabs, but it ensures a very secure closure; once you have completed this step, the box should be very secure.

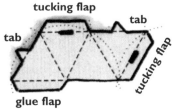

tucking flap

tab

tab

tucking flap

glue flap

Left Basic plan for the pyramid box.

Below You can make your pyramid box to any size. Use plain or foiled light card, or you may even decorate yourself.

GIFT BAGS

These charming little country-look bags take the idea of using bags for awkwardly shaped gifts a stage further—they are perfect for even the most bizarre shapes. Enlarge the size of the template on a photocopier if you want to make a larger bag.

TOOLS AND MATERIALS

* **Tracing paper**
* **White card for template**
* **Ruler and pencil**
* **Check cotton fabric**
* **Paper or card with a textured surface**
* **Fine string**
* **Knife**
* **Scissors**
* **PVA adhesive**
* **Paintbrush**
* **Double-sided adhesive tape**
* **Leather punch**
* **Small buttons with two holes**
* **Thin colored card**

1 *Trace the template (p.241) and transfer all the fold lines accurately. The template shows both sizes. For the bag made of card, cut out a box shape in colored or textured card. For the fabric-covered bag, use thin white card. Score along all dotted lines.*

2 *To make the fabric-covered bag, cut a piece of cloth about 1 in. (2.5 cm) larger all round than the template. Glue the card shape to the fabric, carefully smoothing out any wrinkles and bubbles. Trim the fabric close to the card, leaving 1 in. (2.5 cm) excess at the upper edge. Crease at the fold positions again.*

3 Use double-sided tape to hold the tab to the side edge.

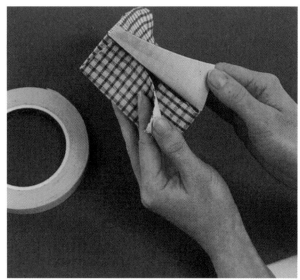

5 If you are making the fabric-covered bag, apply a strip of double-sided tape to the inside of the top edge. Turn the fabric down neatly all round.

4 Fold in the flaps at the lower edge to form the bottom of the bag. Hold the flaps in place with double-sided tape.

6 Make a fastening by using the leather punch to pierce a hole in the center of the bag, about 1 in. (2.5 cm) down from the top edge.

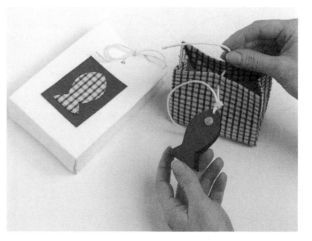

7 *Cut a piece of string about 10 in. (25 cm) long for each bag. Fold the string in half, then thread the ends through the holes in the button and tie a knot. Next, thread the loop end through the punched holes at the top of the bag, then bring the loop around the button at the front. This makes a pretty and secure fastening.*

8 *To make the fish gift tag, trace the template (p.242). Cut one shape from thin colored card. Score and fold it along the dotted line. Pierce a small hole at the head end, using a paper punch. Glue on a small button for the eye. Knot a short length of string and tie up the bag with a neat bow.*

Large Bag

Small Bag

Tab

Gift Bags

**Cut along solid lines
Score and fold along
dotted lines**

Side Edge

Gift Bag Heart Motif

Fold

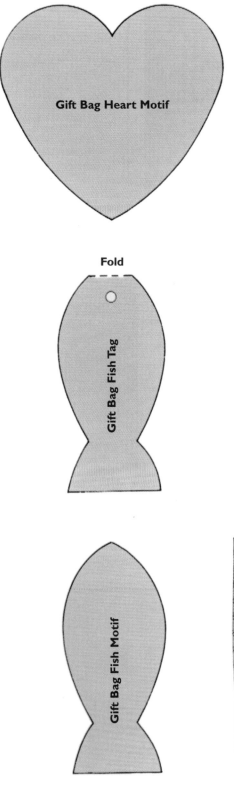

Gift Bag Fish Tag

Gift Bag Fish Motif

9 To make the fish and heart decorations, trace the motifs (LEFT) and cut out the shapes in fabric or card. Fix them to the front of the bag with adhesive or double-sided tape.

COMPLEX BOXES

Flat gift-holder

This type of box is most suitable for flat gifts, such as scarves, ties, and other similar objects. Measure the gift and then make the gift holder the length of the gift, and the width plus the height of the gift (if the gift is solid, allow a little extra). At its deepest point, the curves at the top and bottom of the holder should measure approximately twice the height of the gift.

With these measurements it is now possible to draw the plan of the gift holder (see diagram). The curve can be drawn either with the compasses, placed on the center line, or using a dinner plate of suitable size. Join two sides with one curve and trace this off on to a piece of scrap card—use this as a template to draw the other curves. Cut out and score. Stick the glue flap to the side. Place the gift in the holder and close by turning in the curves.

To make the gift holder extra-special, a shape—such as a butterfly—can be cut and folded from the right side; sinply stick a piece of decorative paper underneath and then lift the cutout.

Above Basic plan for the flat gift-holder.

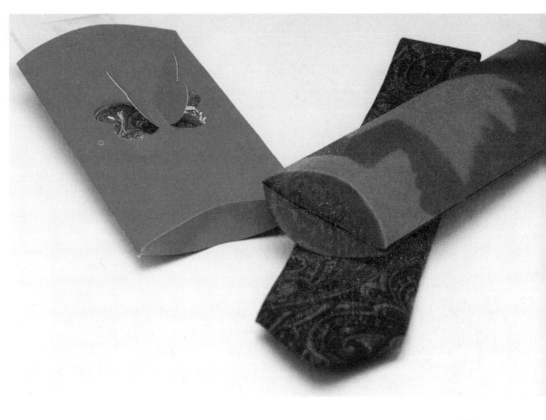

Right The blue gift holder is decorated with a butterfly-shape cutout (see main text). The green one was made with lightweight card decorated with a stenciled design.

CHRISTMAS CRACKERS

Crackers are a traditional part of Christmas, but they do not simply have to contain a little plastic trinket, a balloon, or a paper hat (or even a funny joke!). You could put any small gift—no matter how expensive—in the middle of these bright festive crackers. The first project described here is simply an alternative way of wrapping a small gift. The second one will make your festivities take off with a bang!

TARTAN CRACKERS

1 Cut the thin card into three pieces, one measuring 7¼ x 3½ in. (18 x 9 cm) and two measuring 7¼ x 2¾ in. (18 x 7 cm). Form the two smaller pieces into tubes. Stick paper lace along the short edges of the tartan paper.

TOOLS AND MATERIALS

- **Thin card, 9¼ x 7¼ in. (23 x 18 cm)**
- **Tartan paper, 13½ x 7¼ in. (34 x 18 cm)**
- **About 24 in. (60 cm) paper lace**
- **Clear, all-purpose adhesive tape**
- **Double-sided adhesive tape**
- **Fine string or strong thread**
- **Fine gauge wire**

2 Roll the larger piece into a tube and place it in the center of the paper. Insert the gift and fasten the paper around the tube with tape. Tie the paper with string or thread at the ends of the central tube. Open out the ends and insert the small tubes into the ends.

3 Thread some fine wire through lengths of paper lace. Tie it around the joints in the cracker. Decorate the cracker with paper ribbon bows and sprigs of heather.

TRADITIONAL CRACKERS

TOOLS AND MATERIALS

- ◆ **Tracing paper**
- ◆ **White card**
- ◆ **Metallic-finish crepe paper in colors of your choice**
- ◆ **Scissors**
- ◆ **Pinking shears**
- ◆ **Pencil**
- ◆ **Double-sided adhesive tape**
- ◆ **Three inner tubes from rolls of toilet tissue**
- ◆ **Cracker snap**
- ◆ **Narrow ribbon to match paper**

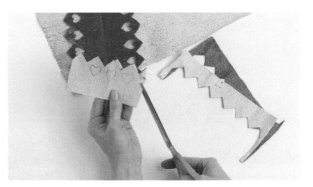

2 *Use sharp, pointed scissors to cut out the shapes from the smaller rectangles.*

3 *Position the contrasting pieces about 1 in. (2.5 cm) in from the ends of the larger piece and stick in place with strips of double-sided adhesive tape.*

1 *Copy a given template and transfer the outline to a piece of white card. Cut a rectangle, 13½ x 7¼ in. (34 x 18 cm), from one of the colors of crepe paper, and two pieces, each 7¼ x 6½ in. (18 x 16 cm), from a contrasting color. Always cut crepe paper so that the grain runs along the length of the cracker. Use pinking shears to trim both ends of the large rectangle. Fold the smaller pieces in half, matching the 7¼ in. (18 cm) sides, and place a template to the fold in the paper. Use a pencil to draw around the template.*

4 *Trim the cardboard tubes so that one is 4½ in. (11 cm) long and the other two are 2½ in. (6 cm) long. Turn over the crepe paper and place the long tube in the center, with the other two tubes about ½ in. (1.5 cm) from the pinked edges. Slip the cracker snap inside the tubes, and place a gift or some wrapped candy in the center tube.*

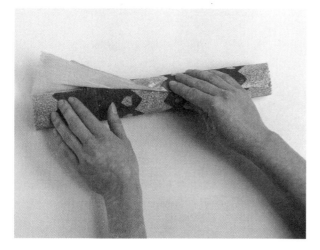

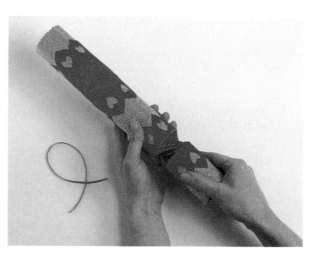

5 Wrap the crepe paper around the tubes, and use double-sided adhesive tape to stick the crepe paper firmly in place.

6 Hold the center of the cracker in one hand and one end in your other hand. Gently twist the cracker clockwise, then anticlockwise. This creases the paper between the tubes and makes it easier to tie in the next step.

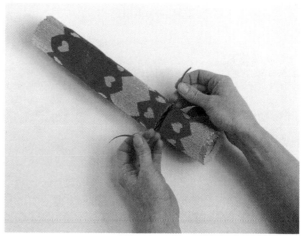

7 Take a short length of matching ribbon and tie the cracker tightly around the creased part. Trim off the ends of the ribbon. Fasten the other end in the same way.

SEE-THROUGH SOLUTION

Here is a practical solution to the problem of wrapping a spherical gift.

1   Place the gift on a large square of brightly colored tissue paper. Then bring the edges to the top.

2   Tie tightly with a piece of strong thread and then spread out the bunched-up paper at the top.

3   Cover the wrapped gift in the same way, but this time with crisp acetate or cellophane. Tie it with thread.

4   Finish off with a bright length of ribbon in a contrasting color and tie a neat bow. Alternatively, add a tassel or attach some beads to a colored cord.

MESSAGE IN A BOTTLE

A corrugated cardboard tube is an excellent way of wrapping a bottle. You can also use any thick, bendable card.

1   Check the circumference and height of the bottle. Cut the cardboard so it is a little taller than the bottle and when wrapped around it, overlap by $\frac{1}{5}$ in. (5 cm).

2   Use double-sided tape to stick the cardboard sides to make a tube. Cut out a round piece of thick, non-corrugated card for the base and glue it to the bottom of the tube.

3   Cut a piece of corrugated cardboard for the lid. It should fit tightly over the main tube, but be loose enough to slide on easily. Glue or tape the edges together to form a tube.

4   Cut a second circle from thick, non-corrugated card for the top of the lid.

5   Put the bottle inside the tube, slide on the lid, and tie with narrow ribbon.

DRESSING UP GIFTS

The cost of shop-bought cards and gift-wrapping paper seems to increase almost daily, and how frustrating it is to spend almost as much on paper and ribbon as on the gift itself, only to be disappointed with the end result. Even if you use shop-bought paper, try to make each gift special by adding your own decoration. One of the secrets of success is to coordinate all the elements of your gifts—wrapping paper, ribbon, tag, and card. Look out for metallic and voile ribbons and for silk flowers, which can be added to a plainly wrapped parcel to make a pretty bouquet. Crepe papers are available in some rich, vibrant colors, and sometimes also with a contrasting color on the reverse, which are especially useful for simple tags.

INDIAN IDEAS

Here are some ideas based on the intricate decorations and vibrant colors of India, for special presents. In keeping with the exotic theme are glowing foils and metallic papers, silk tassels, and metal charms and trinkets.

Although widely available in stationery stores, you can also make your own marbled papers. Fill a plastic dish, about 2½ in. (6 cm) deep, with thin wallpaper paste. Mix two or three colors of oil paint with mineral spirit, until they are of a medium consistency. Drop spots of color on the paste and gently stir with a knitting needle. Place the paper carefully on the surface of the oil, lift it out, and leave to dry.

2 *Use adhesive to cover the tag with small, torn pieces of candy wrappers and sequins.*

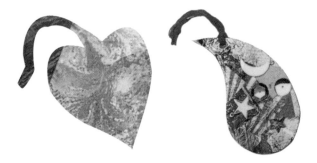

TOOLS AND MATERIALS
- **Medium-weight paper**
- **Scissors and clear, all-purpose adhesive**
- **Selection of candy wrappers**
- **Sequins**
- **Ribbon or sewing thread**

3 *Trim away the excess from around the edges of the tag and punch a hole in the top. Thread through some fine ribbon or several strands of colorful cotton.*

1 *Cut out from the paper the shape of the tag. The tag can be any shape you want.*

Above You will find a wide selection of ornaments and tags for decorating your Indian-style gifts. The colored paper labels were, in fact, made from candy wrappers, but the other ornaments were sold as Christmas decorations.

Above Wrap a narrow strip of hand-marbled paper around a bought paper bag and decorate it with beads and metal charms, threaded on lengths of cotton.

Above When you have wrapped your gift in a single bright color, tie it with metallic or brightly colored silk ribbons, and add some tassels or little fabric birds.

PLEASING PASTELS

Lightweight paper can be used to make flowers and leaves. The effect is really easy to achieve. Pierce holes in the center of simple flower shapes and thread them on to 1 in. (2.5 cm) of rolled-up paper. Glue them to the gift with some paper leaves. You can make simple tags with coordinating papers, all of a similar weight, cut with pinking shears, glued together, and with holes punched in the corners. Decorate them with small flowers. This simple gift of stationery has been made extra special by wrapping decorative strips of colored paper around the central bands. Add a pencil or ball-point pen, decorated to look like a flower or a leaf, to make a simple gift special.

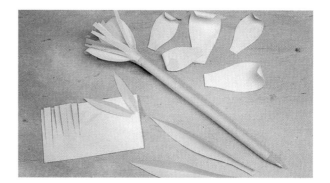

2 *Cut out several petal shapes in paper and curl over the edges by pulling them over the blade of your scissors. Cut a rectangle of paper and make a series of cuts into one side. Wrap the paper around the top of the pencil, and curl back the strips slightly to form the center of the flower. Add some larger petals around the edge.*

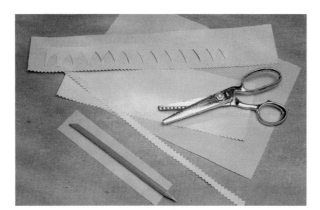

1 *Cut several strips of colored paper, cutting patterns along the edge. Use pinking shears to give a zigzag edge to one side of the strips. Wrap these around the gift. Wrap a pencil or pen in green paper.*

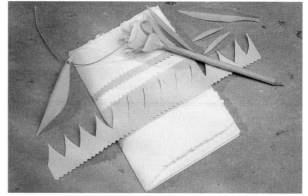

3 *Cut some leaf shapes and glue them to the pencil. Cut a leaf shape for the tag and attach it to the gift with a thin strip of paper.*

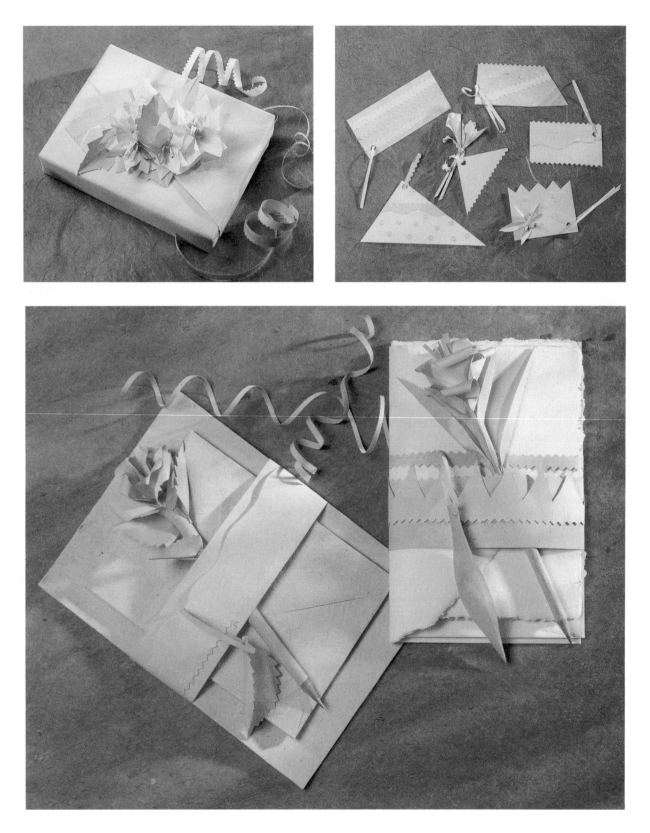

SPATTERING

This is a simple decorative technique but remarkably effective. The gifts are wrapped in brown paper spattered with paint; they are then tied with raffia and string, and decorated with real leaves and paper cutouts, spattered with paint. Dried twigs and berries are added for embellishment.

TOOLS AND MATERIALS

- ✦ **Medium-weight paper or acetate**
- ✦ **Leaves**
- ✦ **Gouache or poster paint**
- ✦ **Old toothbrush or stencil brush**

1 *Use a real leaf to make a template from medium-weight paper or acetate. Mix the paints to a medium consistency and produce shades of green, brown, and gold.*

2 *Dip the brush into the first color and run your finger across the bristles to produce a fine spray effect. Repeat with other colors. Punch a hole and add a raffia or string tie.*

STENCILED LEAVES

The key to stenciling is to use a dry brush—
this will not only give the best results, but will
also help the stencil to last longer. Presents
wrapped in paper decorated with these
natural shapes will look good tied with string,
raffia, or paper ribbon, and you can use scraps
of decorated paper to add interest to a
plainly wrapped parcel.

TOOLS AND MATERIALS

- **Leaves**
- **Medium-weight paper**
- **Sharp, pointed scissors, or scalpel**
- **Stencil or gouache paint in shades of green**
- **Saucer or palette**
- **Stencil brush**

3   *Mix the paint to a thick consistency and keep the brush as dry as possible. Lay the stencil over the paper and evenly dab on the paint.*

1   *Choose an interestingly shaped leaf and draw around it on a sheet of medium-weight paper. If you intend to reuse the stencil for several sheets, use a more robust material such as acetate.*

2   *Carefully cut out the leaf. If you want a perfectly symmetrical shape, fold the paper in half and cut both sides together. In nature, though, leaves are more often slightly asymmetric.*

Above *Real leaves can be used as templates for cutting shapes out of brown paper to use for tags. Paint or spatter the leaf shapes with gouache or poster paint, or leave them brown. Punch a hole in the tag, and thread through string or raffia and tie to the wrapped present.*

FANCY DRESS

Make a plain box a gift in its own right by decorating it to look like something else. Use your imagination to create a costume appropriate to the recipient of the gift, and use any of the paper techniques—pleating, folding, curling, or cutting—to create a truly original wrapping. For a New Year gift, wrapping the gifts in evening dress seemed appropriate.

TOOLS AND MATERIALS
- **Colored and plain white, black, and gray papers**
- **Double-sided adhesive tape and glue stick**
- **Felt-tipped pens**
- **Buttons**

1 *Wrap the box in plain white paper. Cut strips of gray paper about ¹⁄₂ in. (1.5 cm) wide.*

2 *Wrap black paper around the parcel so that it meets at the center front, and turn back the corners for the lapels. Stick the gray stripes along the bottom edge to form the shape of the pocket.*

3 *Cut out two bow-tie shapes and stick them together with a piece of tape. Decorate the tie and stick it in place. Add a flower, buttons, and a label.*

SPICE BALLS

These beautiful and fragrant spice balls make an exotic addition to any gift—not just for Mother's Day. Fill a plain brown box with a selection of cooking spices or potpourri, tie the box with natural colored raffia, and attach a spice ball.

TOOLS AND MATERIALS

- Florist's stub wires
- Polystyrene ball
- Snub-nosed pliers
- Clear, all-purpose adhesive
- Sunflower seeds
- Dried corn kernels
- Raffia
- Dried bay leaves

1 *Push a length of wire right through a polystyrene ball and use pliers to turn a loop in the end. Draw a spiral of glue around the ball and carefully stick on the sunflower seeds.*

3 *Thread some raffia through the loop on the base of the ball. Trim the wire at the other end, if necessary, and turn another loop. Tie on some more raffia and add an extra length for fastening the spice ball to the parcel. Glue on some bay leaves to finish.*

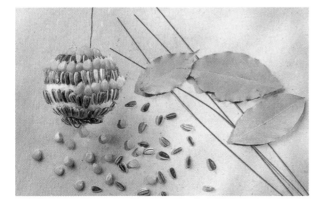

2 *When the glue has dried, draw a second spiral and stick on the kernels. Leave until the glue is dry.*

HEARTS HAVE IT

Decorate a large sheet of paper with a simple pattern of stenciled hearts—nothing could be simpler, and you can make a gift tag to match and finish it off with some pretty curls of ribbon. Do not worry if the stenciled images do not fit perfectly within the edges of the paper. When you wrap up your gift, you may end up cutting off some of the design. This simple decoration is a perfect embellishment to a gift for a loved one.

TOOLS AND MATERIALS
- Scrap paper
- Ruler and pencil
- Heart-shaped stencil
- Acrylic or stencil paint
- Saucer or palette
- Stencil brush
- Large sheet of red poster paper

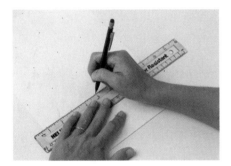

1 On a piece of scrap paper, work out several versions of a grid so that the hearts will be evenly spaced over the paper.

2 Try out a variety of arrangements, spacing the hearts in diagonal patterns or straight lines.

3 When you are happy with the arrangement, plot the same grid on the poster paper. Use very light pencil dots—they should be just dark enough for you to see them as a guide for positioning the stencil, but not so dark that they will detract from your design.

4 Position the stencil on the grid and trace the points of the paper grid on to the stencil using a pencil or permanent marker. This will make it easy for you to position the stencil accurately every time by simply matching the dots.

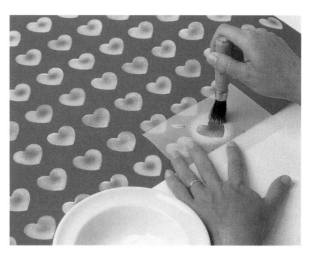

6 As you work, try to make sure that the images are all more or less the same density. Do not try to match them perfectly, however, because the slight differences add to the charm.

5 Now stencil the wrapping paper. Make sure that the brush is absolutely clean before you begin, and remember to remove excess paint on a paper towel.

Below Make some original gift-wrap paper by stenciling white hearts on to some shop-bought red paper. Make a matching red-and-white tag, and tie the parcel with white paper ribbon. For a special treat, add a chocolate heart.

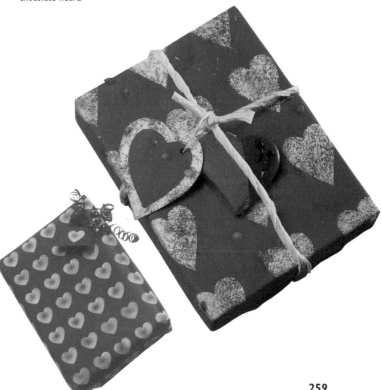

PAISLEY PATTERN PAPER

This striking wrapping paper has been very simply made—it is just tissue paper decorated with a simple paisley-type stamp. Instead of the silver pigment ink, you could use white, but the silver gives a pretty, shimmery effect, which is complemented by the metallic ribbon. This wrapping paper is suitable for all kinds of gifts.

TOOLS AND MATERIALS

- Sheet of turquoise tissue paper
- Silver pigment ink pad
- Floral paisley stamp

1 *Cut the paper to fit the parcel. If you cut it slightly larger than needed, you can hold the paper flat on your work top with small pieces of masking tape in the corners. Ink the stamp and print a row of the motifs, all facing the same way. Re-ink the stamp between each impression. Leave a space of about 1½ in. (4 cm) and print a second row, with the motif facing the same way. Repeat the process until you have reached the end of the paper.*

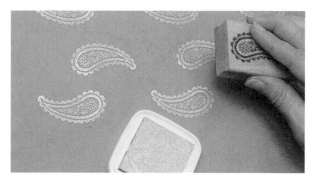

2 *Turn the stamp upside-down, and print further rows, positioning the motifs evenly in the spaces between the existing rows.*

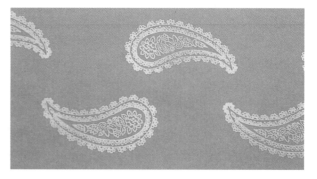

3 *Wait until the ink has dried, before wrapping the parcel.*

BOTTLE WITH A DIFFERENCE

What could be better to welcome in the New Year than a bottle of champagne, and if you are visiting friends or staying with relatives, this decorated bottle would be the perfect gift. The flowers and leaves are silk, and they are attached to the side of the bottle with a small piece of dry floral foam (Oasis), known as a mini-deco. These little semicircular pads are especially designed to allow you to create miniature displays on the sides of bottles or even cakes. You could easily adapt this design to use paper flowers and leaves.

TOOLS AND MATERIALS

- ◆ **Oasis mini-deco**
- ◆ **Selection of assorted silk foliage, including ferns**
- ◆ **Bere grass**
- ◆ **Silk Christmas roses**
- ◆ **Low-melt glue and glue pan**
- ◆ **Gold bow with wire**
- ◆ **Finland moss**

1 *Make sure that the surface of the bottle is absolutely clean. Peel off the circle of backing paper from the mini-deco and press it firmly on the surface of the bottle.*

2 *Insert small pieces of foliage around the edge of the mini-deco, adding some strands of bere grass around the edge.*

3 *Dip the ends of the Christmas roses in glue before positioning them. Dip the wire of the bow in the glue and add it in the center of the arrangement. Put a spot of glue on the ends of the bere grass and bend them over toward the center to form loops. Mask any foam that is still visible with clumps of moss.*

SIMPLE GIFT WRAPS

This is a simple technique for decorating paper, and is suitable for children to try. You can transform sheets of plain, matt construction paper into richly patterned, unusual wrapping paper with very few materials. Gold-and-red or green always looks festive, but you could use silver or red or purple too. For an effective embellishment, remember to finish off the present with matching ribbon.

TOOLS AND MATERIALS
* **Large sheets of plain poster paper**
* **Gold poster or acrylic craft**
* **Saucer or palette**
* **Cloth or tissue paper**
* **Low-tack masking tape paint**
* **Metallic gold spray paint**

2 *Press the paint-coated surface on to the paper to create a mottled pattern. Work all over the surface of the paper with a light, dabbing action. Make sure that you do not smudge the paint as you work.*

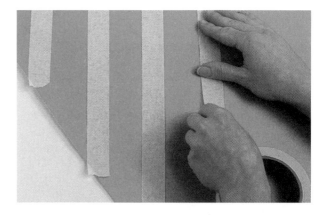

3 *For a striped effect, lay a sheet of plain paper on a flat surface. Place masking tape in diagonal stripes, about 1 in. (2.5 cm) apart, across it.*

1 *Lay the sheet of paper on a flat surface. Pour a small amount of gold paint into a saucer or mixing palette. Take a piece of cloth or tissue paper, about 8 x 8 in. (20 x 20 cm), and crumple it in your hand. Press the crumpled surface on to the paint in the saucer, taking care not to overload the paper or cloth with paint.*

4 *Use the mottling technique described in Steps 1 and 2 to apply random splodges of gold paint over the surface of the paper. Leave to dry before removing the masking tape.*

5 *If you prefer checks, fold a sheet of poster paper concertina style, with each fold about 2 cm wide. To protect your work surface, cover with newspaper. Stretch out the paper a little on your work top and use a metal gold spray paint to coat the paper with a fine mist of paint. Spray from one angle only, so that one side of each fold catches the paint creating a striped effect when the paper is opened out.*

6 *When the paint is completely dry, repeat the process, but this time making the folds at right angles to the first folds.*

7 *Add a special finishing touch to the present with matching gift tags and pretty folded fans.*

PLEATED PAPER

Pleating is a versatile but simple technique to learn. Sections of pleated paper make wonderful gift wraps, and certainly make a change to the gift wrapping papers that you can buy in the stores. Use lightweight paper that can be easily folded. Vary the depths of the pleats and the width of the paper to get different effects, but keep the pleats even and the creases sharp. White, textured, handmade papers look particularly effective.

TOOLS AND MATERIALS

- **Sufficient paper to wrap the gift, plus a piece twice the length of the parcel**
- **Double-sided adhesive tape**

1 Cut a piece of paper about twice the length of the wrapped box. Begin folding over the width of the pleat you require. Make a narrow strip of pleated paper and a very small section for the matching tag.

2 Secure the wide piece of pleated paper at one end. Gently twist the paper until the desired effect is achieved, then stick down the other end. Add the narrower pleated strip in the same way.

PIERCED PAPER

The technique of piercing paper can be used for gift wrap, tags, ribbons, and cards. The delicate effect is achieved by piercing the paper with the fine point of a needle or nail. Although hearts have been used here, any simple motif would be equally effective.

Above Wrap boxes in corrugated card and decorate with pierced paper, ribbon, and tags. Glue some small hearts to pieces of wire and gather them into a bunch to decorate a gift.

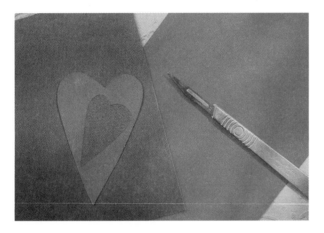

1 Prepare stencils for two hearts, making them different sizes. Cut out a heart of each size from the colored paper.

TOOLS AND MATERIALS

- Acetate or oiled parchment for stencils
- Scalpel
- Colored paper: 2 contrasting shades
- Needles: 2 different sizes

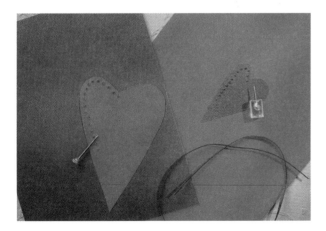

2 Lay the hearts on a soft blanket or something similar, and pierce around the edge of the larger heart with the thicker point.

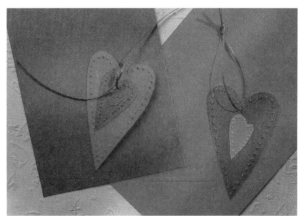

3 Repeat the process with the smaller heart and a finer needle. Pierce a hole through the top of each heart, and thread through a ribbon.

PERFECT PAPER

Paper is a very versatile medium. You can create wonderful three-dimensional and textured effects with simple techniques. Both children and adults will enjoy cutting and folding, creasing and curling, and pleating papers to create original gift wrappings. For these effects, you will need some fine to medium-weight papers in a range of colors, scissors or a scalpel, a cutting mat, and clear, all-purpose adhesive or double-sided tape.

Above Lightly fold plain paper around the box. Lay it flat again, and mark out the circular pattern on two of the box sides only. Cut out the pattern with a scalpel. Wrap the box and decorate with shredded paper and a gift tag decorated in the same way.

A small gift can look effective by cutting a pattern in only part of the paper. Add a similarly decorated tag and matching corkscrews of paper. A colored box showing through the cut paper creates an interesting effect.

Above A simple cutout pattern of little, regularly spaced squares, cut on three sides, gives an interesting effect for little effort. Lightly draw a grid on the reverse of the paper, and carefully cut the squares, making sure that the cut lines do not run into each other.

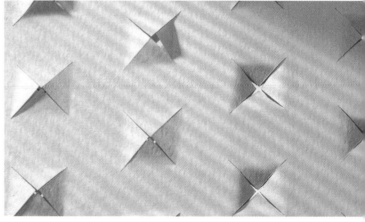

Above A more complicated effect can be achieved by marking a diagonal grid on the reverse of the paper. If you cut the diagonals of the squares, rather than the outlines, you can achieve a rather mysterious effect.

WOVEN PAPER

Weaving is another simple technique that can be used to great effect, whether for small tags or for larger things, such as the bag shown here. Use any type of paper—newsprint, crepe paper, tissue paper, or handmade paper. You can achieve a range of effects by weaving only parts of the paper or by using a mixture of colors and widths.

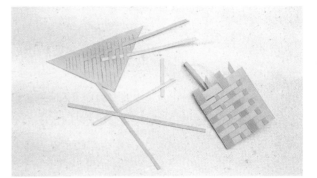

2 *Cut a series of regularly spaced slits in the tag. Weave the first strip over and under the slits, then weave the second strip under and over. Leave the ends different lengths, or trim them off neatly.*

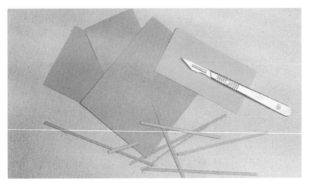

1 *Cut a colored paper into the shape of a tag. Cut several narrow strips in contrasting colors for the weaving.*

Below *To make the woven newspaper bag, fold some newspaper into strips about ¹/₂ in. (1.5 cm) and pin a row of strips about ¹/₂ in. (1.5 cm) apart to a thick piece of cardboard. Weave other strips in and out, alternately, to form a flat sheet. Fold the sheet in half and glue the sides together to make a bag. Tape paper-ribbon handles to the top before filling with raffia, eggs, and your gift. Fill natural and colored woven baskets with shredded tissue, straw and a mixture of hand-painted and chocolate eggs.*

QUILLED GIFT TAGS

The technique of quilling or paper filigree involves using rolled strips of paper to form shapes, which can be glued together and stuck to a base card to make patterns. The designs are especially appropriate for gift tags and small cards. The strips should be about ⅛ in. (0.3 cm) wide, and the length can vary. Some stationery shops sell pre-cut strips, and these are worth looking out for because cutting them by hand is extremely laborious.

Use a cocktail stick, matchstick, or a piece of dowel with a split in the end. Place one end of the strip in the split and turn it slowly and evenly so that the strip remains level. When the paper is completely rolled, squeeze it lightly to make a tight curve before removing the stick.

You can plan patterns in advance or build them up as you go along. It is best to work on a piece of waxed paper so that you can move the designs around as your work progresses. If you are making a decoration for a card and have a good idea of the scheme, glue the center of the shape and place each part of the design carefully in position. A second cocktail stick or a pair of tweezers are useful for controlling the coils. Finished designs can be sprayed with paint or varnish.

__Below__ Plain gift tags can be decorated using quilling. Use the little coils of paper to create some unusual shapes and patterns.

RIBBONS

Adding ribbons is an effective and easy way to turn a plainly wrapped box into an attractively wrapped one. Not all gift boxes need ribbons, though—those that are wrapped in elaborately patterned gift-wrap paper may well be attractive enough as they are, or perhaps with an additional bow or gift tag; Not all gifts will suit ribbons.

Lengths of gift-wrap ribbon can be purchased in gift stores or stationers, and these come in a wide variety of colors. Unconventional ribbons can be found in the fabric departments of stores. Homemade ribbons can be made using strips cut from large sheets of paper. Plaited wools make pretty ribbons, too.

An interesting use of ribbon is to plait or weave together two or more colors. The "under and over" pattern can vary and the

ribbons can either be set square on to the box or set at an angle. Be careful not to cover too much of the gift with ribbons, or it may look over-decorated.

BOWS

Intricate bows can be awkward to make successfully at home. Here, though, is a simple but very attractive bow, sometimes called "My Lady." It works equally well made from gift-wrap ribbon, fabric ribbon, or paper strips, and is an attractive addition to gifts.

1 *Cut a length of ribbon about 22 in. (56 cm) long and twist it as shown, being careful to make both loops the same size. Secure the center with a staple.*

2 *Cut another length of ribbon about 13 in. (33 cm) long and form three loops as shown, beginning with the middle one. Trim off any excess. Check that it will fit between the loops of the other piece of ribbon.*

3 *Staple the second piece of ribbon to the first, being careful to line up all the layers and to centralize the second piece on top. To complete the bow, cut a V-shaped notch into the ends of the ribbon.*

7 GREETING CARDS

Making your own greeting cards is an enjoyable and creative craft,
and giving a handmade design is a much more personal gift than a
store-bought card. The projects that follow can be easily modified
to produce cards for all kinds of occasions.

TWIST-OUTS, CUT-AWAYS, AND POP-UPS

These three similar techniques are exciting ways to create imaginative three-dimensional greetings cards or decorations. They will be best understood if you first follow the instructions explaining how to produce a basic example of each technique. Once you have got the hang of these techniques, you will be able to produce stunning pieces.

TOOLS AND MATERIALS

- ◆ Card
- ◆ A scalpel or craft knife
- ◆ Something to cut on
- ◆ A pair of scissors
- ◆ A pencil and a ruler

Below This technique, once mastered, will produce decorations and sculptural forms of great beauty. Study the examples in the photograph, then experiment with your own ideas.

Twist-outs

Twist-outs are particularly ingenious ways to create three-dimensional cards, suspended decorations, or simply beautiful abstract shapes to be admired. Use thin card for finished examples—paper is too weak, and thick card too cumbersome to bend easily; paper is ideal for practicing, though.

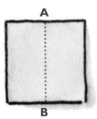

For the basic method, draw line AB down the center of a piece of scrap card or paper.

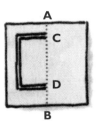

2 With a blade, incise line C to D, so that the incision starts and ends on AB. (Note that AC is shorter than DB.)

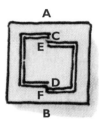

3 Next, incise line E to F, so that the incision once again starts and ends on AB. Note that E is below C and F is below D.

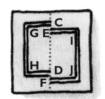

4 Pull edge GH towards you and push IJ away from you, forming short creases between CE and DF.

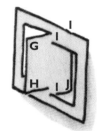

5 The center of the card will twist out from its frame.

Variations

The following are interesting variations of the basic technique. The principle behind these variations is that line AB can be anywhere on a sheet of card. The incisions can be any shape, but they must begin and end on AB, in order that CE and DF can be creased along one uninterrupted line.

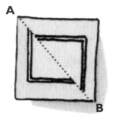 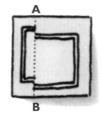 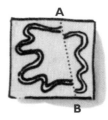

- *Draw AB along a diagonal, so that when incisions are made, the center twists out from its frame along a diagonal axis.*

- *Draw AB towards the left-hand edge, so that the center twists out a long way on the right— but very little on the left.*

- *Draw AB in an arbitrary position and doodle incisions on it at random.*

Cut-aways

This easy technique is an interesting way to make a shape of card project beyond a crease, creating an unusual silhouette. It looks particularly good when used on a greeting card. Use card of thin to medium thickness.

1   *Draw line AB down the middle.*

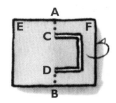

3   *Make a mountain crease between AC and DB, so that corner F bends backwards to touch E. Do not crease between C and D.*

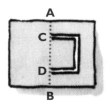

2   *With a blade, incise line C to D starting and ending on AB.*

4   *The card should look like this, with a rectangle of card projecting beyond the crease.*

Variations

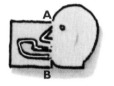 

■ *You could make a cut-away nose and pipe, with the outline of the other half of the card cut to the profile of a head.*

■ *When the top half of the numerals are made to project beyond the crease, the card beyond the bottom half of the numerals can be cut away to complete their silhouettes.*

■ *Here the card beyond the heart has been lost to one side of crease AB.*

Pop-ups

Of the three techniques explained here, pop-ups can become the most technical and therefore the most difficult to learn. This section shows how versatile the simpler pop-up techniques are. If you wish to see more complex examples, look at some of the remarkably clever pop-up books in the children's section of a good bookshop. Pop-ups can be used in combination with the cut-away techniques explained previously, helping to break the symmetry of a pop-up shape. Use thin card, but practice on stiff paper.

BASIC METHOD

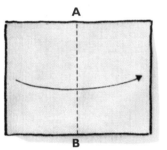

1 *Crease a piece of card along AB and fold the card in half along the crease.*

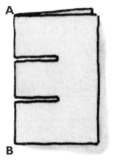

2 *With a pair of scissors, make two cuts from crease AB almost half-way across the sheet.*

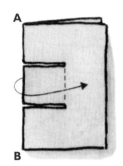

3 *Fold the section between the cuts over to the right, pulling it over as far as it will go, connecting the ends of the cuts with a crease.*

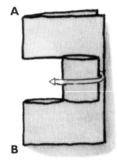

4 *Unfold the center section.*

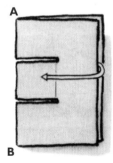

5 *Open the sheet.*

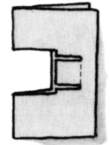

6 Do not flatten the sheet, but keep a valley crease along AB.

7 Lift up the thin belt of card between the cuts, so that the valley crease down the middle of the belt pops up and becomes a mountain crease.

VARIATIONS

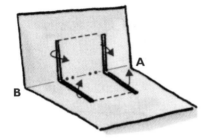

A The cuts do not have to be perpendicular to crease AB, as in Step 2. They can be angled as shown here.

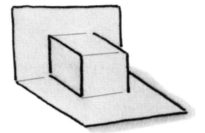

B The crease made in Step 3 need not be parallel to AB—it can be at any angle. The cuts can also be any shape.

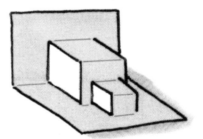

C To make a "second-generation pop-up," follow Steps 1 to 7 of the basic method. Fold the pop-up flat and make two cuts only into the nearside crease (top), then proceed as in Steps 2 to 7. The second-generation pop-up is complete (above). By repeating this process a third generation, then a fourth, etc., can be made to pop up.

MULTI POP-UPS

The pop-up designs made so far have all been built up starting from a central crease AB. However, by starting with more than one crease, you can make decorations that are fully three-dimensional. Here is one suggestion.

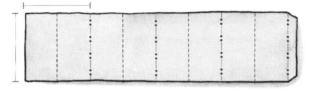

1   *Cut out a piece of thin card four times as long as it is high, with a small tab on the end for glueing. Pleat it into eighths, alternating the mountain and valley creases.*

2   *Make 24 cuts as shown.*

3   *Pleat the strip and glue the tab to hold the pleats in the shape of a cross. Pull out the belts of card between the cuts.*

Below *The cross-shape opened out, with suggested variations.*

WHAT A CRACKER!

Unlike most pop-up cards, here two creases are needed—to mimic the movement of an exploding cracker. To hold the design tight shut during transit, a lock is constructed across the central opening. Note how the four pop-up elements fly off two small rectangular tabs cut from the backing sheet and off two triangles glued to it. The grid is drawn to a scale of 1:2.

TOOLS AND MATERIALS

- **Backing sheet (thin red glossy card),** 12 x 8 in. (30 x 20 cm)
- **Adhesive tape**
- **Blue and yellow glossy**
- **Card (for letters), 10 x 4 in. (25 x 10 cm) in total**
- **Blue foil on white card (for cracker), about 8 x 6 in (20 x 15 cm)**
- **Scissors**
- **Craft knife or scalpel**
- **Clear, all-purpose adhesive**

KEY

Cut along this line

Suggested artwork

Mountain crease

Valley crease

Glue here (sometimes on the underside)

1 Use the template (ABOVE) to cut out the pieces. Incise small square tabs, one on each crease of the backing sheet. Glue the triangular supports against the creases.

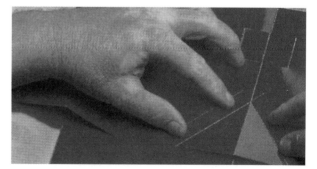

2 Make sure that the creases on the support align accurately with the creases on the triangles.

3 *Glue the letters B and A to the left-hand support.*

6 *Similarly, glue the other half to the right-hand tab. Add the explosions.*

4 *Glue N and G to the other support.*

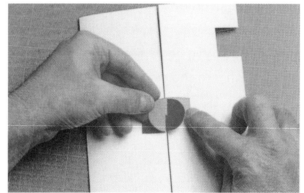

7 *Close the card and add the two halves of the lock, intertwining them. When they are carefully aligned, the lock halves will hold the card tightly shut.*

5 *Glue one cracker half to the left-hand square tab.*

STAMPED HEARTS

It is possible to make stamping tools from a variety of materials, including card, potato, and sponge. For this card corks were used. These, unlike potatoes, do not deteriorate over time, so you can store them away and use and reuse them whenever you want. This particular design is for a wedding card, but stamping tools can be used to make a wide variety of cards. The stamped patterns used here form a circle that is symbolic of fidelity and perpetual renewal. You could incorporate names or dates into the design or, for a really special touch, you could even paste a small photograph into the center of the circle.

TOOLS AND MATERIALS

- ◆ **2 corks from wine bottles**
- ◆ **Fine marker pen**
- ◆ **Craft knife or scalpel**
- ◆ **Pair of compasses**
- ◆ **White crayon**
- ◆ **Blue sugar paper, about 6 x 4 in. (15 x 10 cm)**
- ◆ **Palette or saucer**
- ◆ **Gouache paint: white**
- ◆ **Silver ink**
- ◆ **Silver pen**
- ◆ **White card, about 12 x 8 in. (30 x 20 cm)**

1 *Draw your chosen motif on the corks and use a scalpel or craft knife to remove the areas surrounding the motifs. Do this carefully so that the edge of the pattern stands proud of the top of the corks.*

2 *Use compasses or a small jar to draw a circle on the paper you intend to print on. The circle is a guide for positioning the printed shapes, so do not press on heavily.*

3 *Place some white paint and some silver ink on a palette or on a saucer. Dip one of the cork stamps into the paint and the other in the ink, and carefully apply the stamps around the circle, alternating the patterns. When you have completed the circle of stamps, leave the paint to dry for about 10 minutes.*

4 *Add any further details to the pattern with a silver pen before sticking the pattern to the front of a folded, contrasting piece of card.*

POINSETTIA WREATH CARD

This pretty card has been made by using a simple rubber stamp and by the additional techniques of embossing and hand-coloring with felt-tipped pens.

TOOLS AND MATERIALS

- Embossing pad; clear embossing powder
- Poinsettia wreath rubber stamp
- Cream card, 6 x 4 in. (15 x 10 cm)
- Black embossing powder
- Heat source
- Felt-tipped pens: red, bright green, dark-green
- Embossing ink
- Fine paintbrush
- Turquoise card, about 10 x 6 in. (25 x 15 cm)

1 Ink the stamp with the embossing ink and print the image on to the piece of cream card.

3 Use a hand-held paint stripper to heat the embossing powder. Take care that it does not become too hot.

2 Before the ink dries, pour over the black embossing powder. Tap off any excess powder into a bowl.

4 Color in the embossed design with felt-tipped pens.

5 Use a fine paintbrush to paint a thin coat of embossing ink over the colored areas.

6 Sprinkle clear embossing powder over the surface of the inked area, tap off any excess, and heat carefully. Finish the card by positioning the cream card in the center of the scored and folded turquoise card.

LION IN A CAGE

- *Using a see-through pop-up layer*
- *Drawing up parallelograms to form layers*
- *Creating depth using multiple layers*
- *Hiding the mechanism*

In this pop-up technique, you cut out separate planes and attach them parallel to the base planes. It is one of the simplest techniques used in the earliest pop-up books, but it can be used to create very eye-catching designs. Provided each layer forms a parallelogram, multiple layers enable you to create images of great depth. Theoretically, you could use any number of layers; however, in practice, you are restricted by the amount of paper that allows comfortable closure of the card.

Make sure your base is wide enough to hide the mechanism when the card is closed—or it will spoil the surprise on opening. A multi-layered pop-up is designed to be viewed when the two base planes are at 90°, that is to say, the base would form a floor and a back wall. If you want to view a design from a different angle, turn the base 90° to form a back and a side wall. When you have successfully completed this project, try designing one with twice the number of layers and cutouts. You will find this more difficult, but the effect you will achieve will be worth the effort.

Pop-up greeting cards are particularly good for children's birthdays, but there is no reason why you cannot come up with designs suitable for adults. Once you have mastered the basic principles, there are no limits to what you can accomplish.

The cutout animal makes this simple pop-up mechanism appear more intricate, and a see-through pop-up cage further enhances the effect.

TEMPLATES

The lion templates are actual size and need several pieces of differently colored card, which are assembled before mounting. The cage is a straightforward three-fold construction from a single sheet of card.

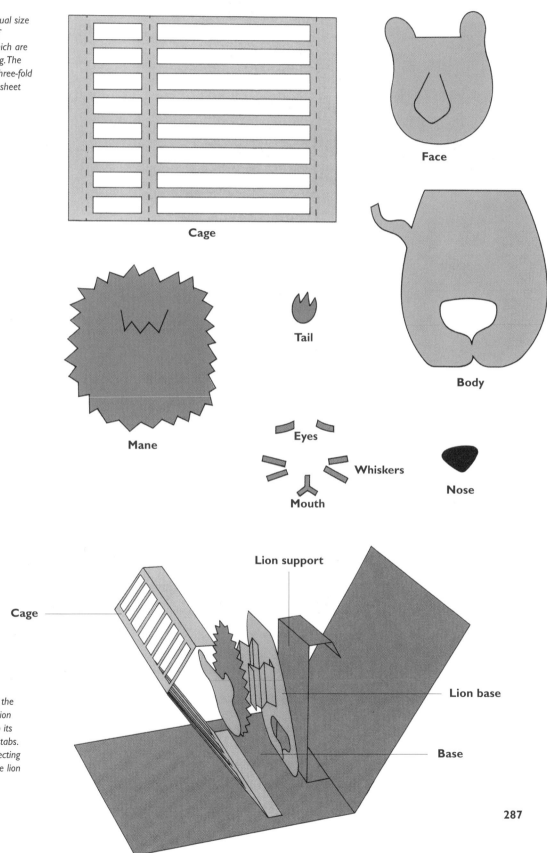

Cage

Face

Lion support

Mane

Tail

Body

Eyes

Whiskers

Mouth

Nose

Concertina head support

CONSTRUCTION

When the card is opened, the cage pops up to reveal a lion whose head is attached to its body by concertina-folded tabs. These keep the head projecting from the body and give the lion added dimension.

Cage

Lion support

Lion base

Base

1   *Trace all the lion templates and transfer them on to thin card: orange for the body and head, and brown for the mane. Cut them out and set aside.*

4   *Paste the plume to the tip of the tail. Then apply glue to one end of each of the concertina head supports and attach them to the body.*

2   *Trace and transfer on to the card the two concertina head supports. Cut them out, score and fold them. Flatten the folds with a straightedge.*

5   *Glue the other two ends of the head supports and fix the head firmly in place.*

3   *Assemble the lion's head, gluing the mane, eyes, nose, mouth, and whiskers. Spear small features with a craft-knife point and apply glue with a toothpick before lowering them carefully into position.*

6   *Choose a piece of card that contrasts well with the lion and cage. Fold it in half. Cut out, score, and fold the lion support, using the same color as the card. The support should be two-thirds of the height of the lion's body.*

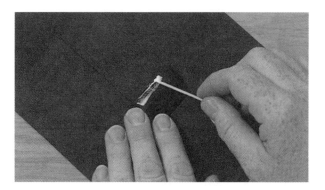

7 *Glue one tab of the lion support up to the card fold. Fold down the tab at the other end, then apply glue to it. Close the card firmly.*

10 *Attach the cage in the same way as the lion support. Glue the cage bottom to the base at the same distance from the fold as the depth of the cage.*

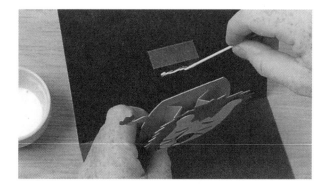

8 *When you open the card, the lion support should pop up. You can now attach the lion to the support. Glue the support and press the lion to it. Be sure that the feet touch the base when the card is open at 90°.*

11 *Fold back the cage top and apply a strip of glue along it. While holding the cage down, close the card and keep pressure on it for a few seconds until the glue adheres.*

12 *When the card is opened at right angles, the lion and the cage should be parallel to the back and the base.*

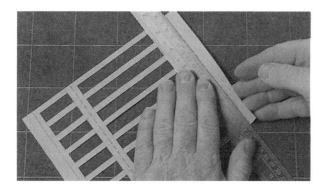

9 *After measuring and drawing the cage on light-gray medium-weight card, cut out the bars, score the folds, and pull them up against a straightedge to fold them without creasing.*

BROWN PAPER CARDS

This technique was discovered while experimenting with inks and brown parcel paper. You can use it to produce one-off pictures or make color copies of your originals to create multiple versions of the design. The card shown here has a baby motif, and it could be used to celebrate the birth of a child.

TOOLS AND MATERIALS
- Pencil
- Brown parcel paper, 3 x 3 in. (8 x 8 cm)
- Fine felt-tipped pen
- Black water-soluble marker pen
- Garden water spray
- Gold marker pen
- Cream card, 8 x 6 in. (20 x 16 cm)
- Clear, all-purpose adhesive

1 *Draw the design in pencil on the brown paper, tracing the template here if you are not confident of your artistic skills. Go over the lines with a fine black pen.*

3 *Use a water spray to mist over the picture. The image will "bleed" around the edges. Dab off excess water with a paper towel, and let it dry for some 20 minutes.*

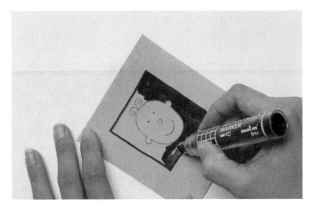

2 *Draw a frame around the design, then fill in the area between the frame and the design with a black water-soluble marker pen.*

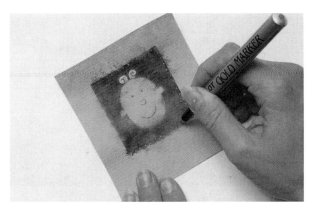

4 *Add any further decoration with a gold marker pen.*

5 *Trim to size, then glue directly to the front of a folded piece of cream card.*

SEASON CHANGE

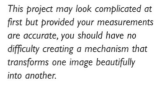

- *Making a sliding mechanism*
- *Dissolving one scene into another*

Sliding mechanisms make it possible to dissolve one scene and create another. The mechanism consists of two pieces: a base with five parallel angled cuts, and a moving section with parallel angled cuts that interweave with the base cuts. Sliding the moving section back and forth reveals either its picture or the one on the base. You will need to use the protractor to create the angles.

This project may look complicated at first but provided your measurements are accurate, you should have no difficulty creating a mechanism that transforms one image beautifully into another.

White cloud

Dark cloud

Sun

TEMPLATES
Minor variations in the size of the sun and clouds are unimportant, but the two pieces that operate the sliding mechanism must be exactly as shown for the movement to work.

CONSTRUCTION
The mechanism underlying the graphics comprises two pieces of card that slide through each other by means of interlocking slits. These are framed by a mask that provides additional decoration. Add glue only at the corners.

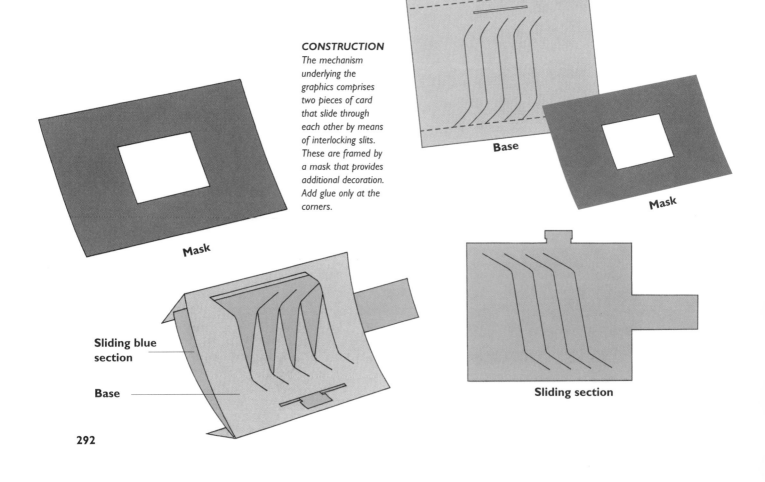

Mask

Base

Mask

Sliding blue section

Base

Sliding section

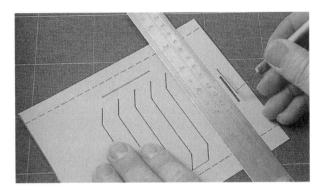

1   *Cut the side and top slits in the pale-gray card. Then cut the four central tabs, leaving them attached at the bottom.*

4   *Cut out the cloud and sun, paste them into position on the blue card and roll them flat.*

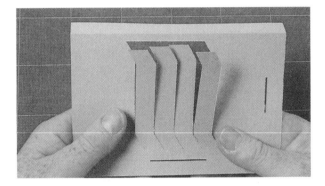

2   *Turn the card over. Score the top and bottom folding lines lightly with a craft knife and fold back. Held up, the card should look like this.*

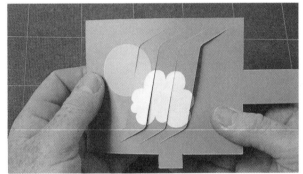

5   *Turn the blue card over and cut the slits again to include the sun and cloud. Check from the right side that you have cut all the way through.*

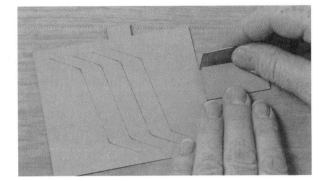

3   *Cut the three central tabs in the blue sliding piece, but leave them attached at top and bottom. Fold the lower tab of the handle up, and the upper part down, to form a triple thickness, and glue into place.*

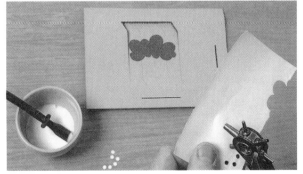

6   *Glue the dark cloud on to the gray card. Punch out some white paper snowflakes with a leather or paper punch, and add these to the gray card.*

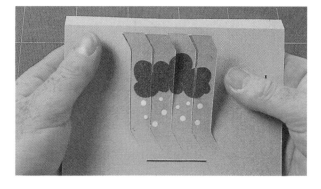

7 Repeat Step 5, cutting the slits through from the back.

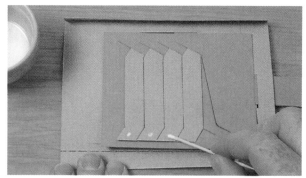

10 With the blue and gray cards in position as shown, put a dot of glue at the end of each gray central tab and fold the gray edge up to attach. Glue and fold the top edge down so that it does not touch the blue card.

8 Holding the gray card reverse-side up, insert the top tab of the blue card into the slot as shown.

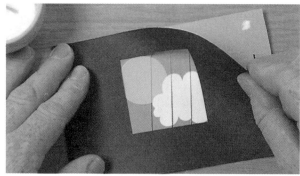

11 Cut a mask to hide the mechanism, and glue it on top of the card at the four corners.

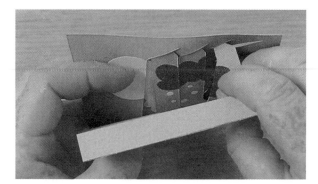

9 Insert the four gray central tabs into the slots of the blue card, one by one, and then place it flat on the table with the reverse-side up.

12 Cutting and gluing everything precisely should ensure that the mechanism operates smoothly. If your paper graphics catch when sliding, try painting them on instead.

BIRTHDAY SCROLL

This card unrolls into a cheerful birthday banner.

Method

1   Cover the white card with orange tissue paper using iron-on adhesive. Mark the card halfway down the long side and measure and mark each of these halves into three equal sections to make six altogether. Fold the card along these lines to form a scroll, with the orange tissue on the inside.

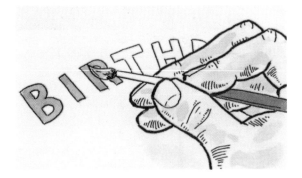

2   On the white side, on the third section from the bottom, pencil the word "happy." The base of the letters should touch the fold. Cut round the top and sides of the letters using a craft knife and cutting mat, but do not cut the bottom edge of the letters—this should remain attached to the fold line. Turn the card over to the orange side and push the letters through and stand up.

TOOLS AND MATERIALS

TOOLS AND MATERIALS
  * **2 white cards, 14 x 8 in. (35 x 20 cm)**
  * **Orange tissue paper, 14 x 8 in. (35 x 20 cm)**
  * **Blue tissue paper, 14 x 8 in. (35 x 20 cm)**
  * **Scrap paper**
  * **Water-based blue paint**
  * **Narrow satin ribbon**
  * **Craft knife; cutting mat**
  * **Iron-on adhesive**
  * **Ruler and pencil**

3   Cut the word "birthday" from white card. Paint blue, allow to dry, and glue to the section of the orange card below the cutout "happy."

4   Put a piece of scrap paper under the stand-up "happy" and paint the letters blue. Allow to dry. Using iron-on adhesive, glue the blue tissue to cover the white side of the card. The "shadow" of the word "happy" is now a transparent tissue window. Roll up the scroll and tie with ribbon.

PRESSED HERB POSTCARDS

Greeting cards made from pressed flowers, herbs, and spices are always appreciated, particularly if the plants that you use have a special meaning.

TOOLS AND MATERIALS

- Selection of fresh herbs, such as sage, thyme, marjoram, parsley, tarragon, and rosemary
- Flower press or telephone directory
- Paintbrush
- PVA glue
- Small rectangles of handmade rag paper

1 Select the best sprigs from each herb and press them in a flower press or a telephone directory for at least two weeks. When dry, remove from the press or telephone directory very carefully—otherwise you could damage the delicate leaves.

2 Using a small paintbrush, paste glue on the herb sprig and carefully press on to the rag-paper backing.

FISH AND STARFISH

Potato printing is one of the simplest of all printing techniques, usually reserved just for young children. However, with a little extra care in planning the design and choosing colors, the results can be surprisingly effective. If your children want to try this, ensure that you supervise them when cutting the pattern.

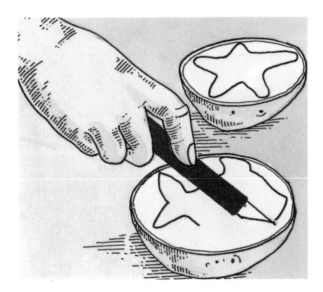

TOOLS AND MATERIALS
- Blue card mount, 12¼ x 8½ in. (31 x 21.5 cm), scored to fold in middle
- Smaller yellow paper for the fish print
- Poster, gouache, or acrylic paints in different colors
- Soft felt-tip pen
- Silver felt-tip pen
- Glass or perspex surface on which to spread paint
- Ink roller
- Potato
- Kitchen paper
- Craft knife or vegetable knife

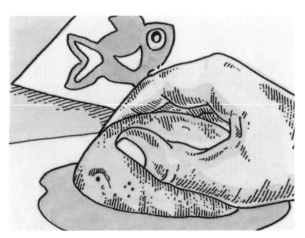

Method

1 Cut the potato in half. Press the halves on to kitchen paper to dry. Draw a fish on one half and a starfish on the other with a soft felt-tip or the point of the knife. Carefully cut away the parts of the design you do not wish to print, ensuring that you keep to the initial outline you drew.

2 Spread out the paint with a roller on to a smooth surface such as glass or perspex, and

dip the raised fish shape into it so that it is covered with paint. Then press the fish shape on to the light-colored paper to make a print. Print other fish all over in a random pattern as if they are swimming, using different colors and ensuring that you clean the potato between each application of color. For a nice and unusual effect, you can use two colors of paint next to each other on the glass for multicolor fish.

3 Trim the print to the size you want, and glue it on to the blue mount.

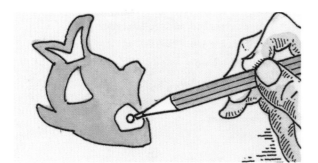

4 Print starfish around the border, using alternating colors.

5 With the silver pen, draw a line around the edge of the fish print, and add silver dots for the fishes' eyes to make them shine.

VARIATION
Print a few fish or starfish on the envelope in which you are sending the card.

WAX RESIST CARD

This is an ideal technique for children, and it works especially well with fairly simple motifs such as flowers, hearts, and animals. It has been used here to make a card to welcome someone to a new home.

TOOLS AND MATERIALS

- White wax crayon or candle
- Watercolor paper
- Paintbrushes
- Gouache paints: orange, red, yellow
- Clear, all-purpose adhesive or double-sided adhesive tape
- Colored card, 12 x 5 in. (30 x 13 cm)
- Scissors

2 *Take a brush loaded with paint and apply it to the paper. For best results, limit the number of colors you use, although it is possible to mix them on the paper to get different shades.*

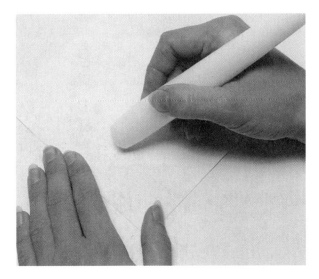

1 *Draw the design on watercolor paper using a candle or white wax crayon. If you tilt the paper slightly in the light, you can see the lines you have drawn.*

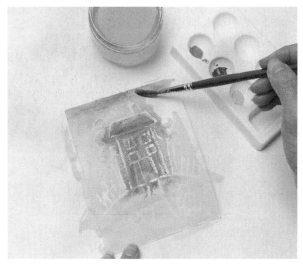

3 *Blend the paints together on the paper with a clean brush and water. Leave to dry for 10-20 minutes.*

4 *When the paint is completely dry, use adhesive or double-sided tape to stick the design to the large piece of contrasting colored card.*

5 *Fold the card in half so that the image appears on the front of the card.*

STRING WRITING

This is an easy way to achieve an embossed metal effect. Have fun experimenting with different thicknesses of string, colored silver paper, and so on.

Method

1 Draw the letters of a name on to the thin card. Apply PVA glue along the outlines and leave to become tacky.

2 Lay the string along the lines of glue and trim the end at the end of each letter. Leave to dry.

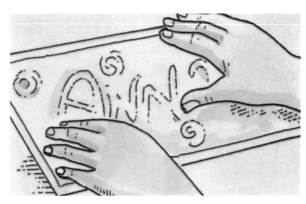

3 Apply PVA glue, thinned with water, to the whole surface of the card. Cover the surface of the card with kitchen foil and smooth this gently over the string, allowing the foil to wrinkle and ensuring that the shapes of the letters are clearly visible through it.

4 Brush thinned paint over the foil and, before this dries completely, rub most of it off, leaving just enough to create an "antique" texture. (Practice first on a spare piece of foil.)

5 Glue the picture to the colored paper, and decorate the border with felt-tip pen.

6 Glue the paper to the card mount.

COLLAGE STAR

A creative painting technique is used to produce richly colored backgrounds on which to build layers of different papers. The end result is an unusual and individual greeting card. Collect foil paper, Christmas wrapping paper, and metallic papers for this project, and choose your paints to complement the foil. The paints used are rich purple and turquoise, and the gold star helps to create an unusual but attractive Christmas card.

TOOLS AND MATERIALS

- Household sponge
- Gouache paint: turquoise, ultramarine, purple
- Palette or saucer
- Garden water spray
- Watercolor paper 11¼ x 8¼ in. (29 x 21 cm)
- Gold ink
- Paintbrush
- Foil papers: various colors
- Scissors
- Clear, all-purpose adhesive
- Gold card
- Ruler and pencil
- White card, about 12 x 8 in. (30 x 20 cm)
- Gold pen

1 *Tear a household sponge into small pieces so that you can use a separate piece for each color.*

2 *Select your paint colors and place them on a palette or saucer. Mist the piece of watercolor paper with water, then apply the paint to the paper using pieces of sponge.*

3 *Mist the painted surface with water again, and use a clean piece of sponge to blend the colors together.*

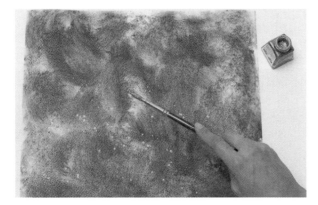

4 *Load a paintbrush with gold ink and tap it over the paint surface for a stippled effect. Let dry for 20-30 minutes.*

5 *Select different colors of foil papers, cut them to the size you want, and crumple them in your hands.*

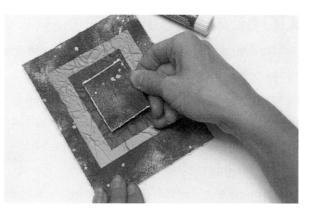

6 *Glue the layers together. The largest piece, part of the painted paper and torn to size, goes at the bottom, with the foil papers next, and a smaller piece on top.*

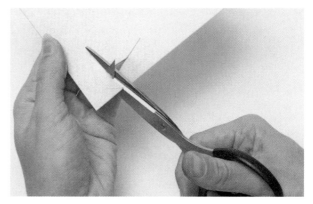

7 *Draw a small star on a piece of gold card, then cut it out and stick it to the center of the collage.*

8 *Glue the collage to a larger card. Fold the card so the collage is on the front. Draw a gold border to finish.*

SHELLS IN THE SAND

It's simple to create your own sand-art designs, using double-sided self-adhesive film. Alternatively, you could use one of the many kits available.

TOOLS AND MATERIALS

- **Card mount, 8¼ x 6 in. (21 x 15 cm), scored to fold in middle**
- **Sheet of 8½ x 11 in. (A4) paper**
- **Double-sided self-adhesive film**
- **Fine sand in a variety of colors**
- **Shells**
- **Colored pencils**
- **Craft knife**
- **Cutting mat**
- **All-purpose adhesive**

Method

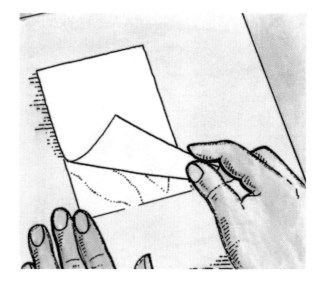

2 Cut a piece of self-adhesive film to the size of your design and transfer your design on to this. Peel the release paper off the back of the film and press the film firmly on to the card mount.

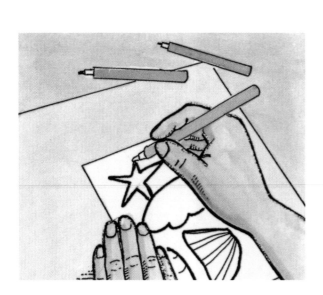

1 Draw your design in color on the paper, keeping it fairly simple—you will be cutting out each area of color.

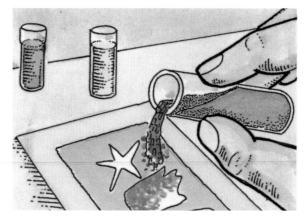

3 Cut around each area of color in your picture with a craft knife, taking care to cut only through the release paper and not through the film itself. Peel off the darkest area of the design and sprinkle the colored sand on to this, shaking off the excess material. Proceed in the same way for each area of the design, unless you want to try something different. You can create interesting effects by mixing the sand colors before sprinkling them on, or by sprinkling one color very lightly on to the film and a little of another on top. Be creative and don't be afraid to experiment.

4 Glue some real shells on to the finished sand picture.

FALL LEAVES

You can produce a wide variety of designs using either natural prints or stencils, and the two techniques are combined in this card, which has an attractive leaf motif.

TOOLS AND MATERIALS

- **Leaves (any fairly flat leaves will do)**
- **Paintbrush**
- **Gouache paint: red**
- **Palette or saucer**
- **Sheets of sugar paper, 11¼ x 8¼ in. (29 x 21 cm): red, cream**
- **Double-sided adhesive tape**
- **Gold spray**
- **Clear, all-purpose adhesive**
- **Cream card, about 12 x 8 in. (30 x 20 cm)**
- **Fine gold pen**

1 *Choose a suitable leaf, then trim off the stalk if necessary. Paint the underside of the leaf, where the veins are prominent, with red gouache paint.*

3 *Carefully peel back the top sheet of paper to reveal the print. This process can be repeated several times, if you wish.*

2 *Place the leaf on a sheet of paper with the painted side facing upward. Put another piece over the leaf, and press down. Rub over the area.*

5 When the paint is dry, carefully remove the leaves from the paper.

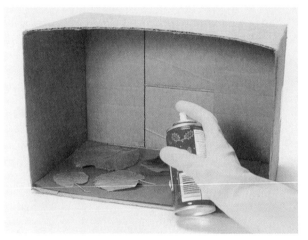

4 Select several leaves of the same kind and place them in a random pattern on a sheet of colored paper. Hold them in place with small pieces of adhesive tape. Spray over the leaves, ideally using an old cardboard box to protect your working area. Leave to dry for 5 minutes.

6 Cut the background to size and glue it to a larger, folded piece of contrasting colored card.

7 Tear the leaf print to size, using a ruler to help tear a neat edge, and decorate the torn edges with a gold pen.

8 Glue the leaf print on to the sprayed background to complete the card.

RIVER FISH

You can create a range of interesting effects by photocopying drawings, prints, etc., on to clear acetate, and layering other papers or fabric behind. The fish-eye rivets hold the acetate to the mount.

Method

1 Make a drawing, or use cutout prints of fish, and arrange and stick the images on to white paper. Photocopy these on to acetate, reducing or enlarging if necessary.

TOOLS AND MATERIALS
- Card mount, 8¼ x 6 in. (21 x 15 cm), scored to fold in middle
- 8½ x 11 in. (A4)-sheet white paper
- Shiny blue paper
- Wave-patterned tissue
- Small pieces of gold card
- Acetate (from a photocopy outlet)
- Black-and-white drawing or print
- Rivets and rivet gun
- Scissors or craft knife
- Cutting mat
- Paper glue

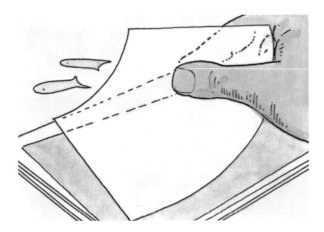

2 Cut acetate to the size of the front of the mount and cut the blue paper and tissue paper into interesting background shapes, and layer them on the mount respectively. Hold the acetate on top to check the position. Cut two fish shapes from gold card.

3 Put the two gold fish behind the acetate in two corners of the mount. Reposition the acetate and fix all the layers together using the rivet gun, with the rivets as fish eyes.

WICKED WITCH

This pop-up design has height and opens with an appropriately large, sweeping movement that will always be remembered. The construction is simple, but the stick supporting the witch must be strong, and the V-angle that it forms at the base must be carefully adjusted so that the witch collapses into the front corner of the card. Children will be particularly delighted at receiving this card. The grid is drawn to a scale of 1:2½.

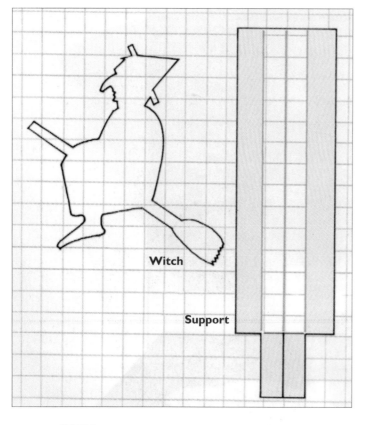

Witch

Support

KEY

cut along this line
mountain crease
valley crease
glue here (sometimes on
the underside)

TOOLS AND MATERIALS

- Backing sheet (thin blue card glued to mounting card), 15½ x 9 in. (39 x 22 cm)
- Adhesive tape
- Thin blue card (for support), about 8 x 2½ in. (20 x 6 cm)
- Scissors
- Thick black paper (for witch), about 6 x 6 in. (15 x 15 cm)
- Medium-weight white paper (for clouds), about 6 x 6 in. (15 x 15 cm)
- Craft knife or scalpel
- Clear, all-purpose adhesive

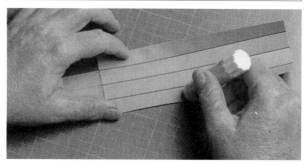

1 Cut the backing sheet in half, place it face down, butt the cut edges together, and stick them together with tape so that it will lie flat after being folded. Use the template (LEFT) to cut out the pieces. Apply glue to the outer, long panels of the support, then fold them inward so that they align with the center crease, halving the width, and doubling the thickness of the support.

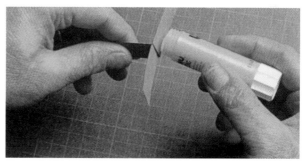

2 Apply glue to the end tabs.

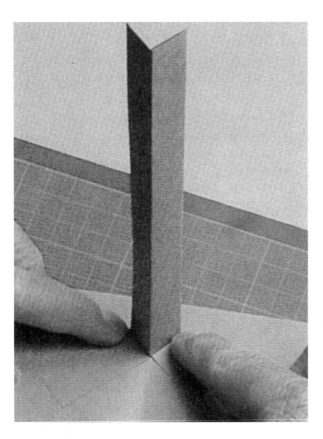

3 Glue the tabs to the backing sheet.

4 Glue the witch to the top of the stick.

5 If the angle of the fold in step 3 is carefully judged, the witch will collapse into the front corner of the backing sheet when the card is shut.

POP-UP SNOWFLAKE

The snowflake motif on the front of this card and the pop-up snowflake inside make a special, personal card for Christmas.

Method

1   Using a compass, draw a circle on one of the pieces of white paper, with a radius of 2¾ in. (7 cm). Next, divide the circle into six segments, marking with your compass the radius around the circumference, and joining the marks through the center with straight lines.

2   Carefully cut out the circle with scissors or a craft knife. Fold the circle in half along one line, then along the other two lines—so you end up with a folded triangle shape with a curved base.

3   With the craft knife and cutting mat, cut geometric shapes within the folded triangle,

TOOLS AND MATERIALS
◆ **Pop-up Snowflake**
◆ **White card mount, 12 x 6 in. (30 x 15 cm), scored to fold in middle of long side**
◆ **2 sheets 8½ x 11 in. (A4) plain white paper**
◆ **12½ x 6½ in. (31 x 16 cm) piece marbled blue paper**
◆ **Newspaper**
◆ **Pearl blue spray paint**
◆ **Compass**
◆ **Scissors or craft knife**
◆ **Cutting mat**
◆ **Double-sided tape**
◆ **Magic tape**
◆ **Fabric/paper glue**

making sure that you leave the two outer straight edges uncut. Unfold your "snowflake."

4   Loosely attach the snowflake to the front of the card mount with magic tape. Place the mount on newspaper to protect the work surface, and spray from a distance of about 12 in. (30 cm) from side to side if you want the paint even, or from the center out if you want a graduated effect as shown here. Leave to dry, then carefully remove the snowflake stencil.

5   Glue the marbled blue paper to the inside of the mount, trimming the edges as necessary. Repeat Steps 1, 2, and 3 to make the snowflake for the inside.

6 Once you have unfolded your snowflake, take one segment, and crease the opposite way in the center. Crease the opposite segment in the same way.

7 In order to attach the snowflake to the card, add two small tabs of paper measuring approximately $\frac{1}{4} \times \frac{1}{8}$ in. (5 x 3 mm) with double-sided tape, or glue. Ensure that you center the snowflake top and bottom inside the card mount. You will need to experiment to get the correct position of the snowflake, depending on how flat you want it to open out—this is really down to your personal taste. First tack one tab to the card, then close up the snowflake, then the card, and press—this way you should be able to attach the snowflake evenly.

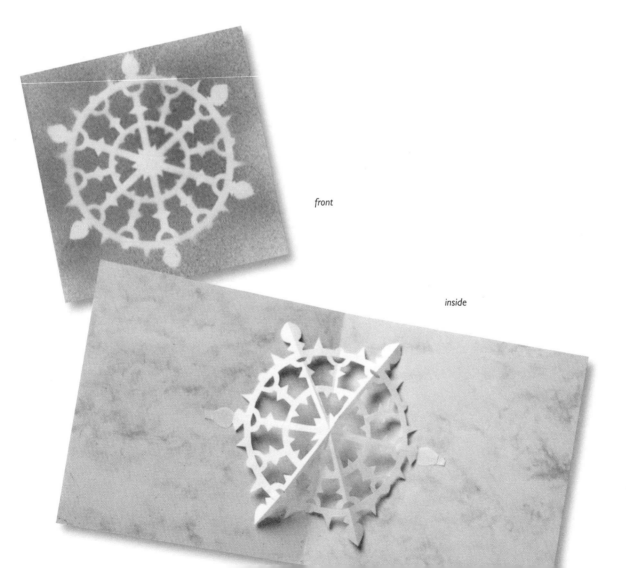

front

inside

FLOWERS AND LEAVES

It has become customary to exchange cards on Valentine's Day, and giving a card that you have made yourself makes the gesture even more personal; the recipient will really appreciate the time and effort you have put in. You can use the flowers and leaves from your garden or from the hedgerows to make your Valentine's card by pressing them, backing them with thin card, then mounting them on colored, fine-corrugated card. Ivy leaves form a charming and natural heart shape—a single leaf could have a little heart cut from it or you could arrange a group of leaves into a heart. Pansies are most appropriate to show thoughtfulness.

TOOLS AND MATERIALS

- **Fresh pansies and ivy leaves**
- **Flower press**
- **Corrugated card**
- **Craft knife; scissors**
- **Double-sided adhesive tape**
- **PVA adhesive**
- **Plain paper**
- **Adhesive pads**

At least two weeks before you make the cards, press the flowers so they can dry completely. Use a flower press or put the flowers and leaves between pieces of tissue paper and place them inside a telephone directory. Place a weight on top and leave undisturbed in a warm, dry place.

2 *To make the pansy ring or the heart of ivy leaves, glue the pressed flowers or leaves to plain paper. When the adhesive is dry, use a craft knife to cut around the shapes. Attach the cut-out shape to the front of the card with adhesive or, if you want a slightly three-dimensional effect, with adhesive pads.*

1 *For the ivy-leaf card, fold a rectangle of corrugated card in half. Cut out a square window. Use double-sided tape to glue the paper behind the window. Glue the leaf to the paper, and use a craft knife to cut out a heart in the leaf. Cut around the leaf so the plain paper falls away.*

3-D STAR

This interesting card had been made with thin card with tissue paper glued to both sides to create an interesting mottled effect. Another way to achieve a similar result is to buy thin card with a texture or pattern. The 3-D effect really sets this card apart from other designs.

Method

1 Making sure that you follow the manufacturer's instructions, use the double-sided film or iron-on adhesive to cover the two sides of the cards with dark-blue tissue.

2 Using a template, cut out two stars from the tissue-covered card. Make a slit in one star from the bottom to the center and in the other from the top to the center, as shown in the template. Slot the two stars together.

TOOLS AND MATERIALS
- **Two squares of thin card, 8 x 8 in. (20 x 20 cm)**
- **Dark-blue tissue to cover**
- **Light-blue tissue for "inside" of card**
- **Packet of small silver stars**
- **Double-sided self-adhesive film or iron-on adhesive**
- **Scissors**

3 Lay the star flat on the work surface. Use the iron-on adhesive to cover just the side facing you (it doesn't matter which side) with the light-colored tissue. The tissue will cover the slits where the two stars join, preventing the two stars from slipping apart, and providing a lighter-colored side on which to write a message.

4 Glue the small silver stars on to the sides covered in dark-blue tissue.

317

A SLICE OF CAKE

If you use reflective card for the backing sheet, the completed card will make it look as if there are several slices of cake. The folds must be accurately marked and creased if the card is to open smoothly. The grid is drawn to a scale of 1:2.

TOOLS AND MATERIALS

* **Backing sheet (thick mirror card),** 10½ x 6½ in. (26 x 16 cm)
* **Adhesive tape**
* **Thin white card (for cake),** 8 x 6 in. (20 x 15 cm)
* **Felt-tipped pens**
* **Scissors**
* **Craft knife or scalpel**
* **Clear, all-purpose adhesive**

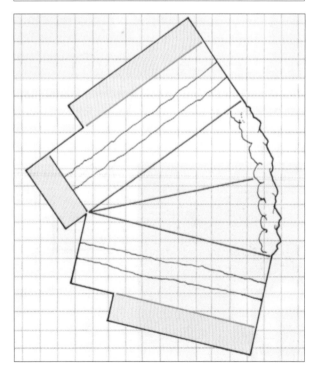

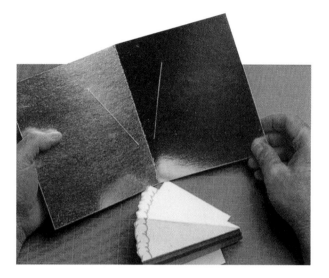

I   *Cut the backing sheet in half, place it face down, butt the cut edges together, and stick them together with tape so that it will lie flat after being folded. Use the template (BELOW LEFT) to cut out the cake. Cut two slits in the backing sheet.*

2   *Fold the decorated cake along the lines and glue the tab on the point of the cake wedge to make the cake three-dimensional.*

KEY

cut along this line
suggested artwork
mountain crease
valley crease
glue here (sometimes on the underside)

3 *Push the tabs along the bottom of the cake through the slits in the backing sheet.*

5 *Use adhesive tape to hold the tabs flat on the reverse of the backing sheet.*

4 *They should fit through them like this.*

6 *The cake is complete. Reflective card will make this slice of cake appear to be many.*

BUBBLY FISH

Pull out the tabs on the right-hand side of this fish, and watch the bubbles coming from the fish's mouth.

Method

1 Draw a fish shape, without a bottom jaw, on the orange card. Draw a bottom jaw with a fin on the end. Both parts should be facing right.

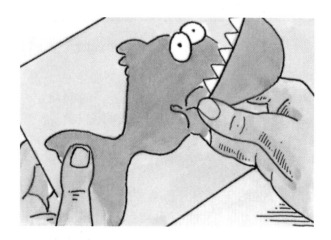

2 Cut out teeth from the white card, and glue to the top and bottom jaws. Glue the main body of the fish to the left-hand side of the blue card. Glue on a pair of eyes, marking the pupils with the felt pen.

3 Using a strong adhesive, attach the binding pin to the back of the bottom jaw, behind the fin. Push the pin through the body of the fish and the card, so that the jaw swings from the fin. Fold the pin legs out behind the card.

4 Using the craft knife and ruler, cut three pairs of vertical slots on the blue card to the right of the fish.

5 Cut three strips of blue card to slide between the slots. They should be slightly narrower than each pair of slots, and long enough to reach from the right-hand edge of the card to the middle.

6 Cut out three circles of white paper, and glue these to the left-hand end of the strips. Cut three tabs of orange card, and glue these to the other end of the strips. Slide the strips into the slots.

7 Glue another piece of blue card as a backing to the main card. Do not attach it on the right-hand edge and take great care not to get any glue on to the slots or the strips of card, or you won't be able to slide the strips in and out.

TOOLS AND MATERIALS
- **3 sheets of blue card, 12 x 8¼ in. (30 x 21 cm)**
- **1 sheet of orange card, 12 x 8¼ in. (30 x 21 cm)**
- **Sheet of white paper or thin card**
- **Binding pin with wide, flat head**
- **Pencil and felt-tip pen**
- **Scissors**
- **Craft knife**
- **Cutting mat**
- **Ruler**
- **All-purpose adhesive**
- **Fabric/paper glue**

OH, TANNENBAUM

This pop-up tree is a fairly easy card to make, and you can involve your children in coloring the tree and tub when you have cut them out. This tree was decorated with felt-tipped pens, but you could stick on little pieces of paper and self-adhesive stars and spangles.

The grid is drawn to a scale of 1:2.

TOOLS AND MATERIALS

- Backing sheet (thin grey card glued to mounting card), 8½ x 8 in. (21.5 x 20 cm)
- Scissors
- Adhesive tape
- Thin grey card (for tree and tub), about 10 x 6 in. (25 x 15 cm)
- Craft knife or scalpel
- Felt-tipped pens
- Clear, all-purpose adhesive

KEY

cut along this line
suggested artwork
mountain crease
valley crease
glue here (sometimes on the underside)

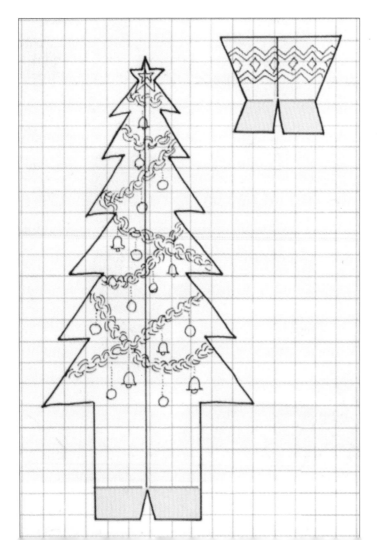

1 Cut the backing sheet in half, place it face down, butt the cut edges together, and stick them together with tape so that it will lie flat after being folded. Use the template (LEFT) to cut out the tree and tub. Decorate them, then apply glue to the tree tabs.

2 Glue the tree to the backing sheet, making sure that the center of the tree aligns exactly with the center of the card base.

3 *Apply glue to the underside of the tub tabs.*

5 *When the card is shut, the tree and tub will tip forward.*

4 *Glue the tub to the backing sheet, making sure to position it a little way in front of the tree.*

FLOWER HEART

The real flower seeds in the center of this card are placed loose in a clear plastic bag, and move as the card is moved. Put the name of the plant inside the card, with instructions for sowing.

Method

1 Attach double-sided film to the front half of the brown paper. Draw a circle in the center and draw petals radiating out from this. Cut out the petal shapes, leaving the center uncut.

2 Carefully peel back a narrow strip of the film at the top of the card and stick this strip to the white mount, ensuring that you place it accurately. Gradually peel back the film, sticking the cut-out flower to the white mount, bit by bit.

3 Cut out the center of the flower through both layers.

4 Put the seeds into the plastic bag and tape this to the inside of the card mount so that the seeds are visible through the hole.

MATERIALS
- **White card mount with a textured finish, 11 x 5½ in. (28 x 14 cm), scored to fold in middle**
- **Brown paper, cut to the same size as the whole card mount, front and back**
- **Double-sided self-adhesive film**
- **Seeds**
- **Small, clear plastic bag**
- **Craft knife**
- **Cutting mat**
- **Adhesive tape**

CARDS FROM NATURE

A relatively simple method of producing unique greeting cards is to collect feathers, leaves, seed pods, or dried flowers, and mount them on to textured, natural-colored papers. Handmade papers are also available, many of which would complement the natural objects used. These cards are very easy to make but look very elegant.

TOOLS AND MATERIALS
- **A feather; chicken or duck feathers are very suitable**
- **Sugar paper in 2 colors; pale beige and pink, 8½ x 11½ in. (21 x 29 cm)**
- **Natural-color blank card, 6 x 8 in. (15 x 20 cm)**
- **Scissors**
- **Craft knife**
- **Masking tape**
- **Cutting mat**

1 *Select your feather and its background paper. Carefully tear the paper to the correct size. A torn edge will give a more interesting effect.*

3 *Slide the shaft of the feather through the slits until the feather lies in the desired position on the paper.*

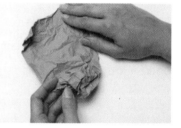

5 *To further decorate the card, select a complementary colored paper for a background. Crumple this sheet of paper in your hands. Flatten out the paper, then tear it to size. Apply glue, then stick this to a larger folded, contrasting card.*

2 *Place the backing paper on the cutting mat and with a craft knife, make two slits in the paper.*

4 *Turn over the paper and keeping the feather in position put a piece of tape over the openings and the feather shaft to secure the feather in place. If decorating with dried leaves, seed pods, etc., mount them using PVA glue and leave to dry for 30-40 minutes.*

6 *To complete the greeting card, glue the paper holding the feather on to the middle of the crumpled-effect background.*

CANNED CHRISTMAS CARDS

These unusual cards are made from pieces of old tin cans. They are fun and easy to make, but take care when you are cutting and working with metal, and always wear protective gloves because the edges can be sharp. When you are punching out the designs, use a thick piece of card to protect your work surface. The metal we used came from the side of a large, empty coffee can. Use tin snips to remove the bottom and top of the can, then cut down the side and open it out to form a flat sheet.

TOOLS AND MATERIALS

- ◆ **Tracing paper**
- ◆ **Pencil**
- ◆ **Ruler**
- ◆ **Scalpel or craft knife**
- ◆ **Colored card, some with textured surface**
- ◆ **Pieces of tin**
- ◆ **Masking tape**
- ◆ **Small hammer**
- ◆ **Center punch**
- ◆ **Tin snips**
- ◆ **Double-sided adhesive tape**

1 *Trace the templates for the cards and motifs, making sure that you transfer all cutting lines and fold lines too. The dots on the motif outlines indicate the positions of the punched holes. Cut the basic card shape, then cut out the windows, using a craft knife or scalpel and a metal ruler. Score and fold the card along the fold lines.*

2 *Choose a motif, then cut a piece of metal about 1 in. (2.5 cm) larger (all round) than the motif. Place the piece of metal on thick card and place the traced motif on top, holding the tracing in place with masking tape. Place the point of the center punch on each dot and tap once or twice with a hammer. The aim is to make a neat dent in the surface of the metal—but not to pierce a hole right through. Continue until the motif is complete, then remove the tracing.*

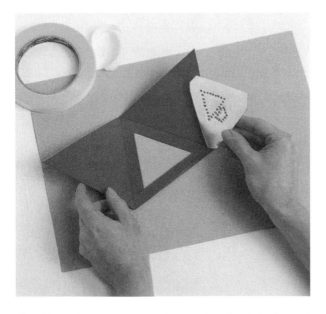 

3 *Using the tin snips, trim the metal so that it is about ½ in. (1.5 cm) larger all round than the window cut in the card. Attach the metal, face down behind the window, using double-sided tape to hold it in place.*

4 *Fold over the left-hand side of the card to cover the back of the metal piece. Hold it in place with double-sided tape.*

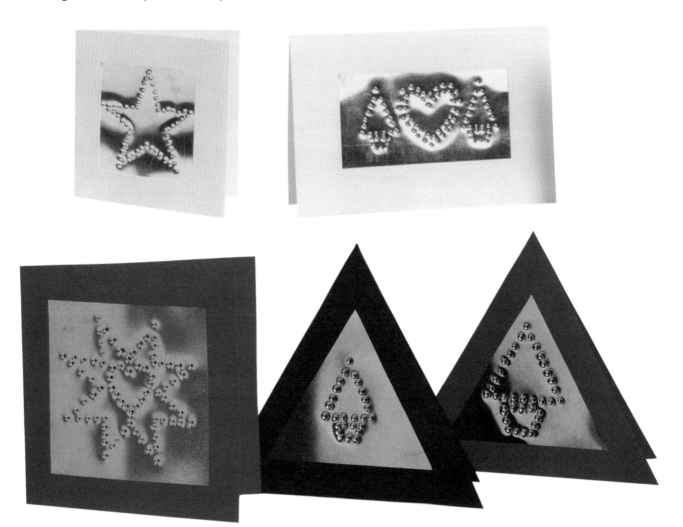

STARFISH

It is easiest to use light or non-printed paper when first making recycled paper pulp. Photocopying or computer paper is the best kind to use for this purpose.

Method

1   Tear the paper into small pieces no bigger than ¾ in. (2 cm) square and soak in a bowl of water for several hours. When soft, macerate the paper in a food processor or blender. Take one cup of paper and two of water at a time and blend until the fibers separate and form a "pulp." Transfer the pulp into a nylon sieve. Allow to drain, but not dry out.

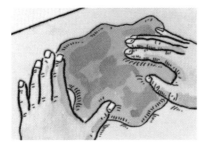

2   Warm and then press out a piece of plasticine so that it is slightly larger than the starfish. It should be about ⅜-¾ in. (1-2 cm) thick. Gently press the starfish halfway into the surface of the plasticine.

3   Cut a strip of strong but flexible card at least 2 in. (5 cm) taller than the height of the plasticine, with the

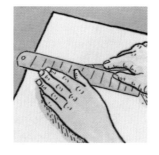

object pressed into it, and large enough to tightly wrap around the plasticine, making a collar. This should then be secured, using either a paperclip or staple. Place on a flat surface on newspaper.

4   Mix the plaster powder to a thick, creamy consistency with water in a throwaway container, then pour carefully over the object. The tight card collar will stop the plaster escaping. (Any leaks can be checked by pressing a spare piece of plasticine against the card.) Tap the card collar to help release any air bubbles. Leave to dry and harden.

5   Remove the card collar and carefully pull off the plasticine. The object should come away quite easily. If it doesn't, release it by carefully easing or levering it out with tweezers. When the plaster casting mould is completely dry and hard, brush a very thin layer of waterproof PVA over the casting surface. This should then be left to dry.

7 With a blunt, flat knife ease the paper pulp cast off the plaster mould. Leave in a warm place to dry, preferably on a wire-cooling rack. Mount on the card with an adhesive.

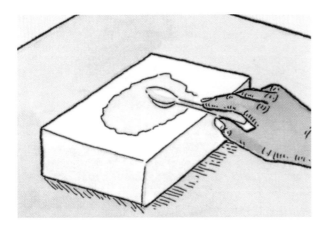

6 Spoon a small amount of the drained paper pulp on to the casting surface of the plaster mould. Using the back of a spoon press the pulp into and over the mould. Use an absorbent cloth to press down firmly on the pulp, removing all excess water and pushing the pulp into the shapes on the casting surface.

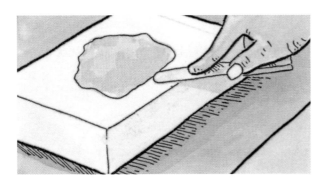

TOOLS AND MATERIALS

- **Card mount scored to fold in middle**
- **Strong, flexible cardboard**
- **Paper for pulp**
- **Plaster of paris**
- **Starfish for casting**
- **Plasticine**
- **Mixing pot and stirrer [throwaway]**
- **Food processor or blender**
- **Nylon sieve**
- **Scissors**
- **Paperclip or stapler**
- **Newspaper**
- **Tweezers**
- **Brush**
- **Metal spoon**
- **Absorbent cloth**
- **Blunt, flat knife**
- **Wire-cooling rack**
- **Waterproof PVA**
- **All-purpose gluecard mount scored to fold in middle**

BIG-MOUTH HIPPO

Open this card, and this hippo will stick out his tongue at you. This is a great card to give to children.

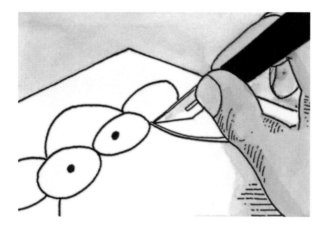

Method

1 Fold the card in half lengthways. Draw a hippo's head on the front. Give him a great big nose and a pair of jutting-out teeth. Using a craft knife, cut around the hippo's head through both layers of card.

2 Paint the front and back of the head gray, adding the details of eyes, nostrils, and ears, and outlining in black.

3 Fold the pink paper. Using the hippo head as a template, draw around it on to the pink paper. Cut out two pink paper shapes, and glue to the inside-front and back of the head—or just paint the inside pink.

4 With the ruler and blunt edge of the scissors, score a line across the front of the face, about $\frac{1}{4}$ in. (5 mm) below the eyes. Fold the lower part of the face back up from this line. Draw a pencil line along the fold, on the other half of the card.

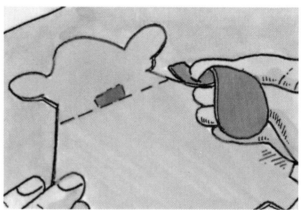

5 Cut out a tongue from the red paper. Glue it to the inside of the mouth, just above the pencil line on the back card.

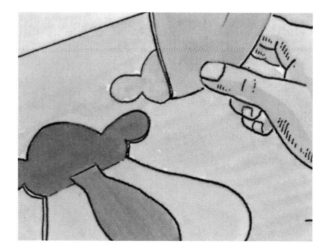

6 Spread glue on the inside of the head, as far down as the pencil line. Press the two top halves of the head together, enclosing the top of the tongue, but leaving the mouth open.

7 Paste white paper teeth inside the mouth (and on the back of the jutting teeth). Cut out a black paper epiglottis and glue in place, or paint a black epiglottis.

TOOLS AND MATERIALS

- Piece of card, 12 x 5 in. (30 x 12 cm)
- Pink paper, same size as card, or pink paint
- White paper
- Red paper
- Black, gray, and white paint
- Paintbrush
- Scissors
- Craft knife
- Cutting mat
- Ruler
- Fabric/paper glue

NEW HOME, SWEET HOME

This is a complicated card to make, but it looks so good that you will want to try it if you have successfully attempted any of the other pop-up designs in this book. The house is made in the form of a box, as is the fence. The telegraph pole is attached to the fence, and the chimney is not attached to the roof, but to the backing sheet, which increases the three-dimensional effect. The grid is drawn to a scale of 1:2½.

TOOLS AND MATERIALS
* Backing sheet (white mounting card), 12 x 8¾ in. (30 x 22 cm)
* Adhesive tape
* Scissors
* Thin green, brown, dark-green, gray, and white card (for all other pieces), about 12 x 10 in. (30 x 25 cm) in total
* Craft knife or scalpel
* Clear, all-purpose adhesive
* Masking tape

KEY

▬▬▬▬	cut along this line
▬▬▬▬	suggested artwork
▬▬▬▬	mountain crease
▬▬▬▬	valley crease
☐	glue here (sometimes on the underside)

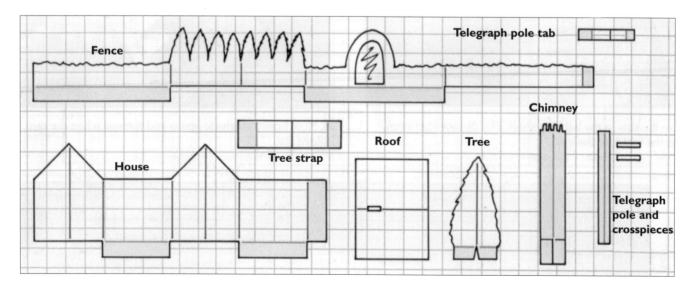

Fence

Telegraph pole tab

House

Tree strap

Roof

Tree

Chimney

Telegraph pole and crosspieces

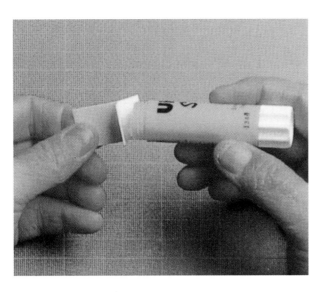

1   *Cut the backing sheet in half, place it face down, butt the cut edges together, and stick them together with tape so that it will lie flat after being folded. Use the template (OPPOSITE PAGE) to cut out the pieces. Apply glue to both ends of the tree strap.*

3   *Glue the tree to one end of the strap.*

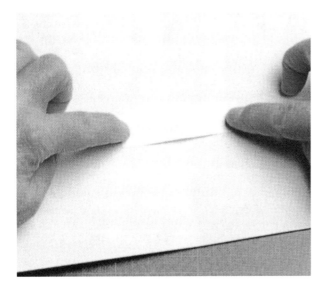

2   *Glue the strap across the central crease on the backing sheet. The strap folds up when the card is closed.*

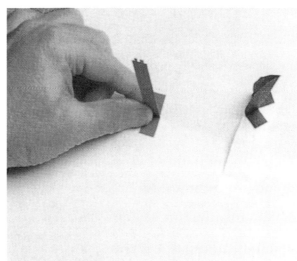

4   *Glue and fold the chimney so that it is double-thickness, and glue its tabs to the backing sheet, each side of the central crease.*

5   *Glue the tab at the end of the house to the other end to make it three-dimensional.*

6   *Add masking tape to the long top edges of the house, then lower on the roof. Fix it in place so that it rests in the correct position. This may take several attempts, and you will need to open out the house to check that you have got it right.*

7   *Apply glue to the underside of the house tabs.*

8   *Glue them to the backing sheet, taking care to lower the house over the chimney and to pull the house fully open.*

9   *Similarly, fold and glue the fence to the backing sheet. Stretch it so that it is square.*

10   *Glue the telegraph pole to the fence and backing sheet. Assemble the telegraph pole and crosspieces, and glue to the front of the tab.*

11   *When the card is closed, all the separate pieces collapse.*

AMAZING
PAPERCRAFT

MAKING HANDMADE PAPER

Papermaking itself is a gratifying occupation. No previous experience is necessary—you can start right away and be pleased with what you produce. Moreover, papermaking by hand actively recycles, and the cultivation of the fresh plant ingredients has an almost entirely benign ecological impact.

Having made it, what will you do with it? You may want to send special messages on personally crafted paper, such as seasonal greetings, love letters, and even poems. You can create presents with it, cover boxes, embroider it, or wrap jewels in it. You can even print images on it – recycled paper blended with plant material takes ink beautifully from linocuts and wood blocks.

PAPER RECIPES

The main ingredient of paper pulp is plant cellulose, and although paper can be made from any plant, the higher the ratio of usable cellulose in the plant, the stronger the pulp and the better the paper. Pulp is a carrier, a fibrous web to which you can add any decorative plant material.

This section contains a range of diverse and exciting paper "recipes," which add various plant materials to the paper pulp. Some of the more adventurous recipes create a pure plant pulp, rather than adding ingredients into a base of paper pulp. The selection of recipes here is based on readily available ingredients, most of which can be found in the home, grown in the yard, or collected from plants in the wild.

PAPERMAKING TECHNIQUES

A great attraction of hand papermaking is its accessibility. Abundant materials, inexpensive equipment, and modest space requirements are matched by recipes that are as straightforward and hassle-free as an elementary cookbook. The basic technical skills are easily acquired. You will achieve ever-more distinguished papers, but you will not have to clear any very difficult technical hurdles along the way.

Scooping and couching

Many people are discouraged by their inability to make sheets from pulps with the consistency of lumpy porridge or with unsuitable fibers, such as from newsprint. Make sure your pulp is of a fine consistency. Secondly, the smooth action necessary for scooping and couching the wet pulp sheet on to a post of felts is a knack that comes with experience, so don't become frustrated and angry with yourself if you don't pick up this technique immediately.

Keeping things simple

When you first start making paper, it is a good idea to air-dry all your sheets on the mould, avoiding the need to couch and press the papers between felts. You can make enough frames to make a number of cockle-free sheets with attractive surface textures. This is a technique used right around the world; indeed it is in fact the traditional way of making paper in Nepal.

Even experienced paper makers use the air-drying technique, in particular for very fine papers made from pure plant pulps. If you fail during your first attempts at papermaking, do not be dismayed. The material is not wasted—put it back in the vat and you will be able to get it right next time!

SIMPLE AND INTERMEDIATE TECHNIQUES

These recipes all work on a standard quantity of paper pulp, based on eighteen 8$\frac{1}{2}$ x 11 in. (A4) sheets of wastepaper, mixed with 8 pints (4.5 liters) of water. This quality will make 12 new sheets of 6 x 5 in. (15 x 12.5 cm). Before you start work, cover your surfaces with capillary matting or other water absorbers.

PREPARING RECYCLED PAPER PULP

1 To filter the water, wrap several thicknesses of net around a tap before filling a bucket or kitchen bowl.

2 Soak eighteen 8$\frac{1}{2}$ x 11 in. (A4) sheets of wastepaper in the water overnight, making sure it is completely covered.

3 Tear the soaked paper into small pieces, about 2 in. (5 cm) square. Separate the torn paper into six batches of equal size.

4 Fill a 2-pint (1.2-liter) kitchen blender jar to three-quarters and add a batch of torn paper. Blend for 20 seconds, or until no undigested pieces of paper remain.

5 Pour into the vat and repeat. The vat should be three-quarters full. Keep the sixth batch to top up the vat later.

6 For writing on the paper, add size to the pulp. Use 2 tbsps of white craft glue (P.V.A.) or laundry starch, mixed with $\frac{1}{2}$ pint (300 ml) of warm water. Stir gently.

MAKING A MOLD

1 *A store-bought embroidery frame can be made into a papermaking mold with net curtaining, held tautly in place. Patterned net will emboss the paper.*

2 *Stretcher frame kits can easily be assembled with a small amount of waterproof glue at the joints. Tap into place with a hammer.*

3 *Fold net curtaining over the edges and fix in place with stainless steel staples. Align the mesh squarely on the frame and it will be easier to get the tension even all over.*

SHEET FORMING

1 *Dampen 13 felts, twice as long as the mold and a little wider. Fold one into a small pad, to help release the pulp from the mold. Place another felt so the pad sits centrally under one half of its length: the other half will be folded over the sheet.*

2 *Stir the pulp and wait for the waves to subside. Grasp the mold by the shorter sides and lower it vertically into the vat, at the side furthest from you.*

3 *Tilt the top end of the mold downward and pull it towards you until it is horizontal below the surface of the pulp.*

4   *Still holding the mold horizontally, raise it out of the vat. It will emerge covered with a layer of pulp, while water drains back into the vat through the net. Try to complete this scoop in one continuous motion.*

5   *Check the sheet for unevenness. If the sheet is uneven, turn the mold over and gently place it back on the surface of the mixture. Raise the mold and the pulp will drop back into the vat. Stir and scoop again.*

COUCHING

1   *When you have an even covering of pulp, hold the mold over the vat for a few seconds to drain. Then position the mold over the couching pad at one end of the felt, turn it over, lower, and press down on the post.*

2   *Press a damp sponge into the exposed net to remove more water. Rock the mold from side to side to loosen the sheet before lifting up the mold. After the first few sheets you will be able to couch in one continuous motion.*

3   *Fold the other half of the felt over the sheet, making a sandwich. Lay a fresh felt on top of the post and repeat until you have completed four sheets. Refill the vat with half the reserve pulp. Make four more sheets and refill the vat with the remaining pulp.*

4   *Before completing the final four sheets, allow the pulp to settle and skim over the top with a jug to remove the thin pulp. Sieve the contents of the jug, and return the solids in the sieve to the vat. Stir, let settle, then form and couch the final four sheets.*

STORING PULP

Sieve the pulp and leave to dry. To use it, soak for two hours and re-blend with water. Wet pulp can be kept in refrigerated airtight containers for a week, longer in a freezer.

ADDING DRIED PLANT MATERIAL

In some recipes, plant material is positioned on the surface of a sheet. Form and couch the first sheet. Use tweezers to place the plant material as you wish. Fold over the felt.

PRESSING

1 Once a post—a pile of sheets and felts—is built, it must be pressed to expel water and help the fibers bond. Cut two pieces of capillary matting and two boards slightly larger than the felts.

2 Place the pieces of capillary matting at the base and top of the post, and place the post between the boards. Put the post into a press and tighten as much as possible, until no more water is squeezed out.

3 To press sheets with bulky additions, or that stain the felts, form and couch one sheet and place the single sheet-and-felt sandwich between several newspapers. Press, and dry by the newspaper method (see p.345).

DRYING AND FINISHING

All handmade paper needs to be restrained in some way while it dries. If the pressed sheets were to be removed from their felts while still damp, and left to dry naturally, they would shrink unevenly and cockle, so restraining is a necessary stage in the papermaking process.

Different methods of drying are appropriate to different types of paper. You cannot use the board-drying method for papers made with bulky ingredients, but newspaper drying is perfectly suited to them. The air-drying method is used for delicate papers that are difficult to couch.

HANGING

Indoor *Pick up each felt by the open ends and hang them vertically, with clothes pins (pegs), on a washing line or clothes-drying rack. Leave until the sheets are nearly dry (the exact time will depend on how warm and well-ventilated the place is) and then finish off by ironing.*

Outdoor *To make sheets with an "elephant hide" appearance, hang the felts outside in a breezy spot. Only do this when rain is not forecast, or invest in a rain alert, a device designed to let blind people know when it starts to rain. Once dry, do not iron.*

NEWSPAPER DRYING

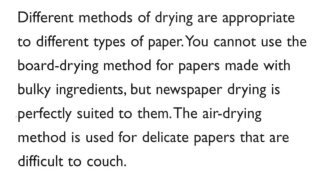

Place two felt-and-sheet sandwiches side by side on a whole newspaper, not just a single sheet. Cover the felts with at least six sheets of newspaper and position the next two felts on top. Continue to build up a post, finishing with a final whole newspaper. Leave for several hours. Either repeat the process with dry newspaper until the sheets are completely dry, or finish the drying by ironing.

Below *A sheet of paper that was dried by hanging outdoors, giving a characteristic "elephant hide" appearance.*

PHOTOGRAPHIC PRINT DRYER

This is great for delicate paper. Partially dry the sheet between newspapers, and lay it face up on the metal plate. Clip the cover down. Your sheet will be dry in two hours.

BOARD DRYING

Use a melamine-face board, dampened with water. Unfold the felt and place it sheet down on the board. Brush the felt with a paint-brush, working from the center outward. Remove the felt and leave the exposed sheet to dry, away from direct sunlight. If the edges curl, spray-mist the sheet with water and sponge the edges back against the board. Once dry, release the sheet with a pointed palette knife.

AIR DRYING

1 *Form a sheet and wipe the pulp off the frame. Let it drain flat until it is only damp. Place it on dry newspaper at an angle so the underside can dry. Finally, stand upright in an airy place, not in direct sun.*

2 *When the sheet is completely dry, carefully insert a pointed palette knife where the sheet looks thickest. Support the knife from under the net. Work the blade around the sheet's edges and carefully lift it off.*

IRONING

Ironing finishes a sheet of paper and helps the final stages of drying. Sandwich sheets of dry or semi-dry paper between two sheets of brown paper. Work with a domestic iron on "dry" setting, keeping it moving until the sheet is dry. Use moderate heat for papers with flowers, or it will affect their colors. For a smooth surface, sprinkle the sheets with talcum powder before ironing. Alternatively, mist the sheets with spray starch: this will also help size the paper (see p.341).

SPECKLED SHEETS

You may think, and with reason, that it is a little odd to tear up a piece of paper, only to reconstitute it so it looks pretty much the same at the end!

If these are your thoughts, look at the following creative suggestions. It is at this point that papermaking becomes an open-ended art form, where the only limitation is your imagination. Assume no rules, no right or wrong, just enjoy it. You will be surprised how often a silly idea, or indeed a silly mistake, can give a beautiful result.

3 *Form the sheet on the mold as before (with or without a deckle), then couch, press, and dry. The sheet will be white with orange and gray speckles.*

1 *Make a bowl of white pulp. Blend a small quantity of orange paper in a little water for about 10 seconds, so that it is not quite pulped, but shredded into small speckled pieces, and pour it into the white pulp.*

2 *Repeat the previous step with a similar quantity of gray paper.*

4 *Try speckling the paper with white speckles in a colored pulp, or with any other combination of colors. As an alternative, blend tea leaves in a little water and add them to a white or colored pulp. You could also add small objects directly to the pulp without blending them: seeds, short lengths of hair or colored threads, confetti, small scraps of fabric, colorful flower petals, or autumn leaves, all make an attractive effect when embedded in the paper.*

LAID-ON EFFECTS

1   *Couch a white sheet. Then tear up strips or cut out shapes from sheets of colored tissue paper and lay them on top of the couched sheet. As the sheet dries, the tissue will remain stuck to it.*

2   *To achieve subtle colored effects try this. Couch a sheet and lay paper on top. Form another sheet using the mold only and couch it exactly over the top of the first sheet. This traps the colored items between two layers of pulp, but they will still be faintly visible.*

TIPS

Try creating laid-on effects with thin and thick pieces of colored paper. With thick pieces, press and dry the paper on the couched sheets, then peel it off. Some of its colored pigment will have run off on to the main sheet to form a colored shadow (see left). Other interesting laid-on effects can be created with tickets, wool, petals, leaves (see left), sand, etc.

SHAPED PULPS

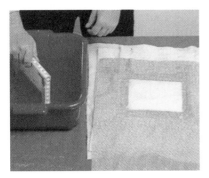  

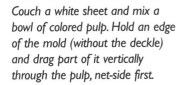

1	*Couch a white sheet and mix a bowl of colored pulp. Hold an edge of the mold (without the deckle) and drag part of it vertically through the pulp, net-side first.*
2	*Remove the mold from the pulp – the pulp will be deposited on to only part of the mold. Couch it over the top of the white sheet.*
3	*The colored pulp will cover part of the white pulp. Press and dry as before. Various effects can be achieved (BELOW).*

TIPS

Try mixing up a few differently colored pulps and couching them on the same sheet, or dragging a corner of the mold through the pulp, in order to change the shape of the pulp on the mold.

To achieve more complex shapes of colored pulp, stick a paper shape to the top of the net, leaving holes where the pulp has to couch. Put all the mold under the pulp in the conventional manner. Pull it out and remove the paper shape, taking part of the pulp with it. Those parts of the net that were not covered with the paper will have retained pulp. Couch on to a previously couched sheet.

EMBEDDING USING LAMINATING

The technique of laminating (also known as "multiple couching") involves couching one or more sheets of paper on top of each other. The fibers of each layer of paper bond together during pressing and drying to create a single sheet. You can use this relatively simple technique to produce a number of subtly interesting effects.

Try using layers of different colors to make a double-sided sheet, or several overlapping layers to create a softer effect. Here, feathers are embedded between two laminated sheets.

TOOLS AND MATERIALS
- Cotton linters pulp
- Feathers
- Mold and deckle
- Press

2 *Place another sheet of couched paper directly on top. Place a felt and then the heavy blanket over the sheets, and proceed with the pressing operation. Embed and press one sheet at a time; otherwise, you will get impressions of the embedded material on the other sheets as they are pressed.*

After couching a sheet of paper, arrange the feathers in a pleasing composition on its surface.

USING A WIRE MESH

Paper can be embossed either by forming it on a textured surface, or, as demonstrated here, by pressing a textured surface against it. By virtue of the paper used in this technique being thicker, the wire mesh can actually be pressed quite firmly down into the paper. The pressure of the relief element applied against it quite dramatically alters the surface of the paper to form a satisfying textured pattern. If you want to achieve more subtle embossing patterns, you could try pressing a dishcloth, tea towel, piece of lace, or embroidered cloth on to the paper, remembering to cover it first with a felt.

TOOLS AND MATERIALS
- **Formed sheet of paper**
- **Wire mesh**
- **Press**

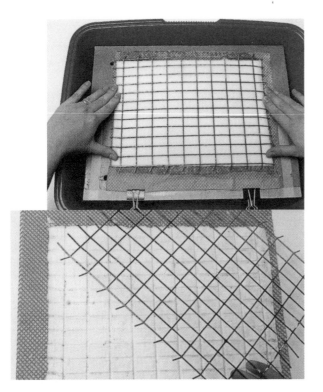

1 *Couch a thick sheet of paper and place the wire mesh on top, pushing well into the surface. Lay a felt and a heavy blanket over the top and press. Leave the layers in the press for at least four hours, with the wing nuts tightened.*

2 *Remove the sheet and mesh, and let the paper dry on the felt. The paper will shrink, so remove the mesh before the paper is fully dry, leaving an impression of the mesh on the surface of the sheet.*

COLORING PULP

You can get exciting colors by adding a dye to the pulp before you start to form a sheet of paper. Cold-water fabric dyes are easy to obtain and use, or you can purchase specialist dyes. Make sure that the color is fast and will not run, especially when laminating wet sheets of colored paper. It is worth experimenting, too. Try using tea or coffee, the juice from berries, food colorings, and spices.

2 *Leave the pulp to soak in the dye for a while, then pour it into a colander lined with fine net. Run water over and through the pulp to wash away excess dye.*

TOOLS AND MATERIALS

* **Pulp**
* **Cold-water fabric dyes**
* **Rubber gloves; barrier cream**
* **Plastic container**
* **Fine net**
* **Colander**
* **Mold and deckle**
* **Plastic tub**

3 *Start with the bold primary colors – red, blue, and yellow – and then mix them in order to obtain an exciting range of colors.*

1 *Mix the dye and pour it into the pulp. Mixing well will help obtain a consistent color.*

4 *Place the colored pulp in the tub and mix it well. Form the sheet, and press and dry it in the normal way. Make sure you wear rubber gloves and/or a barrier cream to prevent your hands from becoming the same color as the sheet of paper.*

MARBLING

Marbling is used after the paper has been made. It is a relatively simple technique, which originated in Persia in the 16th century, and helps you to get some amazing effects.

Marbling is based on the fact that oil and water do not mix, so an oil-based color will float on the surface of water. The colors can be mixed into patterns that are picked up on paper, but cannot be reproduced exactly.

TOOLS AND MATERIALS

* **Oil paints**
* **Wallpaper paste**
* **Ox gall**
* **Handmade paper**
* **Newspaper**
* **Mineral spirits**
* **Shallow tray**
* **Small dish**
* **Small paintbrush**
* **Dropper**
* **Knitting needle or toothpick**

1 *Squeeze some oil paint into a small dish.*

2 *Add a small quantity of mineral spirits and then mix well together.*

3 *To test for the correct consistency, dip a brush into the mixture and hold it above the dish. The paint should slowly form a drop and fall off. If the paint drops too fast, add more paint. If it does not drop at all, add more solvent.*

4 *To thicken the water, add a small amount of pre-mixed wallpaper paste and stir it in well.*

5 *Add a drop or two of ox gall to the paint mixture to aid the dispersion of the paint across the water surface.*

6 *To test for the right amount of ox gall, drop some paint on to the surface of water. It should quickly spread across the surface, forming interesting patterns. If it fails to spread, add more ox gall.*

7 *Repeat Steps 1 to 6 to mix the colors. Drop paint on to the water surface in a test bowl. It should spread well and indicate how the colors look together.*

8 *Dragging a strip of folded newspaper across the water surface will break its surface tension. This should be done before starting the marbling as well as to clean the water surface afterwards. As you drag the strip across the water, the paper picks up the remaining paint.*

11 *Holding a paper at diagonal corners, lay it on to the water surface. Start with the corner farthest from you. Remove the paper when the water begins to soak through the back.*

12 *Holding the corners of the paper, lift it up vertically from the water surface. Lay the sheet flat on top of a thick pad of newspapers and let it dry. The dry sheets can then be ironed.*

9 *Hold the brush loaded with paint horizontally above the water surface and tap it gently so that drops of paint disperse across the surface.*

13 *For a more controlled pattern, try the traditional marbling technique known as "combing." Drop two colors on top of the water, and with a knitting needle, drag through the water along the length of the tray to produce parallel lines.*

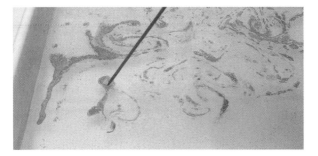

10 *Repeat with another paint color, then use the point of a knitting needle to move the areas of paint into one another – until you have a pleasing design.*

14 *Lift the sheet carefully from the water and lay it flat to dry. Always clean the surface of the water before marbling another sheet of paper.*

AROMATIC PAPER

- *Incorporating natural objects*
- *Creating scented paper*
- *Combining color, texture, and scent*

Handmade scented paper is both attractive to look at and delightful to smell. These sheets are ideal for using as notepaper for a special letter, or even for folding into envelopes. Sprinkle scented ingredients into your pulp for a textured, lightly perfumed effect, or blend scent into your pulp for a stronger fragrance. Your choice of scented ingredients is limitless, but be careful when using artificially dyed products, because they tend to bleed. Test for this by wetting the material. If the color runs, the dye is not fast and it will leak into your paper. This is less important if you are pulping your ingredients, and indeed you may want to create the effect deliberately.

Right *These delicate, scented sheets will be treasured by the recipient of a letter written on them.*

SCENTED PAPER

Select the dry ingredients that you want to include. If you are using flowers on stems, such as lavender, shake the flowerheads off and discard the stems.

2 *After making a batch of pulp and coloring it to match your scented ingredients, mix the pulp with water in the vat.*

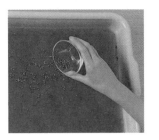

3 *Sprinkle the lavender flowers evenly into the pulp.*

4 *Agitate the pulp with your hand to ensure that the flowers are mixed well.*

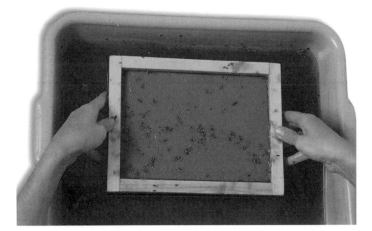

5 *Form, drain, and couch your sheet of paper. The texture will add visual interest to the delicate smell.*

POTPOURRI PAPER

1 *To make a more strongly perfumed sheet, use scented pulp. Liquefy a potpourri of scented wood shavings in an electric blender three-quarters full of water.*

2 *Add the scented mixture to some colored pulp in the vat and mix well.*

3 *Form the sheet. The sheet will have a more regular surface than the lavender paper. Couch your sheet on top of the first lavender sheet.*

SHAPING PAPER

- *Creating unusual shapes*
- *Masking areas on the mold*
- *Embedding objects within layers*

Once you have mastered the basics of forming and couching, you can adapt those techniques to create more unusual pieces. Make your own irregularly shaped deckles, or utilize other craft frames, as we have done here. Masking areas on the mold gives further flexibility of shape.

Simple deckle shapes can be cut from plywood with a jigsaw. You can also use biscuit cutters, cake molds, or a product called Buttercut (available from papermaking suppliers). If you are making stationery papers, an envelope-shaped deckle is convenient. Experiment by creating hearts, stars, animal shapes, and festive figures such as angels.

Here, three separate couched sheets were layered. There are two benefits to this technique: the varying thicknesses of the pulp over different areas gives a pleasing effect; and if you want to use heavy items as embellishments, they can be anchored between the layers.

Below *To preserve this fragile creation from dust and damage, it will need to be placed in a deep frame with a glass front.*

1   To make a basic circular mold and deckle, stretch a piece of nylon curtain over a 12 in. (30 cm) diameter embroidery frame. Tighten the outer ring and then trim off any excess nylon to the edge of the hoop.

4   Form your sheet. You will notice that pulp will not adhere to the masked area, and so a hole will appear in the center of the sheet.

2   Using a template, draw two semicircles on waterproof tape. Cut these out. Use the same template and a soft pencil to draw a circle on the center of the screen. Stick the tape in place using the pencil mark as a guide.

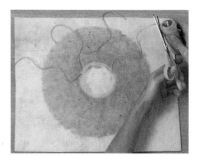

5   Couch the sheet. While it is still wet, apply lengths of string from the middle ring to the outside edge and beyond. As it becomes wet, the natural color of the string will be absorbed into the paper and leave a 'printed' line.

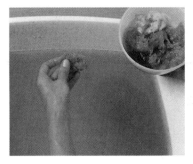

3   Use two or three different pulps. This will give an unusual effect to the finished piece. Add all the pulp to the vat and agitate well. A combination of half-stuff and pulp made from natural fibers was used here.

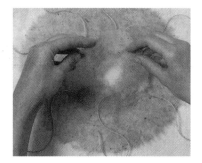

6   Make a small circular sheet in the same way as the first one, using a 5¹/₂ in. (14 cm) embroidery hoop mold. Mask the center. Laminate this sheet on top of the first one, trapping the string. Brush out with a soft brush.

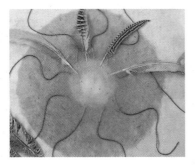

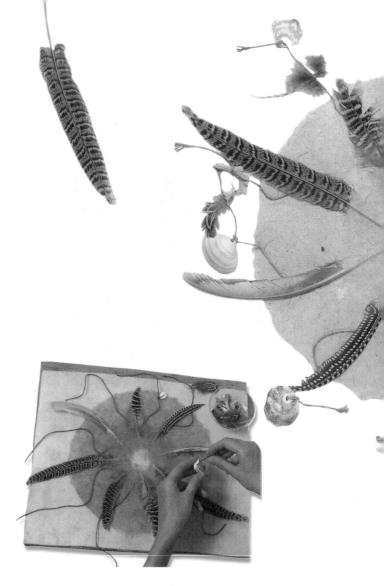

7 *Add feathers to the wheel, positioning them in such a way as to make a pleasing design with the string.*

8 *Form another circle of paper using the smaller mold, but do not mask the center. Place this solid circle over the center of the wheel, covering the base of the feathers. Take care when handling, as the circular sheet is fragile.*

9 *Use the soft brush to secure the feathers, and sponge off any excess water. You can now add decoration, such as knotting the ends of some of the strings or attaching tiny shells.*

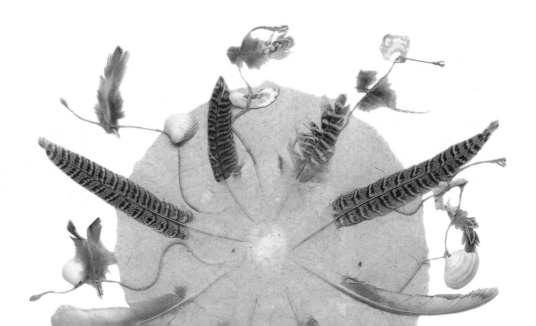

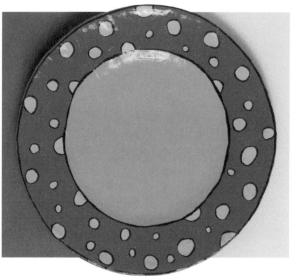

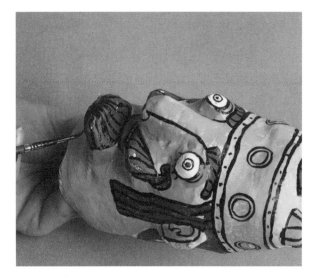

PAPIER MÂCHÉ

Papier mâché is French for 'chewed-up paper,' referring
to the two methods of making papier mâché: from roughly torn
paper strips or from a paper pulp. The first method
is more common, because it uses basic household
materials and needs no preparation.
Papier mâché can be made into bowls, jewelry,
wall ornaments, dolls, and masks. It can also be a
substitute for traditional sculpture. Shape an armature
of chicken wire to your chosen form, and layer it with
papier mâché. Or cast your sculpture from a clay model
or existing mold, such as a fruit or shell.

A papier mâché object is made by building up layers of glued paper strips on a mold or by using papier mâché pulp. When the layers are dry, the form is eased from the mold and decorated. Newspaper is an ideal material for papier mâché, because it remains flexible when wet with glue. The layering and the paste give it strength, and its tendency to discolor does not matter because it will be painted. The newspaper must be torn, not cut, since the slightly irregular edges blend with less obvious seams when the strips are pasted down. To make objects from papier mâché you will need to make a mold. The easiest way of doing this is first to make a model from modeling clay, then to cast a mold in plaster of Paris. There is no limit to the range of molds you can make.

When the form is released from the mold, it can be trimmed and bound with additional torn paper. After preparing the surface with paint primer or gesso—a mixture of chalk, white pigment, and glue—you can decorate your finished piece with poster colors or acrylic paint.

TOOLS AND MATERIALS

- Hand blender
- Paintbrush
- Small scissors
- Craft knife
- Plastic buckets and bowls
- Rubber gloves
- Sieve
- Waterproof tape
- Modeling tools
- PVA glue
- Wallpaper paste
- Vaseline
- Modeling clay
- Gesso
- Acrylic paints
- Varnish
- Plaster of Paris
- A variety of newspapers and wastepaper torn into strips

LAYERED DECORATION
These colorful pots and dishes were decorated with paint and cutout paper shapes. The artist layered the cutouts directly on to the pots and sealed them under a coat of varnish.

HELPFUL HINT . . .
Cover your work top or table with old newspaper to prevent it getting marked with splashes of glue or paint. Best of all, use a plastic sheet, which can be wiped clean when you have finished work for the day.

HELPFUL HINT . . .
Wash your hands when you have been tearing up newspaper. You will be surprised at how much ink comes off the paper!

HELPFUL HINT . . .
Knives, especially craft knives, can be dangerous. Always hold what you are cutting very carefully, and cut away from you. Better still, ask an adult to help you.

HELPFUL HINT . . .
Wear a plastic apron or a pair of overalls when you make papier mâché—it can be quite messy.

HELPFUL HINT . . .
Don't be tempted to leave papier mâché to dry in strong sunlight—it may well become warped.

TECHNIQUES

Before you start any of the projects, read through all the instructions carefully to check how long the project will take you—many stages need to dry out overnight, so it is best to plan ahead.

Tearing paper

The length and width of your paper strips will vary according to what you are making. Pieces up to 3 in. (7.5 cm) wide can be used if you are covering large, flat surfaces, but for a lot of other projects you will often find that you need much smaller pieces, some only as large as postage stamps.

When you are tearing up paper, bear in mind that it has a grain, rather like material, and it will tear much more easily in one direction than the other, usually—though not always—from the top to the bottom. When embarking on a papier mâché project, never cut paper into strips with scissors; this will give a blunt, hard effect, which will show up when your object is painted and varnished.

Right Tear along the correct grain of the paper, as in the top picture. You can see, in the bottom picture, what happens if you do it the wrong way!

Gluing

Your strips of paper should be covered on both sides with wallpaper paste or watered-down PVA adhesive. You can use your fingers or a brush to apply the glue, but don't put too much on—or your object will take a long time to dry.

Using a mold

All sorts of objects can be used as molds for papier mâché. Bowls, plates, and dishes are ideal. Always smear petroleum jelly over the mold before you use it, or it will be very difficult to remove the dried paper shape. Cardboard is also a good "mold" or base—but it will be left inside the paper as a permanent part of the structure. Several layers can be built up on top of cardboard to make a good, strong base.

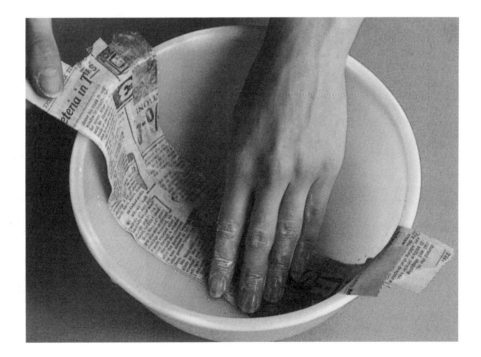

Drying

The time each piece will take to dry will depend on its size and the number of layers of papier mâché you have used. Usually, 24 hours is adequate for a cardboard shape with two or three layers of paper on it, but a balloon with eight layers of papier mâché may take up to 3 days to dry. If you can, use an airing cupboard to dry your papier mâché—it is an ideal place.

Sanding

When your papier mâché is dry, you should lightly rub down the surface with fine sandpaper. This will remove any wrinkles in the paper and give you a smoother surface to paint on.

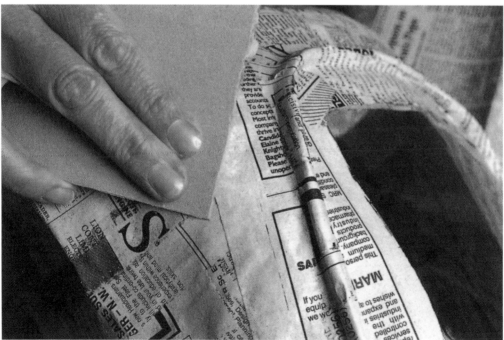

Priming

Use two coats of white paint to prime the surface of your papier mâché. This will cover up newsprint effectively, give a bright ground to paint on, and make your colors seem more luminous. You must let the first coat dry before adding the second, or the paint may crack badly. If this happens, let the paint dry, sand it back to the paper, and start again. Always use non-toxic paint.

Decorating

When you have finished priming the papier mâché object, it is finally ready to decorate with poster paint. You will have to thin the paint with water, and you will probably need to use two coats to achieve a good, deep color. Black Indian ink, which is waterproof, can be used to accentuate the painted designs. Apply it with a thin paintbrush and use a non-toxic brand.

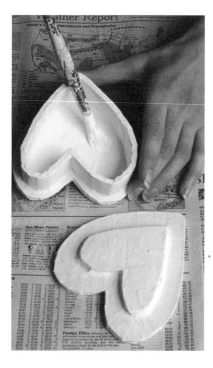

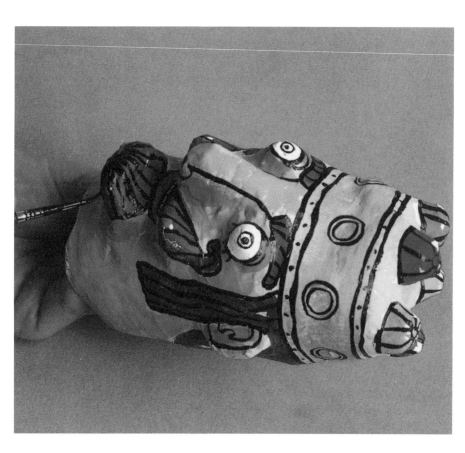

PLATE

This is a very simple project to teach you the basics of papier mâché, and it involves the process known as layering, by which strips of paper are laid on top of one another to form a strong paper shell.

The plate is decorated in bold, cheerful colors, and it is sealed with two coats of clear gloss varnish. Although you should not put wet things on it, the plate would hold fruit or something similar, or it could be hung on a wall as a decorative plaque. You could make several, painting them to match the color scheme of a bedroom or the kitchen.

TOOLS AND MATERIALS

- A plastic plate
- Petroleum jelly
- Paper
- Wallpaper paste or watered-down PVA adhesive
- Blunt knife or palette knife
- Scissors
- Fine sandpaper
- Poster paints
- Black Indian ink
- Clear gloss varnish

MAKING THE PLATE

1 Grease the plate you are using as your mold with a thin layer of petroleum jelly. This will make it easy to release the finished plate shape from the mold when it has dried. Tear the paper into strips about 1 in. (2.5 cm) wide and long enough to stretch across the plate with about 1 in. (2.5 cm) hanging over the edge at each side.

2 Coat the first strip of paper with wallpaper paste or watered-down PVA, and lay it in the mold, taking care to smooth out any creases or air bubbles. Continue to lay pasted strips of paper across the plate, covering the edge of the last strip you have put in position with the new piece.

3 *When you have completely covered the mold with the first layer of pasted paper, lay a second layer of strips across the plate, in the opposite direction to the first. This will ensure that the papier mâché is good and strong. Continue to cover the plate with layers of pasted paper in this way, until you have completed eight layers. Then leave your plate to dry for 48 hours in a warm, dry place.*

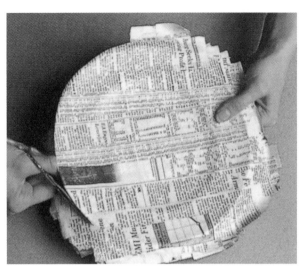

5 *When the papier mâché is dry, use a pair of scissors to trim the edge neatly back to within 1/4 in. (5 mm) of the rim.*

4 *When the papier mâché is dry, put the blade of a blunt knife or of a palette knife under the edge of the paper where it meets the rim of the mold, and gently prise it away. Because you greased the plastic plate with petroleum jelly, the paper should come away quite easily. Your paper shape will probably be a bit damp underneath, so lay it down in a warm place to dry for a few hours.*

6 *The cut edge will need sealing. Take a strip of paper about 1 in. (2.5 cm) wide, cover it with paste or glue, and carefully wrap it over the edge, tearing it off at the other side. Repeat this process until you have sealed all around the edges of your plate. Leave the plate to dry overnight on a wire cake rack.*

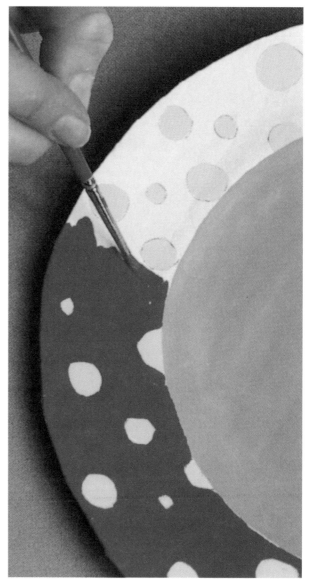

7 *Rub down the dry plate gently with fine sandpaper, paying special attention to the sealed edge, which may be a bit lumpy. When it is smooth, give your plate two coats of white paint, allowing the first coat to dry before you add the second. Let the paint dry for an hour or so after the second coat is applied.*

8 *Draw a design on the plate with pencil and start to fill in the color. You will probably have to use two layers of paint to get a good, deep color. Don't forget to paint the back as well!*

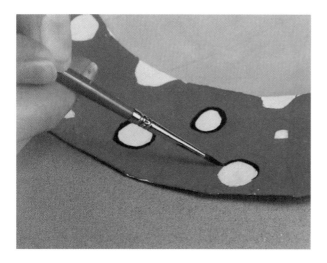

9 *Allow your painted plate to dry for 4 hours, and then outline your design with black Indian ink. Let the plate dry overnight.*

10 *Give the finished plate two coats of clear gloss varnish. You will probably have to paint the front of the plate and let it dry before you can varnish the back. Allow the first coat of varnish on each side of the plate to dry before you add the second. Remember to wash your varnishing brush with soap and water when you have finished.*

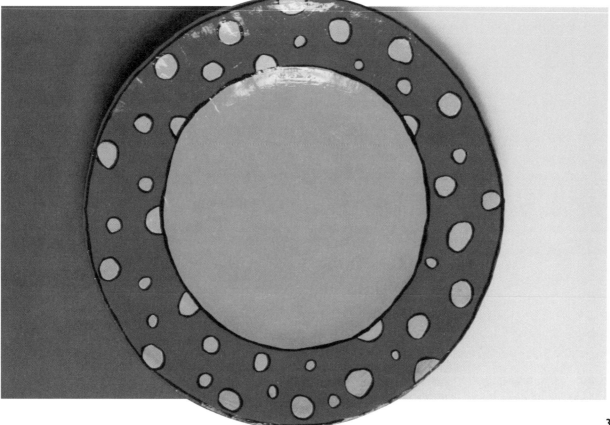

EARRINGS

These bright flower earrings look very attractive. Although they are quite large, these earrings are very light, and you could make them even larger or longer without weighing your ears down. Other motifs that would look good include hearts, stars, and fish.

The earrings are attached to the ears by clips, which are stuck to the backs of the yellow discs with strong glue.

Earrings Templates *(Thin card)*

MAKING THE EARRINGS

1 *Trace the earring shapes from the pattern above and transfer them to the thin card.*

2 *Cut around the shapes with a craft knife or scissors. Paint your cutout shapes with one coat of watered-down PVA adhesive. Lay them on a wire cake rack for 4 hours to dry.*

TOOLS AND MATERIALS

- ◆ Tracing paper
- ◆ Thin cardboard approximately 4 x 4 in. (10 x 10 cm)
- ◆ Craft knife or scissors
- ◆ Wallpaper paste or watered-down PVA adhesive
- ◆ Paper
- ◆ Fine sandpaper
- ◆ Poster paints
- ◆ Black Indian ink
- ◆ Clear gloss varnish
- ◆ Darning needle
- ◆ PVA adhesive
- ◆ 2 pairs of earring hooks and eyes
- ◆ Strong, clear glue
- ◆ 1 pair of clip fastenings
- ◆ Small pair of pliers

3 *Using strips of paper about ¹/₂ x 2 in. (12 mm x 5 cm), cover the earring shapes with three layers of pasted paper. Work around each petal, ensuring that your papier mâché does not get too lumpy. Lay the papered shapes on a cake rack to dry for 24 hours.*

4 *Smooth the shapes down with sandpaper and coat them with two layers of white paint, allowing the first to dry before adding the second. Draw the center of the daisy. The petal outlines and swirls will be drawn freehand on top of the poster paint later with black Indian ink.*

5 *Fill in the colors. The petals were painted light-blue, and when this coat was dry, they were painted again with violet, with the light-blue allowed to show through in patches. The discs have been given two coats of yellow paint. Allow the pieces to dry for 4 hours.*

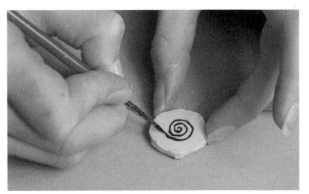

6 *Then, using a fine paintbrush, carefully draw in the black outlines and swirls. Let the earrings dry overnight, then varnish the fronts with clear gloss varnish. Lay the pieces (varnished side up!) on a wire cake rack to dry. Varnish the backs and allow them to dry again. Repeat the process so that the fronts and backs have two coats of varnish.*

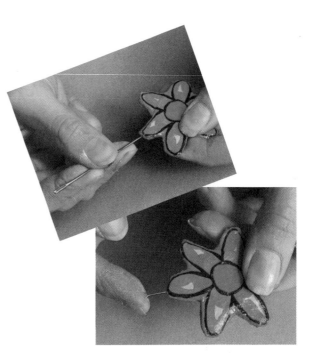

7 *When the second coat of varnish is dry, make a small hole with a darning needle in the top of the petal section and in the bottom of the disc. Dab a little undiluted PVA adhesive into the holes. Push an earring-hook section into the hole in each flower and an eye into each disc.*

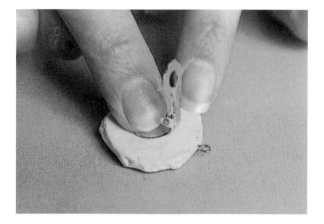 

8 Dab some strong, clear glue on to the earring clips and position one on the back of each disc. Press the disc and clip together firmly, and let all the earring pieces dry overnight.

9 Loop the hook into the eye, so joining the disc and the flower, and close the opening with a small pair of pliers. Your earrings are now ready to wear!

MAKING THE JEWELED BOX

1 *Measure the dimensions from the diagrams opposite and transfer them to the cardboard. Cut them out and form a square out of the wall pieces, holding the pieces together with masking tape. Smear the underside of the walls with PVA adhesive and stick the rectangle squarely on to the box base, securing it with masking tape. Then glue the lid insert on to the underside of the lid, holding it in place with tape. Leave everything to dry for a few hours, and then give both sections a coat of watered-down PVA. Leave to dry out overnight.*

2 *Cover both pieces of the box with three layers of papier mâché. Use strips of paper approximately 1 in. (2.5 cm) wide. When you have finished papering, leave the box to dry for 24 hours on a wire cake rack.*

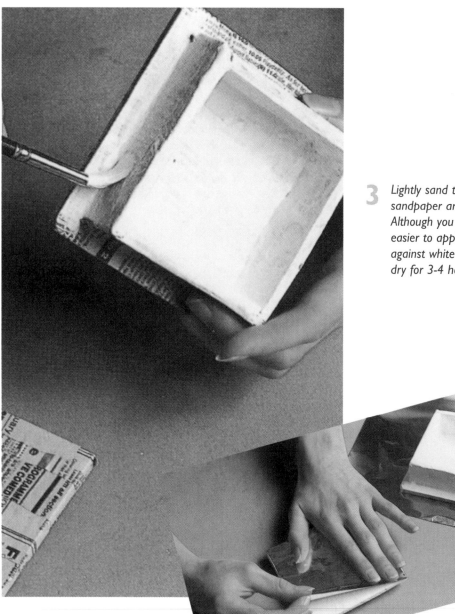

3 Lightly sand the surfaces of your dry box with fine sandpaper and give it one coat of white poster paint. Although you will not see this paint, it will make it easier to apply the foil, which will show up better against white paint than newsprint. Let the paint dry for 3-4 hours.

4 When the paint is dry, the box is ready to be covered in foil. The easiest way is to use long, thin pieces of foil to go around the walls of your box, and large pieces to cover the lid, base, and inside of your box. Cut all the pieces of foil to size before you start sticking it in place. As foil will mold itself to the shape of your box, it is a good idea to fit all the pieces of foil around your box as a trial run—to ensure they are the right shape and size. Use strong, clear glue to stick the foil down.

5 *Once you have stuck the foil to your box, leave it to dry for an hour or so before you add the "gemstones." Give some thought to the pattern you want to create and try a few variations before you stick the stones down permanently. When you have decided on the arrangement, smear a little strong, clear glue on the underside of each stone, and press it firmly on to the box. Let the box dry for 24 hours before you use it.*

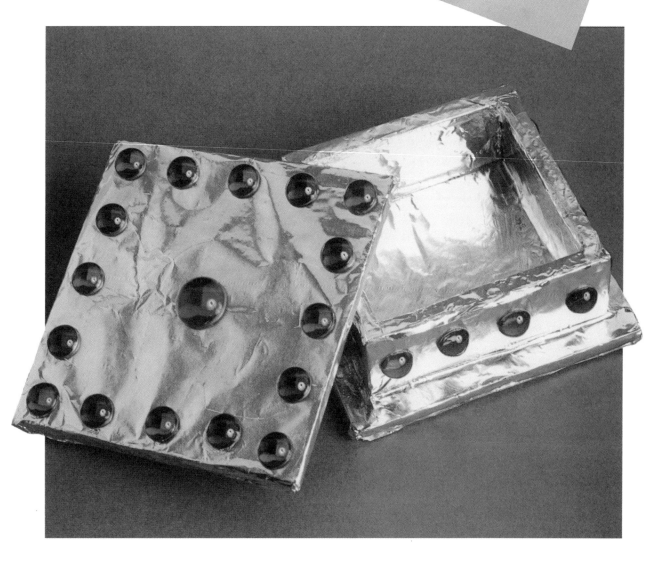

CHRISTMAS CUTOUTS

These cheerful cutouts can be used as decorations to brighten up your Christmas tree, but you need not stop there—they will lend a festive atmosphere to any part of the house and will look especially decorative displayed at a window.

Once you have painted and varnished them, you might like to add sequins or fake gemstones to give them an extra sparkle!

TOOLS AND MATERIALS

- Tracing paper
- Thin cardboard, approximately 10 x 10½ in. (25 x 26 cm) for each decoration
- Scissors
- Wallpaper paste or watered-down PVA adhesive
- Paper
- Fine sandpaper
- Poster paints
- Black Indian ink
- Clear gloss varnish
- Darning needle
- PVA adhesive
- Metal-screw eyes, one for each decoration
- Thin colored cord, approximately 8 in. (20 cm) for each decoration

Christmas Decorations Templates (*Thin card*)

BOW

STAR

ROBIN

MAKING THE CUTOUTS

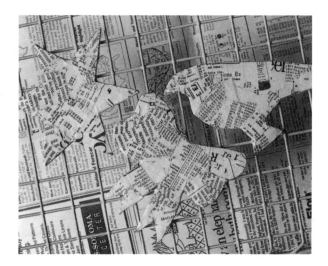

1 Trace the decoration shapes from the book and transfer them to your thin cardboard. Cut out the cardboard shapes with scissors. Give each decoration a coat of watered-down PVA adhesive and let them dry on a wire cake rack for about 4 hours. When they have dried somewhat, start to cover your pieces with pasted paper, using strips about 1/2 in. (12 mm) wide and 2 in. (5 cm) long.

3 When the shapes are dry, smooth them lightly with fine sandpaper and give them two layers of white poster paint; allow the first coat to dry properly before you add the second. Let the paint dry for 4 hours.

2 Cover each decoration with three layers of papier mâché and place them on a wire cake rack to dry for 24 hours.

4 Draw in the features or patterns on your decorations with pencil and start to apply the color with your paints. You will probably have to use two coats of paint to cover the white paint properly.

5 Leave the paint to dry for 4 hours, then use black Indian ink to outline and emphasize the details. Let the decorations dry overnight.

6 When they are thoroughly dry, paint your decorations with two coats of clear gloss varnish, allowing the first coat to dry properly before you add the second. Remember, as always, to clean your brush in soap and water when you have finished with it.

7 When the varnish is dry, ask an adult to help you to make a hole in the top of each decoration with a darning needle. Dab a little PVA adhesive into each hole and screw the metal eyes into each hole as far as they will go. Be careful to keep the screws straight so that they do not emerge from the sides of your decorations. Leave the decorations to dry for a few hours until the glue has set. All that remains to do is to tie the thin cord to the top of each metal eye. Tie a loop in the top of each length of cord once it is fastened to a decoration, and hang it from your tree.

SQUARE FRAME WITH HEART-SHAPED OPENING

This frame has a distinctive heart-shaped opening. It has a hinge and is fastened at one side with a thin ribbon bow.

Although this design would be good to give as a Valentine's Day present, you could make the opening any shape you like and make the frame as large or as small as you please. You could even have several openings in the frame and keep a variety of pictures or photographs in it.

TOOLS AND MATERIALS

- Thick cardboard, approximately 14 x 14 in. (36 x 36 cm)
- Craft knife
- PVA adhesive
- Masking tape
- Wallpaper paste or watered-down PVA adhesive
- Paper
- Fine sandpaper
- Cotton tape, approximately 1 in. (2.5 cm) wide and 8 in. (20 cm) long
- Thin cotton ribbon, approximately 8 in. (20 cm) long
- Strong, clear glue
- Poster paints
- Black Indian ink
- Clear gloss varnish
- Black felt, about 7 x 7 in. (17.5 x 17.5 cm)
- Scissors

Square Frame with Heart-shaped Opening Template *(Thick card)*

FRONT BACK

6.9 in. (17.5 cm)

6.9 in. (17.5 cm)

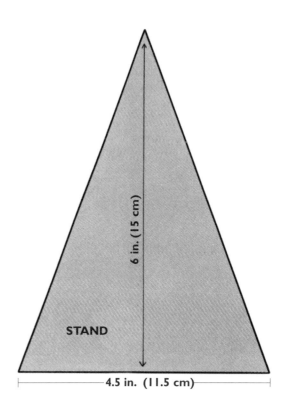

6 in. (15 cm)

STAND

4.5 in. (11.5 cm)

MAKING YOUR FRAME

1 Mark out the measurements for the front and back of the frame on the cardboard. Be sure to transfer the measurements correctly. Ask an adult to help you cut out the frame and stand pieces with a craft knife, because the knife will be very sharp.

2 Measure a point halfway along the top and bottom edges of the back. Use a ruler to join these two points with a pencil line. Smear one long edge of the stand with PVA adhesive and place it along the line on the back. Hold the stand firmly in position with masking tape and leave the glue to set for a couple of hours.

3 Give the frame pieces a coat of watered-down PVA adhesive, and let them dry on a wire cake rack for 4 hours. Cover all the pieces with three layers of papier mâché. Make sure that you do not knock the stand out of position. Let the frame pieces dry on a wire cake rack overnight.

4 Lightly rub down the dry pieces with fine sandpaper. Fold the tape you are going to use as the hinge in two lengthways and spread undiluted PVA adhesive on half of it. Stick the tape to the right-hand edge of the inside of the front of the frame. Smear glue on the other half of the tape and stick it to the edge of the back. While the tape is drying, prop the frame slightly open so that it doesn't stick to itself.

5 When the tape is dry, open the frame. Measure two points, one halfway down the inside of the left-hand side of the front of the frame, and one halfway down the right-hand side of the back. Mark these points and stick half the length of thin ribbon to each with strong clear glue. Hold the lengths of ribbon in place with masking tape. Cover the edges of the hinge tape and the thin ribbon with two layers of papier mâché. Leave the frame to dry for 24 hours.

  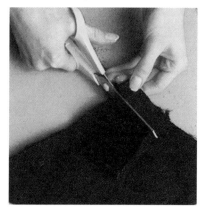

6 *Lightly sand the extra papier mâché and give your frame two coats of white poster paint, allowing the first coat to dry before you add the second. Leave to dry.*

7 *Draw a design on the frame with pencil and fill it in with color. Don't forget to paint the back too. Allow the paint to dry for 4 hours and then add detail to your design with black Indian ink. Let the frame dry overnight and then apply two coats of clear gloss varnish.*

8 *Take the piece of black felt and use scissors to cut it to the same size as the back. Smear it with undiluted PVA adhesive, and stick it carefully to the back so that it covers the edge of the thin ribbon. Let your frame dry overnight before you use it.*

DECOUPAGE

Decoupage is the art of decorating surfaces with applied paper cutouts. The word "decoupage" comes from the French *decouper*, which means "to cut out." Motifs are cut from paper and glued flat on to a surface and heavily varnished so that the edges blend in with the background, almost as if the motif was painted on to the surface. One of the primary goals is to get the motifs as smooth and flat as possible.

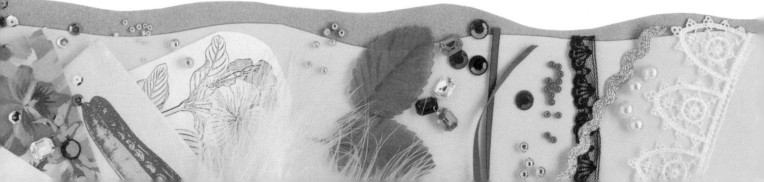

INTRODUCTION

The term "three-dimensional decoupage," then, seems to be a contradiction in terms, since the paper motifs are freestanding and not a part of the surface as they are in traditional decoupage. Unlike two-dimensional decoupage, three-dimensional decoupage gives an effect of depth and volume—in effect, a "trompe l'oeil," a trick of the eye. The composition looks almost lifelike, and has a richness and realism that a flat design would find it impossible to compete with.

There are differing opinions on the history of decoupage. Some sources say that it is an European art, dating from the 12th and 13th centuries. Others, however, believe it originated in 15th-century Germany, when

Above Buttons, beads, scraps of fabric, and tiny cloth dolls decorate these small notebooks.

printed decorative borders simulating the complex Tarsia wood inlay were produced for use on furniture, so that from a distance it looked real.

Many eminent authorities on the subject remain convinced that it was the demand for heavily lacquered Chinese furniture, or Chinoiserie, that began the trend towards decoupage during the late 17th century. The furniture was very fashionable and much sought after, but prohibitively expensive. In response to this huge demand, Venetian craftsmen decided to use decoupage to emulate the handpainted and lacquered effects of Chinoiserie, thereby creating a more accessible and affordable version. They created their own designs that they painted, cut out and pasted on to items of furniture, which were then varnished heavily.

Above This attractive painted box is embellished with colorful beads and felt scraps.

MATERIALS AND TECHNIQUES

There are often many elements in a 3D decoupaged object, and it is important that the composition of all the different parts work together. When working on a design using only paper motifs, one has to decide which parts of the image will stand out in relief. Flowers are an eduring and popular subject for 3D decoupage. Taking at least two identical copies of a floral print, cut out the separate petals and fit them back together again. The identical partners of these petals are then overlaid.

Working with other elements like beads, cords, charms, and three-dimensional paint, leads to a slightly different composition as these things can be added to frame a particular motif or to accentuate points.

Selecting motifs

There are many sources for decoupage motifs, from prints of Old Masters to trendy wrapping papers. Search out old prints and books in second-hand book shops, thrift stores, and libraries.

Use a color photocopier to copy the images and experiment with sizes and density of the colors. Although color copying can be expensive, it is preferable to cutting up old books.

Wrapping papers are a great source; they range from classical images to modern abstract designs. Postcards and greeting cards are also fine.

Prints, cards, and papers can be used on personal items, as long as one is not planning to sell them, as the images are usually copyrighted. Some illustrated books, though, can be used specifically for these purposes.

Cutting out motifs

Before you begin to cut out the motifs, examine the picture and consider the parts that will be the farthest away and those that will be the nearest, in relation to how you will build up the picture. The number of identical copies of the image will determine the layers of your final picture.

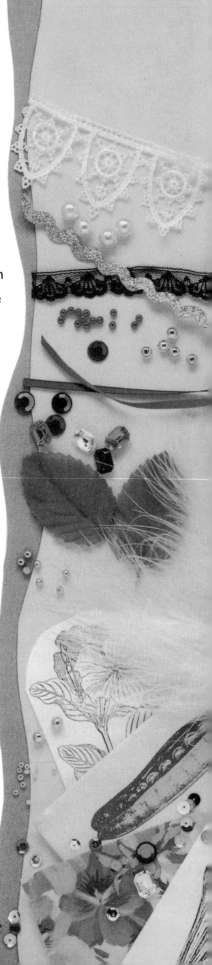

Contouring

When you look at your chosen motif, you will notice that the two-dimensional picture has a degree of perspective; however, through gentle shaping you will be able to give the picture more realism.

It is important to remember that when you contour parts of the motif, the piece will look smaller than its identical base motif, which will lie below it. The contoured elements will be the second layer of decoupage.

The most straightforward and effective method to contour motifs is by curling over edges with your fingers. Roll things like leaves and petals into a tube and then flatten them out again. Glue them down only at certain points so the edges can curl up and stand above the background. This will give a really eye-catching effect.

To emphasize creases and folds, fold the lines sharply against the edge of a metal ruler, and run your thumb along the creases to make them sharp.

Laying the base print

There are two ways in which to lay down the base print: either glue the back of the paper motif before arranging it into position, or glue the actual surface and then lay the motif down on to it. Try both methods to see which one you prefer.

Smooth over the glued motifs using either your fingers or a soft cloth. If any air

Left Use small, sharp scissors to cut out intricate flower scraps.

Left Pleating paper fans gives a three-dimensional effect.

Left Using both glue and foam tape adds depth and dimension.

bubbles appear, simply pop them with a pin. Once the motif is fully stuck down, check if the edges adhere to the surface. If not, then apply glue around the edges and wipe away any excess while it is still wet.

MESSENGER'S LETTER RACK

A blank letter rack with heart cutouts has been painted in a soft blue and then embellished with three-dimensional paper forget-me-nots and roses. The final touch are the swallows, who are traditionally used as messengers.

TOOLS AND MATERIALS

- **A pressed-wood blank letter rack**
- **Light-blue latex paint**
- **Paintbrush**
- **Pink puff paint**
- **Floral and bird decoupage scraps**
- **Scissors/craft knife**
- **Cutting mat**
- **Foam tape; glue**
- **Blue satin ribbon roses**

2 *Cut out the flowers to fit around the top and lower heart cutouts. Arrange them around the hearts as you cut, building up a composition.*

3 *When you are satisfied with the composition, glue the base decoupage down. Then, using pieces of foam tape, begin to layer the flower motifs on top of the base.*

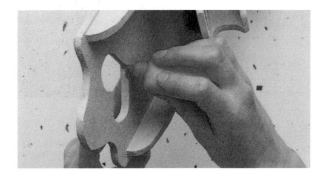

1 *Paint the letter rack with the light-blue paint; do two or three coats to give a smooth and even finish. If after the second coat it looks lumpy, sand it down lightly before doing the third coat. Pierce the top of the puff-paint tube with a pin, and carefully pipe the paint around the insides of all four of the hearts. Pipe dots around the center of the two hearts that will not have decoupage around them.*

4 *Cut out the birds, cutting a second identical set of wings for each. Attach the second set of wings to each cutout with foam tape, so that they look three-dimensional. Once you have achieved the right look, glue them into the correct place.*

5 *Finally, add a couple of blue satin ribbon roses to the decoupaged flowers on the top and lower hearts. Secure them with glue.*

FOLIAGE FRIEZE

This frieze emulates the grand hand-painted floral swags that are seen in some of the grand houses of Europe. It is perfectly suited for a bedroom or a living room.

TOOLS AND MATERIALS

- **Wallpaper/wrapping paper or any source material with foliage**
- **Small, sharp scissors**
- **String and chalk**
- **All-purpose glue**
- **Acrylic varnish**
- **Small sponge**
- **Watercolors**

1   Select your source material, and cut around the foliage details using a pair of small sharp scissors. You will need smaller pieces of foliage for the ends of each swag, but you can use larger groups for the center areas.

2   Measure the length of one wall that you are covering with the decoupage. Determine the number of swags you would like to feature, and divide the wall measurement by the number of swags to determine the width of each swag. Mark these points with chalk along the wall.

3   Tape a length of string between two points, allowing it to swag in the middle. Use chalk to draw this curve on the wall, then remove the string and repeat between the other points, making sure the drop of each swag is the same.

4   Apply the glue to the wall and rub gently with your finger until it is silky smooth. Press the pieces of foliage on to the glued surface and wipe off the excess glue with a small piece of sponge squeezed out in warm water. Continue with this process until each swag is completed. Allow to dry; then lightly tint with watercolors.

Below Chalk is used to figure out the measurements for these elegant grapes and vine leaves.

OTHER IDEAS

For a softer look, you could use flowers as well as foliage within the swags.

SAIL AWAY

The handpainted effect on this hook is in fact created from an ordinary photocopy that has been repeatedly worn away with sandpaper and hand-tinted until the look has been achieved. The overall look is very convincing.

TOOLS AND MATERIALS

- Small piece of wood or pegboard
- Sailing-ship picture
- Plain white paper
- All-purpose glue
- Adhesive brush
- Water-based paints
- Brush
- Sandpaper
- Sealer (fixative)
- Acrylic varnish
- Drill with wide bit
- Dowel pegs
- Wood glue
- Rope

OTHER IDEAS

Glue the sailboat photocopy to a piece of driftwood for an original look.

Below *Torn paper can be used to suggest the sea and sky. Experiment with different techniques.*

1 Photocopy the picture of the sailing ship on white paper. Cut the wood to size if necessary: the photocopy and the wood should be approximately the same size. Spread glue on to the surface of the wood and paste on the whole photocopy sheet. Smooth the copy with your fingers, from the center outward to avoid trapping air bubbles.

2 When dry, tint the photocopy with thin washes of color. Allow the color to dry, then use fine sandpaper to "distress" the surface of the copy. You will notice that the sandpaper rubs away some of the color also, so reapply and continue this process until you reach the effect you are happy with.

3 Allow the paints to dry thoroughly, then seal with a layer of charcoal, pastel, or watercolor fixative (available from art suppliers). Once this layer is dry, apply at least five coats of acrylic varnish, allowing each coat to dry thoroughly before applying the next.

4 Drill holes at the base of the decoupage picture to about half the depth of the wood. The diameter of these holes should be equal to the diameter of the dowel pegs. Squeeze a little wood glue into each hole before twisting in the dowel peg.

5 Using the same drill bit, drill right through the wood at top right and top left of the picture, if required, to hold rope ties. Insert a length of rope through the holes and knot it neatly at the front of the picture.

LIGHT AND LACY

This basic lampshade is one of the easiest projects in the book and one that has a really professional look.

TOOLS AND MATERIALS
- **White paper or "plastic"**
- **8 in. (20 cm) tall lampshade**
- **Water-based blue paint**
- **1yd (1 m) each of 1³⁄₄ in. (4 cm) and 2³⁄₄ in.- (7 cm-) wide cream paper lace**
- **Wallpaper paste and brush**
- **Scissors**
- **Water-based quick-drying matte varnish**

1 Apply two coats of blue paint to the lampshade, allowing each coat to dry. Measure around the lampshade and divide the top and bottom edges of the shade into eight equal sections. Make a small pencil mark at the top and bottom edges. Measure the paper lace against the height of the lampshade, cutting four pieces of lace in each width that are just long enough to fold over each edge to make a neat finish.

2 Mix a small amount of wallpaper paste, and spread sparingly on the back of one piece of the narrow paper lace and on the lampshade. Position the lace on the lampshade, making sure it is straight. Smooth it gently with your fingers, removing any excess glue or air bubbles, and make sure the edges are stuck down.

3 Following the pencil marks, paste the second piece of narrow lace exactly opposite the first piece and the remaining two in between, thereby quartering the lampshade. Now paste the wider paper lace between the narrower strips. Smooth the strips down carefully and pay particular attention to turning under the edges and sticking them to the inside of the lampshade. This produces a very neat finish. Allow the paste to dry thoroughly.

4 When the shade is completely dry, apply two or three coats of water-based matte varnish, allowing each coat to dry completely before applying the next.

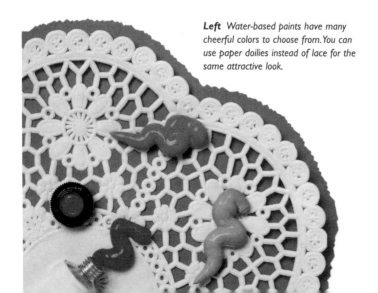

Left *Water-based paints have many cheerful colors to choose from. You can use paper doilies instead of lace for the same attractive look.*

OTHER IDEAS
If paper lace is difficult to find, you can use doilies, although you may have to vary the shapes of the lace pieces. The color of paint you choose will determine the look of the shade, making it pastel-pretty or rich-looking.

BIN IT

For a lasting memento of a foreign vacation or business trip, paste receipts and low-denomination paper money on to a plain wastepaper bin—a witty and unusual receptacle in which to jettison those unwanted bills!

1   Select a variety of old travel receipts and mix the wallpaper paste according to instructions. Apply a thin layer of paste to the surface of the wastepaper bin and the back of the receipts. Starting at the edge of the bin (top and bottom), lay them on to the bin at slanting angles and smooth out air bubbles or ripples in the paper with your fingers. Work toward the middle of the bin until the whole surface is covered. Use the largest receipts first, leaving the smaller ones to fill in any gaps. Make sure that all the edges are well stuck down.

2   With a sharp craft knife, carefully trim away any pieces overlapping the edge and tuck them under the rolled rim of the bin. If the bin does not have rolled edges, trim the paper level with the top and bottom edges.

3   Paste paper money over the background of receipts. Space them well apart and at different angles. Allow to dry.

4   Apply two or three coats of matte polyurethane varnish to the finished collage, allowing each coat to dry before applying the next. Before applying the final coat of varnish, lightly sand the bin with fine sandpaper to create a smooth finish. Dust with dry brush and then apply the final coat of varnish. To give the bin an interesting aged effect, add a small amount of raw umber oil paint to the final coat of varnish.

TOOLS AND MATERIALS
- **A selection of notes and receipts**
- **Metal wastepaper bin**
- **Wallpaper paste**
- **Craft knife**
- **Matte polyurethane varnish and brush**
- **Oil paint in raw umber (optional)**

Left As an alternative, use Chinese or Japanese printed papers for an exotic, oriental effect.

OTHER IDEAS
Collect interesting packaging and labels from foreign trips, or newspapers with unusual type, and paste these on to the wastepaper bin as a variation.

COMPACT STORAGE

Modern plastic packaging is efficient but it is often unsightly. You can hide away compact discs in boxes decorated with sheet music or pictures of your favorite musicians.

TOOLS AND MATERIALS
- **Plain CD box**
- **Sheet music**
- **Small, sharp scissors**
- **Craft glue and brush**
- **Clear matte varnish**
- **Very fine steel wool**
- **Varnishing wax**
- **Polishing cloth**

I Choose a selection of sheet music and carefully cut them into pieces with small, sharp scissors. Arrange the paper pieces roughly on the blank box to make sure you have enough material, before sticking them down.

2 When you are fully satisfied with the arrangement, carefully glue the pieces in place. To ensure that everything has been stuck down, use a brush to spread the glue right to the edge of the pieces. Smooth the paper on to the box with your fingers to remove any air bubbles, then carefully wipe off any excess glue with a lightly dampened cloth. Ensure that your fingers and the cloth are both clean so that you avoid smudging the paper. When the box is dry, check the corners and if necessary, carefully re-stick them. Allow to dry.

3 Apply clear matte varnish to the outside of the box and allow to dry overnight in a dust-free place.

4 When dry, lightly sand the surface of the box using very fine steel wool, removing any lumps and bumps of varnish. Dust with a clean, dry brush. Revarnish and, when dry, sand smooth again.

Right *Comics and old books with black-and-white illustrations are fun to use as source material—match the theme to the subject.*

OTHER IDEAS
The boxes could be themed with different pictures of pop stars or posters so that the contents of the boxes are instantly recognizable. To give the box an interesting crazed effect, you could use crackle glaze varnish after step 4.

GRECIAN VASE

Create your own museum piece using a classic-shaped terracotta pot decorated with Greek illustrations.

1 If the surface of your terracotta pot is rough, sand it smooth using sandpaper. Dust with a clean, dry brush.

2 Photocopy the black-and-white illustrations on white paper. Cut out images and position them on a large sheet of white paper and glue using a dry glue stick. Re-photocopy them.

3 Brush a wash of terracotta-color waterproof drawing ink over the images and allow to dry. This helps achieve a more authentic "ancient" look. Cut out the tinted images using small, sharp scissors.

4 If the vase/urn is glazed, apply a coat of vinyl silk paint; if it is unglazed, use black India ink. Leave to dry.

TOOLS AND MATERIALS
- Terracotta vase/urn
- Medium-grade sandpaper
- Clean, dry paintbrush
- Greek vase illustrations
- White paper
- Scissors
- Terracotta-color drawing ink
- Craft glue; dry glue stick
- Black India ink or vinyl silk latex paint
- Clear matte varnish and brush
- Very fine steel wool
- Varnishing wax; polishing cloth

5 Apply craft glue to the selected images and stick to the painted vase/urn, wiping off any excess glue with a lightly dampened cloth.

6 Apply clear matte varnish to the vase/urn and allow to dry overnight. Lightly sand using fine steel wool and dust with a brush. Revarnish and allow to dry. Sand again with the steel wool.

7 Dust with a brush and apply oil color varnishing wax. Buff with a soft cloth.

OTHER IDEAS
If the pot or vase is made of plastic, paint it with black vinyl silk paint instead of India ink. Visit museums to get more ideas about the colors and images to use.

Left Classical Greek patterns included acanthus leaves, squares, and spirals.

PAPER SCULPTURE

No two papercraft enthusiasts would give exactly the same
answer. It has been variously described as relief illustration,
drawing with light and shadow, and as a catchall term
for forms of paper art that are not paper engineering, origami, or
modelmaking. The term 'paper sculpture' means different things
to different people.
This book adopts a wide definition, presenting
step-by-step instructions for projects that are in
relief and fully three-dimensional, expressive and
geometric, decorative and practical, so everyone
will find something of interest to make.

PAPER SCULPTURE

Sculpture can be made from virtually any paper —recycled office paper, packaging or junk mail, or the standard and special papers at art supply stores. As you will see from the works in this section, a diverse range of extraordinary sculptures can be created in myriad colors and textures. However, the epitome of this art form is still considered to be white sculpture, with its graceful modeling of light and shade. Such pieces are often constructed from top-quality handmade watercolor papers whose high cotton-rag content gives strength and malleability.

Unlike traditional sculpture materials, paper cannot be shaped into a compound curve, that is, a form that curves in two directions. When the second curve is made, the first curve springs back. However, you can create a similar effect by gluing two pieces of paper together. Most of the other restrictions inherent in paper can be overcome by careful cutting, curling, scoring, and shaping; indeed, once you have mastered the basic techniques of paper sculpture, you will come to realise that it is an excellent medium for this form of art.

Mastering the following techniques is crucial to success in this art form. Practice them thoroughly as a sound basis for your own creativity.

TOOLS AND MATERIALS

- **Large and small scissors**
- **Craft knife**
- **Cutting mat**
- **Pencils 2B and 6H**
- **Scoring tool**
- **Craft knife**
- **Wooden sculpting tools**
- **Eraser**
- **Stapler**
- **Small wooden skewers**
- **Tracing paper**
- **Wooden dowel**
- **Polystyrene**
- **PVA glue**
- **Silicone glue**
- **Various papers**

SHADOW AND HIGHLIGHTS
This delicate, all-white sculpture captures the elegance of paper sculpture in its purest form. Here the shapes are given life by the way each piece interacts with light and shade (White Wreath, Joanna Bandle).

Above COLOR ENHANCEMENTS

To create this sculpture the artist used colored papers and then embellished some pieces further by adding painted color to create a gradated tone, or a spattered background. These techniques further enhance a composition, giving an added illusion of depth in areas that may not be naturally modeled by light (Sally Jo Vitsky).

Below THREE-DIMENSIONS

To create a three-dimensional effect the artist has cut and curled printing papers and then added texture with pastels. The frame becomes part of the composition (Wood duck, Bill Finewood).

Above TEXTURED PAPER

A subject that is popular in any illustrative medium is the cat. Here simple, graphic shapes are given more interest by the use of fur-texture embossed paper (Rousseau's Cat, Clive Stevens).

Basic Shapes

Most paper sculpture shapes are created by cutting, scoring, folding, and curling. Using combinations of the basic shapes demonstrated here, you will be able to construct more complex pieces.

Scored lines are indicated on the diagrams by dotted lines. When scoring, it is best to bend paper away from the scored line. When scoring alternating valley and mountain folds, you will need to turn the paper over to score the correct side.

TIPS FOR PAPER SCULPTING

Work methodically from background to foreground so that each piece you add hides the gluing points of the previous piece.

Paint the paper components before you sculpt them, since water-based paints tend to flatten sculpted shapes.

Keep your hands clean and free of pastel dust. Dirty finger marks will ruin a sculpture.

Avoid water-based glues when working with thin paper. They will soak in and leave wrinkles. Use a clear household adhesive.

When raising paper components with blocking, make sure that it remains neat and carefully hidden.

When using PVA glue, keep it in a small, flexible plastic container lid. This will bend and allow you to remove hardened glue easily.

If you decide to make a limited edition of a particular image, cut out all the pieces and then use them as templates to trace out identical pieces for the edition. Be sure to label all your templates clearly.

When working on an all-white sculpture, it is helpful to place a desk lamp in the position of the final light source. In this way, you can gauge the effect of the light on each piece as you add it to the sculpture.

U-SHAPE

Cut out a large letter U and score a valley fold in the middle with a mountain fold on either side. Pull one side of the U over the other and glue in position.

ZIGZAGS

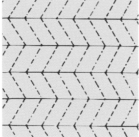

On a rectangular-shaped piece of paper, score five vertical marks, then score eight zigzag horizontal lines with alternating valley and mountain folds.

WAVY LINES

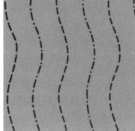

Cut out a rectangle with top and bottom edges as wavy lines. Score six horizontal wavy lines with alternating valley and mountain folds.

SWEEPING CURVE

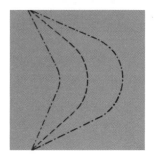

On a rectangular piece of paper score a curve from side to side to create a valley fold. Then score a corresponding curve on either side to create two mountain folds.

SCORED CONE

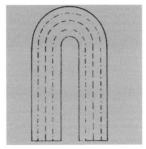

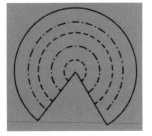

Cut out a circle and score four circular lines, as shown, to create alternating valley and mountain folds. Cut out a segment, pull the edges together, and glue.

CONE

Cut out a circle and remove a quarter segment, then bring the ends together to form a cone, and glue.

TRIANGLE

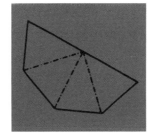

Draw four joining triangles, as shown, and score the dividing line between each. Fold along the scored lines and glue the fourth triangle behind the first.

CUBE

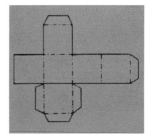

Draw the six squares, as shown, with glue tabs attached to them. Cut out and score all the joining lines and tabs. Fold together and glue tabs to attach.

STAR

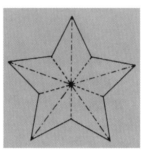

Cut out a five-pointed star. From the center to each point, score a mountain fold. From the center to the joint between each point score a valley fold.

FOUR FOLD

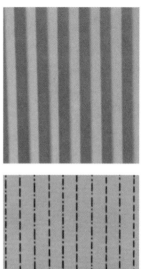

On a square piece of paper, score a series of equidistant horizontal lines for alternating valley and mountain folds. This is also called a fan fold.

CYLINDER

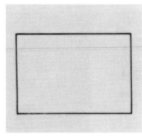

Take a rectangular piece of paper and curl over the edge of a table to form a tube. Open up and glue one edge. Bring the other end over to attach them together.

LEAF

Cut out a leaf shape and score an S-shaped line along the central axis. Fold back to create a mountain fold.

SWAN

The combination of a graceful shape, white cardboard to maximize light effects, and delicate scoring to show the curve of the wings, makes the swan an irresistible subject for paper sculpture.

The construction technique can be adapted to create cygnets, ducks, geese, and any nesting bird, just by changing the proportions. Experiment until you get the effect you are after. To use the design in a relief—perhaps a pond scene—simply cut the free-standing swan in half. A little extra-scoring may be necessary down the neck and along the tail.

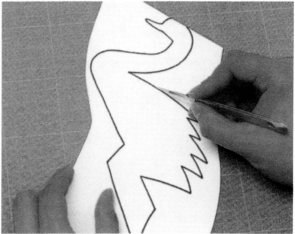

Fold the cardboard in half to make a double thickness, then cut out the shape through both layers. Note that the center crease lies between the layers, across the top of the head. Be especially careful to make flowing cuts along the neck.

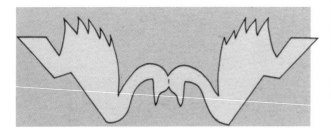

When unfolded, your cutout shape should look like this.

TOOLS AND MATERIALS
- Knife
- Adhesive tape
- Yellow and black fiber-tip pens
- White cardboard 7 x 16 in. (18 x 40 cm)— folds in half to become 7 x 8 in. (18 x 20 cm)

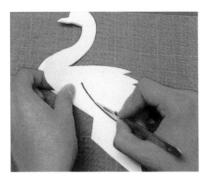

2 Cut through both layers along a curved line that follows the bottom edge of the wings.

3 With the back of the blade, make several creases from the cut (in Step 2) to the tip of the wing feathers. Pleat the creases, starting with a valley at the top.

4 Crimp each wing, overlapping the bottom edge slightly with the cardboard to create a shallow cone, the tapered point of which is at the end of the wing cut. Hold the crimp in place with adhesive tape.

Below Add the beak and eye markings with fiber-tip pens. You can use colored cardboard to achieve such finishing touches—and purists might insist on it. But the markings here are so delicate that they would be difficult to make from cardboard, so pens are a prudent choice.

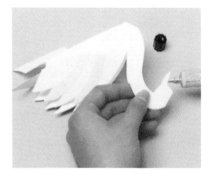

5 Place a dab of glue between the two layers of the beak, and glue to form a solid double thickness.

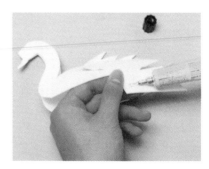

6 Fold the two tail halves inside the swan. Glue them along the top edge, so the bottom edges detach and hold the swan upright.

FALL LEAVES

Fall leaves are a perfect subject for paper sculpture: they resemble paper and their veins can be reproduced by creasing. The natural decay of leaves in the fall makes them slightly ragged, so—conveniently for us—they do not demand precision. In fact, a carefully constructed paper leaf can look unconvincing, so loosen up for this project.

Roughly draw the outline of a leaf. You can use a template if you are mass-producing them. Then cut out the shape somewhat imprecisely, so that no two leaves are identical.

TOOLS AND MATERIALS

- **Knife**
- **Adhesive**
- **Adhesive tape**
- **Foamboard**
- **Cardboard**
- **Dark-brown cardboard: 12 x 10 in. (30 x 25 cm)**
  - **Each leaf 4^5/$_{16}$ x 3^1/$_2$ in. (11 x 9 cm)**
- **Maroon cardboard: 12 x 12 in. (30 x 30 cm)**
  - **Each leaf 5^1/$_2$ x 2^3/$_4$ in. (14 x 7 cm)**
- **Mid-brown cardboard: 12 x 10 in. (30 x 25 cm)**
  - **Each leaf 4^3/$_4$ x 3^1/$_2$ in. (12 x 9 cm)**
- **Light-brown cardboard: 6 x 6 in. (15 x 15 cm)**
  - **Each leaf 2^3/$_4$ x 1^3/$_8$ in. (7 x 3.5 cm)**
- **Dark-green cardboard: 10 x 10 in. (25 x 25 cm)**
  - **Each leaf 4^5/$_{16}$ x 2^3/$_{16}$ in. (11 x 5.5 cm)**

PIECES TO CUT

Frame 16^1/$_2$ x 12^5/$_8$ in. (42 x 32 cm)

The frame's decorative waves are cut from the central panel removed from the frame (i.e., no extra card needed)

Background 16^1/$_8$ x 12^1/$_4$ in. (41 x 31 cm)

2 Score the leaf to create veins. Their exact location is unimportant, provided that they fan out from the stem. The position of the scores should vary from leaf to leaf, and some should be slightly curved.

3 Bend the scores, as shown, so that they alternate in a mountain/valley pattern to create a pleated effect. Note the gently curved scores at the center.

Left Glue and tape the windswept pile of leaves into position before framing. Some leaves may be added later to overlap the frame. Separate the frame from the background with foamboard to increase the depth of the image. They are quick and easy to make, so family and friends could help you mass-produce them. The same leaves in shades of green could be part of a spring or summer relief scene.

BIRD IN FLIGHT

Relief sculpture achieves its illusion of depth by using shapes cut out in perspective and elaborated at varying levels to create a natural shadow when the work is lit. This method has become popular in modern advertising and book illustration as an alternative to painting or drawing. Some contemporary paper sculptors will use only white paper to create the classic works that capture the essence of the medium and rely on light and shade to model their graceful lines. Others exploit the full range of colored and textured papers, or use recycled materials, such as corrugated cardboard, newspapers, paper towels, and cardboard tubes.

Your choice is virtually unlimited. If flimsy paper would achieve a particular effect but is too light to shape, laminate it to a heavier material, such as watercolor paper—remnants of this are sometimes available in art supply shops.

Polystyrene sheet is one of the most convenient methods for elevating components, because it is light, easy to cut, and glue, and holds its shape. Mount your sculpture on a backing board and frame it to last for years.

This project for a bird in flight is a stunning example of this form of paper sculpture. The feeling of depth is really accentuated by the way it is mounted.

- ***Creating a relief sculpture***
- ***Scoring and curling in sculpture***
- ***Constructing a sculpture over a drawing***

Right The finished sculpture can be mounted on a backing board and then framed.

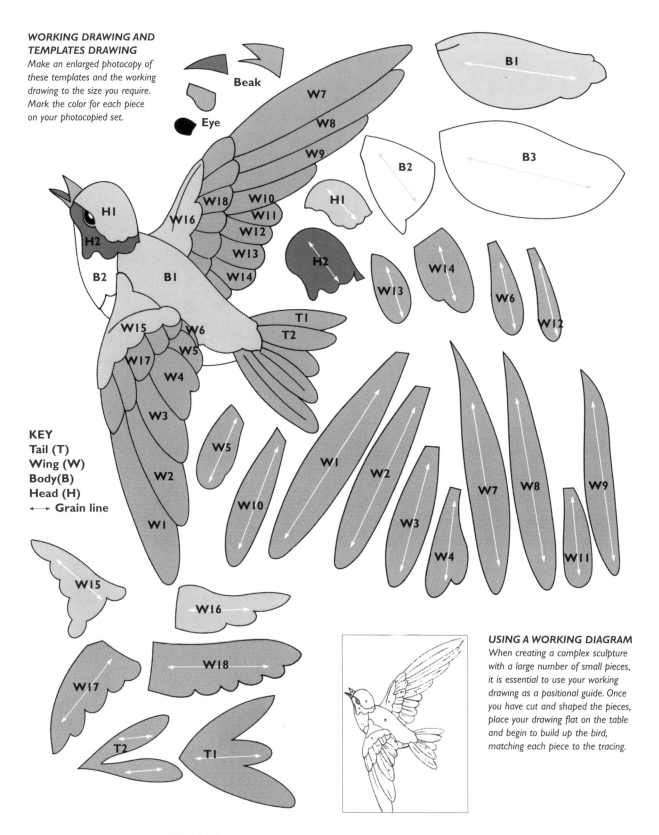

WORKING DRAWING AND TEMPLATES DRAWING

Make an enlarged photocopy of these templates and the working drawing to the size you require. Mark the color for each piece on your photocopied set.

Beak

Eye

W7

W8

W9

B1

B2

B3

H1

H1

H2

W18

W10

W16

W11

W12

W13

W14

W14

W13

H2

W6

W12

B2

B1

T1

T2

W15

W6

W5

W5

W17

W4

W3

KEY
Tail (T)
Wing (W)
Body(B)
Head (H)
←→ **Grain line**

W2

W1

W5

W10

W1

W2

W7

W8

W9

W3

W4

W11

W15

W16

W18

W17

T2

T1

USING A WORKING DIAGRAM

When creating a complex sculpture with a large number of small pieces, it is essential to use your working drawing as a positional guide. Once you have cut and shaped the pieces, place your drawing flat on the table and begin to build up the bird, matching each piece to the tracing.

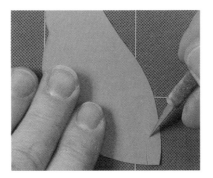

1   *Trace the diagram from an enlarged photocopy, and mark the colors.*

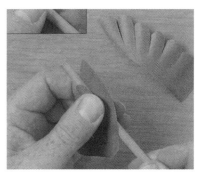

4   *Cut the main body slit as indicated on the template. This is the connecting slit that fits around the bird's neck.*

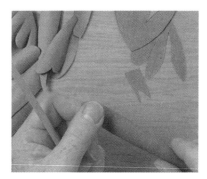

7   *Cut and shape the red head piece, and then the gray wing parts. Curl each feather in the wing piece over the dowel.*

2   *Turn the tracing face down on a blue paper, and trace the wings' outline with a hard pencil. Leave enough overlap for the back wing to hide under the body.*

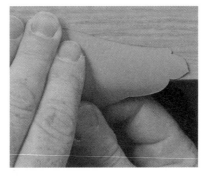

5   *Curl the main blue body part over the edge of a table two or three times to ensure an even curve.*

8   *Cut the remaining gray pieces, and curl each one lengthwise.*

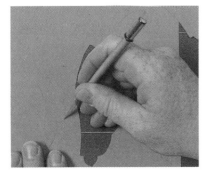

3   *Trace all of the blue parts. Cut them out and put them aside.*

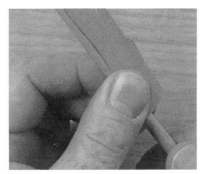

6   *The smaller pieces are easier to curl around a dowel.*

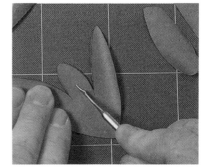

9   *Take the gray tailpiece and score a central line along each feather. Bend the lines back to form a mountain fold.*

413

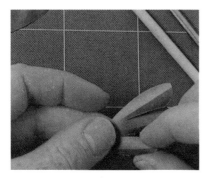

10 Repeat the scoring and folding process on the wing feathers.

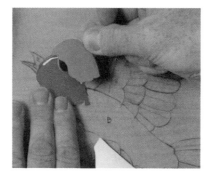

13 Secure the blue cap with eye to the red head piece. Apply a strip of glue around the top edge, so the head does not sit too flat.

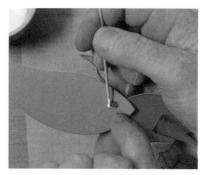

16 Turn the assembly over and glue the back of the red tab. Hold in position for a few seconds to adhere.

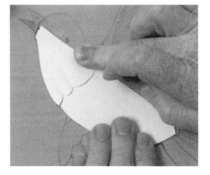

11 Cut and shape the white breast and body pieces. Glue the top straight edge only and adhere to the white body.

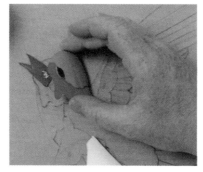

14 Assemble the beak parts and attach to the underside of the head, as shown.

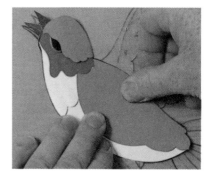

17 Glue the top straight edge of the white body part and attach the blue body and head, smoothing the glued area with your thumb.

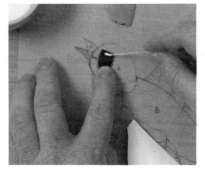

12 Cut and shape the black eye piece. Glue the top edge and attach the blue head piece.

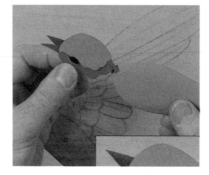

15 Slide the main body part and the head together, ensuring that the tabs interlock.

18 Cut out a tiny white oval, and glue it to the top of the eye to indicate the reflection of light.

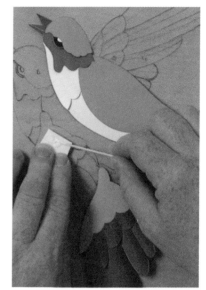

19   *Glue the top edge of the gray back wing feathers and secure the blue front feathers to it.*

21   *Glue the two feathered tail parts on top of the three feathered pieces. Slide the assembled tail between the blue and white body parts, and glue the tail into place.*

23   *Glue a 1 x ¹/2 in. (2.5 x 1.3 cm) block of polystyrene to the underside of the front wing. Then glue the other side of the block and attach it to the body.*

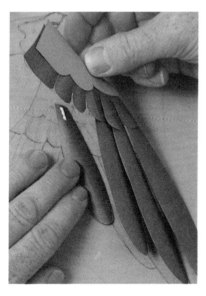

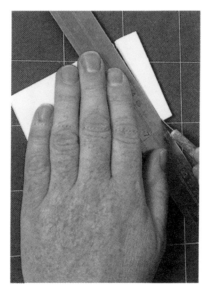

20   *Glue the end of each gray primary feather in turn and attach to the underside of the wing assembly. Use your tracing as a position guide.*

22   *Cut some tapered lengths of 6 mm (¹/4 in.) polystyrene sheet to act as blocking for the wings.*

24   *Glue a similar block to the front of the back wing and attach the wing to the body.*

ROOSTER

The *curved crease technique* is ideal for creating feathers, and is used extensively in this project. Construction is simple, because it is not necessary for you to position the feather pieces with complete accuracy when you assemble them. The brilliant colors of the plumage play a strong decorative role, and the plain, contrasting background keeps attention on the rooster.

PIECES TO CUT
- Dark-blue background 14 x 16 in. (35 x 41 cm)
- **YELLOW PIECES:**
  – *All can be cut from a sheet 8 x 8 in. (20 x 20 cm)*
- Head: $2^{3/4}$ x $2^{3/4}$ in. (7 x 7 cm)
- Neck: $3^{15/16}$ x $4^{5/16}$ in. (10 x 11 cm)
- Legs: $4^{5/16}$ x $3^{1/8}$ in. (11 x 8 cm)
- Orange piece: $5^{1/2}$ x $7^{1/2}$ in. (14 x 19 cm)
- **RED PIECES:**
  – *Can be cut from a sheet 8 x 10 in. (20 x 25 cm)*
- Tail: $5^{15/16}$ x $6^{11/16}$ in. (15 x 17 cm)
- Back: $3^{1/8}$ x $5^{1/2}$ in. (8 x 14 cm)
- Comb: $1^{1/2}$ x $2^{1/2}$ in. (4 x 7cm)
- Crop: $1^{1/2}$ x $3/4$ in. (4 x 2 cm)

TOOLS AND MATERIALS
- **Knife**
- **Adhesive**
- **Masking tape**
- **Cardboard or paper**
- **Dark-blue paper 14 x 16 in. (35 x 41 cm)**
- **Yellow paper 8 x 8 in. (20 x 20 cm)**
- **Orange paper 5½ x 7½ in. (14 x 19 cm)**
- **Red paper 8 x 10 in. (20 x 25 cm)**

Head

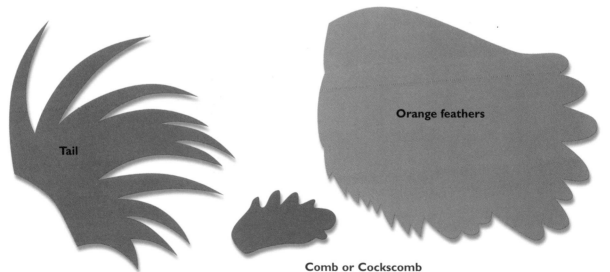

Tail

Comb or Cockscomb

Orange feathers

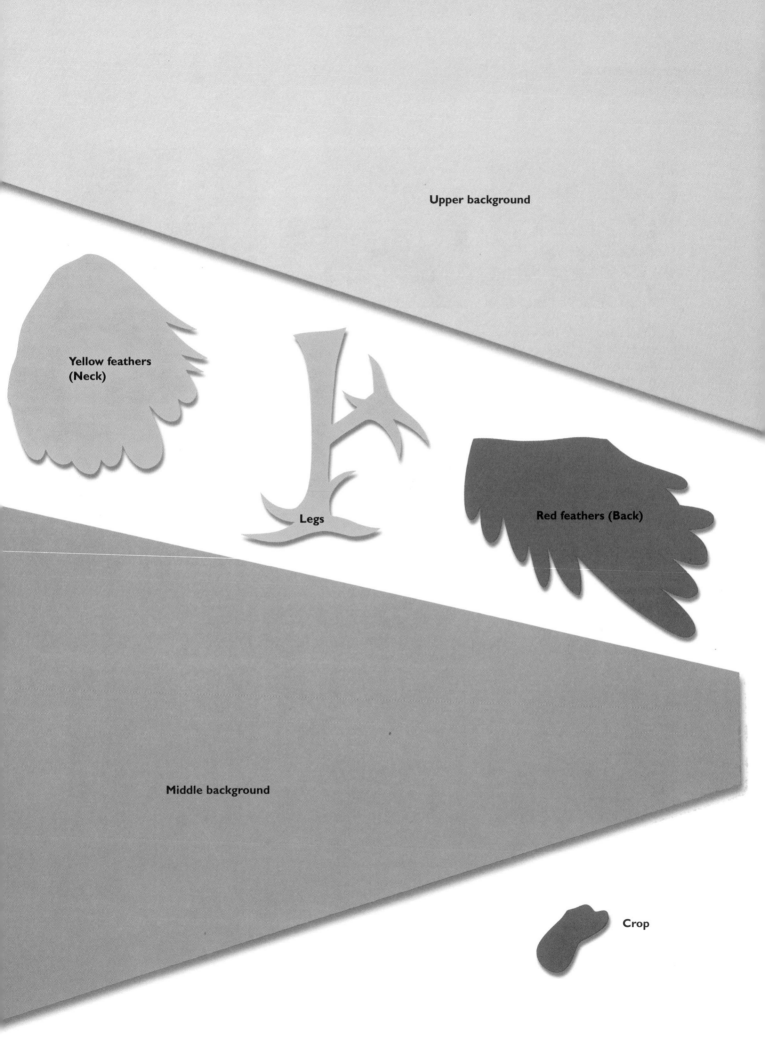

Upper background

Yellow feathers
(Neck)

Legs

Red feathers (Back)

Middle background

Crop

1 Cut out each piece. This piece sits on the top of the back. More than precision, it is important to give the impression of feathers.

4 Secure the overlap with a small strip of masking tape. Be careful not to make the cone too pointed – it is an easy mistake to make.

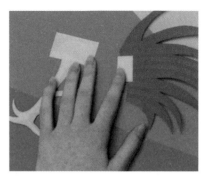

7 The feather pieces can now go into place. Begin with the tail, judging its position in relation to the feet.

2 With an upturned blade, crease all of the feather pieces. You do not need to place every score exactly. Gently pleat the creases.

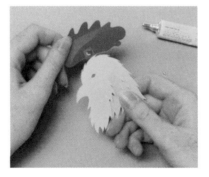

5 Turn the head piece over. Curl the V cuts upward. Glue the tab of the comb piece behind the top of the head.

8 Add the orange feather units, taping each layer in turn.

3 Cut a pattern of small V shapes in the head piece, and a line of jagged "feathers" from the bottom edge to near the eye, as shown. Overlap across the cut line to create a shallow cone.

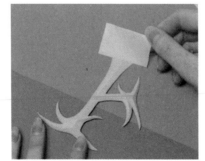

6 Score the leg piece as shown. Tape it to the assembled background. The technique is similar to that of scoring in the Nameplate project.

9 Attach the red body feathers in the same way.

10 *Glue the head and neck to the background, and add the red crop piece beneath the beak.*

Right *The Rooster is an example of the classical style of relief paper sculpture, owing more to drawing and collage than to engineering or constructional skills. You can use the same layering technique to make other birds, or omit the pleating to create the fur of cats or shaggy dogs. The only tricky part is designing the head, but if you do this last, you will find it much easier.*

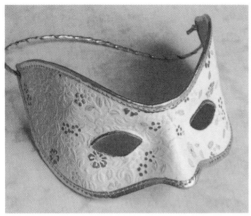

72 MASK MAKING

The cave paintings at Lascaux in France, done by Stone Age man, showing him wearing masks of the animals he hunted, are among the earliest records we have of masks. By wearing the mask a hunter could take on the spirit of the animal and enact the scene he hoped to bring about.

For thousands of years different cultures across the world have made masks for celebrations, to ward off evil spirits, to commemorate seasonal events, for religious and pagan rituals, for dance, and for self-defense. The forces of evil, power, and love have all been symbolized as masks. Often made from found, local materials, masks have been carefully crafted and sculpted to become beautiful and fantastic objects.

INTRODUCTION

Children find wearing masks great fun, loving to surprise and scare, while believing themselves to be hidden. Children can also make masks with enthusiasm, beginning with a simple eye mask or paper-bag mask, and moving on to more complex papier mâché masks. Their designs can be innovative and imaginative, as they create a favorite animal or a dragon.

Techniques

The masks in this section are to a great extent suitable for most people. In a few cases the masks have been specially designed to suit children or adults, but in general the masks can be adapted to accommodate various sizes.

If you have never made a mask before, it would be wise to start with one of the simpler styles. However, it is quite unnecessary to work through all the methods in the technique section before starting on a mask. This section is intended to operate as a reference area for the various ways in which masks can be created.

There are some general rules about faces which apply to everyone. Look at the face of any adult and you will see that the eyes are situated approximately halfway between the top of the head and the chin. In young children the eyes are a little lower. You will notice that the bottom of the nose lies halfway between the eyes and the chin, with the mouth coming halfway between nose and chin. The ears fit between the levels of the eyes and the bottom of the nose. Bear these facts in mind when creating the masks.

Below Left African antelope skin masks were produced by gifted craftsmen following ancient traditions.

Below Center Each mask of the Commedia dell'Arte represents one of the standard group of characters.

Below Right Wooden masks from Africa display striking and often intricate carving.

Right and Below Southeast
Asian masks using eye holes (below)
and slits below the eyes (right).

Positioning eye holes in
the mask is one of the most
important and difficult things to
do. They should not be made
too large because too much of
the wearer's own eyes would
show and this might detract
from the effect of the mask. On
the other hand, if they are too
small the wearer will be unable
to see properly. In some masks,
notably in Mexico and South America, the eye
holes of the masks are slits cut into the mask
at a place to suit the wearer—but they bear
no relation to the design of the mask, which is
elaborately decorated. One way of minimizing
the effect caused by large eye holes is to
make a feature of them by sticking net across
the space. This will enable the wearer to see
quite clearly, but will shield the eyes and
expression from the audience.

Gloriously colored paints are a
characteristic of several Southeast Asian
masks.

METHODS OF FIXING MASKS

There are several ways of fixing masks so that they can be worn comfortably. Sometimes the type of mask dictates the method of fixing, as with the Rider mask (see p.436), but as a general rule, the best way to choose a method is to experiment with all the ways of fixing and then select the one that suits you the best.

Elastic, string, or ribbon attached to the mask at about the level of the eyes is the easiest and most common way of fixing the mask.

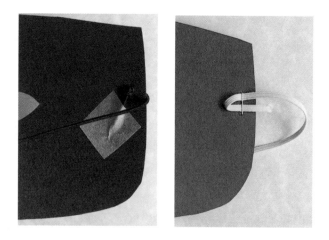

Method I—Elastic

If fixing the elastic by piercing a hole and tying, always strengthen the area of the mask where the hole has been made so that the weakness caused by the hole is reduced. This can be done by sticking masking tape over the hole area on the inside of the mask, so that the decoration of the mask is unaffected. Alternatively, staple the elastic in position and cover the staples with layers of adhesive tape for the wearer's protection.

The most suitable and comfortable type of elastic to use is hat/millinery/round cord elastic. However, thin, flat elastic can be used if this type is not available.

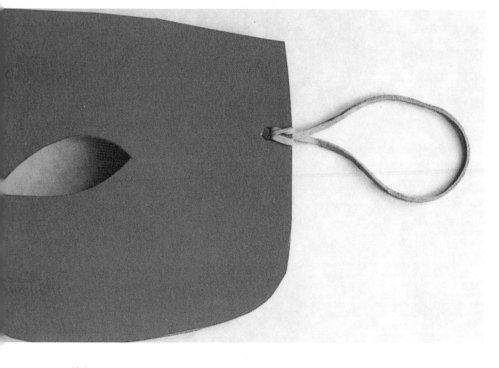

Two elastic bands looped through the holes in the mask, and stretched around the ears, can be used as an impromptu fixing—although this may not be comfortable to wear for a long period of time.

TIP

If there are spots where a mask rubs the face or otherwise feels uncomfortable, it is quite easy to stick a piece of soft material, such as stockinette, to the inside of the mask using glue or tape.

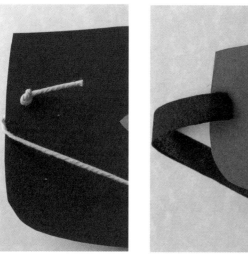

Method 2—String

If you decide to use string, make sure that the knot securing the string to the inside of the mask is larger than the hole, or use staples. In either case, stick a piece of adhesive tape over the ends to keep them in place. The string can be painted to match or contrast either with the hair of the wearer or with the design of the mask.

Method 3—Ribbon

Thin black cotton ribbon was traditionally used in Victorian masks, but more exotic ribbons can be used as part of the decorative effect of a mask. The ribbon can be held in place with staples, but make sure the ends are covered with tape so that they do not scratch the face.

Method 4—Sticks

This is a useful way of fixing a mask when it does not need to be kept permanently in front of the face. There are two ways of using sticks.

Style A If the mask is a flat whole-face mask, such as the Dragon mask (see p.438), a flat piece of wood can be attached centrally to the chin area of the mask. The stick should be stuck in place with glue and the glued end covered with adhesive tape. This method is good for young children.

Style B If the mask is an eye/domino mask, a small round stick is normally used. This can be fixed with glue and/or tape at the side of the mask or slotted through two holes (see diagram). The stick can be painted or decorated to suit the mask.

In both instances the length of the stick will depend upon the person carrying the mask, but it is wisest to make the stick too long and cut it down to size as required.

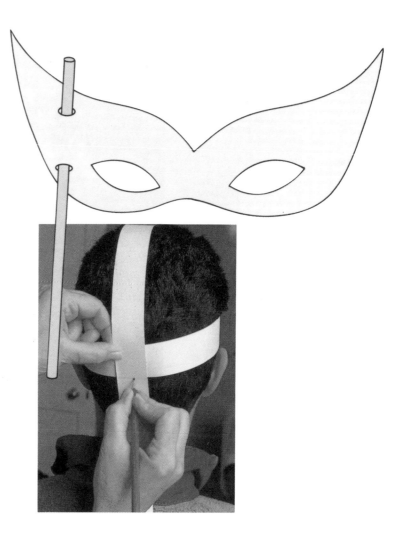

Method 5

When making an oversize mask, such as the Dragon mask on page 438, a different method is required. A quick and easy way is created by using strips made from lightweight card.

Take a strip of card about 1 in. (2.5cm) wide and fix this around the head of the person who will be wearing the mask, and secure this ring with adhesive tape.

Next, fix another strip at right angles to the ring and place the ring back on the head. The second strip should be at the center-back.

BAG PEOPLE

*Paper-bag people are very easy and quick to make. The more
varied your paper bags, the more interesting the crowd will be.*

CARD FRAME SPECTACLES

Another spectacle disguise can be achieved by making frames from card and decorating them in whatever style appeals to you—this could be severe and heavy-looking, or it could be stylish and extravagant.

Many different decorative materials can be used and the only limitation is your imagination. The exotic styles shown here are simply extensions of the basic shape. You could experiment with the basic shape yourself to create your own styles.

TOOLS AND MATERIALS

- ◆ **Pencil**
- ◆ **Tracing paper**
- ◆ **Stiff card for the basic shapes**
  17 x 5 in. (42 x 13 cm), or
  7½ x 4 in. (18 x 10 cm)
- ◆ **Craft knife**
- ◆ **Glitter pens, sequins, feathers, net, tissue paper, pipe cleaners, etc.**
- ◆ **Clear glue and adhesive tape**

The butterfly glasses are cut from card of 7½ x 5 in. (18 x 12 cm). They have been decorated with glitter paints, strung sequins, and sequins. Adding net "lenses" aids the delicate style. A toning pipe-cleaner has been pushed through the middle of the top and twisted so that it stays in place.

PREPARATION

1 *Trace the pattern from the template and draw it on to the card. If you are using foil card, draw on to the wrong side. Cut out the card frames.*

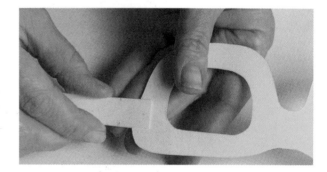

2 *If you are using the shorter piece of card, it will be necessary to fix the arms with adhesive tape. This should be done before decorating so that the tape can be hidden as much as possible—decoration can be stuck over the tape.*

3 *Now begins the fun of decorating. The basic shape has been adorned with strung sequins as they can be glued in curls and twists quite easily.*

EYES AND EARS MASK

The two masks shown here are both made from the same basic
pattern and you will probably think of other animals that can be
created from the same template. The important thing to remember is
that you are trying to represent the essentials of the animal—a mouse
has large ears with pink inside, and a black cat often has green eyes.

PREPARATION

TOOLS AND MATERIALS

- Pencil, scissors, and craft knife
- Tracing paper
- Light- to medium-weight card in gray and black 11³⁄₄ x 8¹⁄₄ in. (29 x 21 cm)
- Scraps of pink, pale-gray and green paper or card
- Glue
- Elastic or ribbon

2 *Cut out the ear linings from the colored paper.*

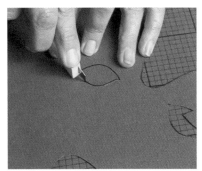

4 *Cut out eye holes using the craft knife on a protected surface.*

3 *Stick the ear linings in place centrally on the ears.*

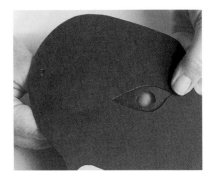

5 *For the cat, cut green scraps to stick behind the eye hole, and a smaller hole in the centers. Make holes on the sides of the mask to fit the elastic and tie.*

1 *Trace the patterns from the template. Draw the pattern on to the appropriate card and cut out carefully, trying to make the curves as smooth as you can.*

HARLEQUIN MASK

This style offers ample scope for use of decorative materials. Here, a variety of paper and card has been used including foil and fluorescent, and patterned paper. The leather and fabric pieces are a great way of using leftovers from other projects. Traditionally the Harlequin is dressed in patchwork, so the costume features differently colored squares.

PREPARATION

TOOLS AND MATERIALS

- ♦ **Pencil and ruler**
- ♦ **Scissors and craft knife**
- ♦ **Tracing paper**
- ♦ **Card for mask, about 20 x 20 in. (50 x 50 cm)**
- ♦ **Clear glue and adhesive tape**
- ♦ **Materials for decorating**
- ♦ **Strips of card 1 in. (2.5 cm) wide for head fixing**

1 *Trace the pattern from the template and enlarge using the grid system. Draw the pattern on to the wrong side of the card and cut out very carefully.*

If you are using foil card for the basic shape, it will be necessary to cut the face area from some plain white card first, and then stick the foil in position on the main shape. If you are using plain card, you will only need to mark this area with a pencil.

2 *A diamond grid with the shapes 1½ in. (4 cm) apart has been used here. Mark your design on to the right side of the card. Then cut up pieces of decorative materials so they fit within the grid.*

3 *When sticking the shapes in place, continue right to the edges. Cut away the excess areas from the wrong side when you finish.*

4 *To give a neat appearance, braid or other materials may be stuck over the joints between the shapes.*

5 *After the decoration, the nose piece can be fixed. Score along the line marked on the pattern, and then curve the nose gently and stick in place on the rear side of the face piece.*

6 *Glue the face piece in position on the mask.*

7 *Now cut out the eye holes. Finally make the head fixing.*

CROWNS AND CORONETS

TOOLS AND MATERIALS

- Lightweight white card
  9 x 6 in. (23 x 15 cm)
- Lightweight metallic card in gold, silver,
  or bronze 13 x 7 in. (33 x 20 cm)
- Craft knife
- Hole punch
- Adhesive tape
- Double-sided tape
- Glue
- Sequins, sequin strips, beads, jewels,
  colored papers
- Paints and paint brush
- Thin ribbon for mask fastening
- Soft white net or silver foil film
  for a veil (optional)

PREPARATION

1 *Draw the round coronet part on to the wrong side of the metallic card and cut it out. Draw round face piece on to white card and cut it out. Then cut out the eyes. Try on this part of the mask and make any necessary adjustments. Paint in the facial details.*

2 *Cut thin pieces of sequin strip, about 3 in. (8 cm) long, to make a fringe. (You can use paper strips for this, even curling some of them.) Put double-sided tape along the top of the face part and carefully lay the sequin strip on this.*

3 *The coronet can be decorated in many different ways. Treat each segment in a uniform way. The princess will want simple decoration, some silver-sprayed flowers (use small silk flowers or flower-making components), plastic pearl beads, and some filigree along the edges.*

4 When you have finished decorating, lay the coronet over the face part; then making sure it is in position, gently press it down. The double-sided tape should hold it in place while you turn it over and tape it firmly on the back. Attach some ribbon to the back of the mask for the fastening.

Above Give a king strong bold eyebrows and eyes. You might want to put a few wrinkles around his eyes or give him a moustache using face paints. On his crown use big plastic gems, or stick on cut pieces of colored foil card and scrunched tissue paper, sprayed gold and silver.

Above If you want to make the princess more magical and fairy-like, you could give her a veil. Real bridal net is very expensive, but you could use cheap dress net. The quantity will depend on the size of the princess and how long you want the veil. Lay the net on top of the head and let it hang down the sides and back. Put the mask on and fasten it over the net.

Above To make an Ice Maiden, drape silver foil film over the head, like the net, and place a silver or blue metallic card coronet over it.

ZEBRA

The template can be scaled up or down to fit the size of the wearer's head. Make it rather larger than the actual face, as it will curve slightly when it is fastened.

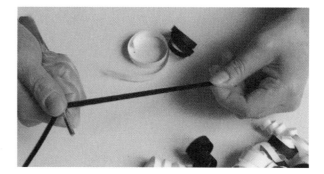

2 *Make paper curls ¹/₄-¹/₂ in. (5-10 mm) wide in black-and-white paper.*

TOOLS AND MATERIALS

- ◆ **Medium-weight white card**
- ◆ **Pencil**
- ◆ **Cutting knife**
- ◆ **Black paint and thin brush**
- ◆ **Black-and-white paper**
- ◆ **Glue**

3 *Stick them to the top of the head.*

PREPARATION

| *Draw round the template on to the card and cut out the shape. Cut out the eyes, nose, and mouth. Draw in the zebra's stripes, in pencil, making them about ¹/₃ in. (1 cm) wide. Paint a thin black line around the eyes, nose, and mouth. Paint in the stripes and leave to dry.*

RIDER MASK

This mask simulates the sixteenth- and seventeenth-century Italian rider's masks, worn to protect the face from branches when riding through wooded countryside. They were cut from thin sheets of metal and formed a type of armor. The designs could be quite decorative, however, and they inspired the simple cutout mask shown here.

PREPARATION

TOOLS AND MATERIALS

- ◆ **Paper and pencil**
- ◆ **Silver foil card or white card and aluminum foil 11 x 9 in. (28 x 23 cm)**
- ◆ **Craft knife**
- ◆ **Elastic, string, or ribbon**

2 *If you have made the mask from white card, it should now be covered with the aluminum foil. Lay the foil over the mask and cut roughly to size allowing enough to turn over the edge. From the wrong side, cut a slit through each open area. Turn to the right side and bend all the edges to the back, making sure no excess shows. Hold the mask up to the face and mark the position of the holes for the elastic, string, or ribbon. Pierce the holes, thread and tie.*

1 *Trace the basic mask shape. Either draw your own design or choose the rider mask pattern shown. If the mask is for an adult, take it to a photocopy shop and ask them to enlarge the pattern by 20 per cent. Trace the design on to the back of the foil card and then cut away the shaded areas with a craft knife. Make sure the work surface is protected either by a cutting mat or scrap card. Turn the mask over and smooth the cut edge where the knife may have caused a slight burr. If you are using white card this may not be necessary.*

DRAGON

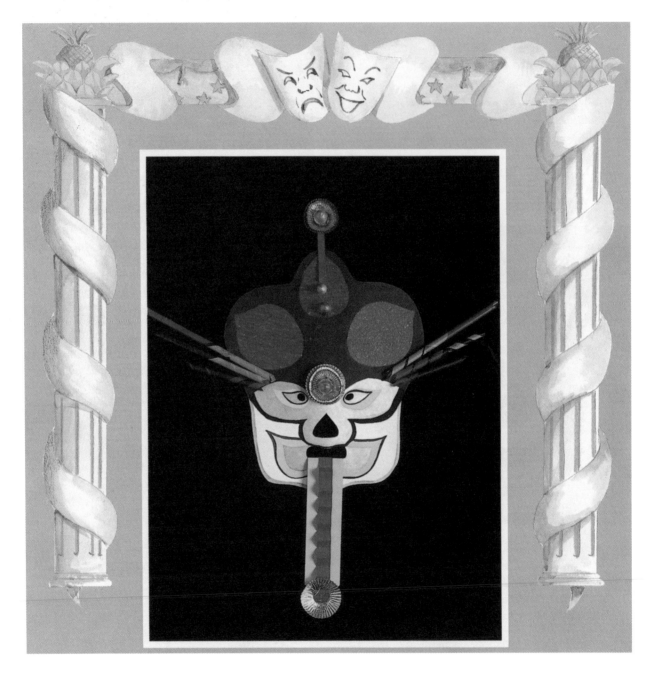

A very important symbol in all parts of Asia—especially China, Hong Kong, Tibet, Sri Lanka, and Indonesia—the dragon is a colorful and crucial element in many celebrations and festivals. Often the dragon is made into a large whole-head mask, sometimes with a large mouth, articulated jaws, huge bulbous eyes, and a large mane of colored hair.

The dragon is a flat mask and is very simple to make. It can be as ornate and decorative as you want depending on the materials you have available. The mask can be made to wear on the face or attached to a stick to wave in front of the face when appropriate.

TOOLS AND MATERIALS

- **Medium-weight white card 14 x 12 in. (35 x 30 cm)**
- **Black or dark-colored paper 12 x 8 in. (30 x 20 cm)**
- **Colored papers in 2 lengths of contrasting colors 2 x 12 in. (5 x 30 cm)**
- **Gold or silver metallic marker**
- **Paints and thin brush**
- **Pulp shapes**
- **Lollipop sticks**
- **Colored translucent paper or tissue paper**
- **Colored, crinkle foil paper**
- **Various metallic and colored fondant cases**
- **PVA glue**
- **Pencil**
- **Craft knife**

TIP
The wearer's nose could be painted a color—white or deep-red.

PREPARATION

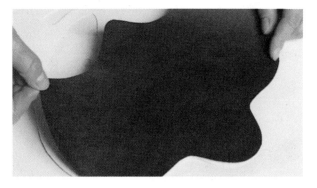

1 Draw round the template on to the white card and cut it out. Draw round the head-dress area on to the black or dark-colored paper and cut it out. Stick this shape on to the white card.

2 Draw in the facial features with silver or gold metallic markers. Make the eyes and mouth big and bold.

3 Add the final details of the face with red and black paint.

4 When decorating the head-dress, stick lots of brightly colored materials on to the black paper area. Do not be afraid of having lots of different colors and textures, but do aim for some symmetry to avoid ending up with a mess. Cut out three bright shapes from the crinkle foil and stick them on to the head-dress.

6 Make the tongue with paper 2 x 8 in. (5 x 20 cm). Fold over one end and make a point at the other. Pleat a piece of paper 3/4 x 12 in. (2 x 30 cm) in contrasting color, making each pleat about 1/2 in. (1.5 cm) wide. Put glue on alternate concertina fold edges and stick it down the middle of the previous strip of paper.

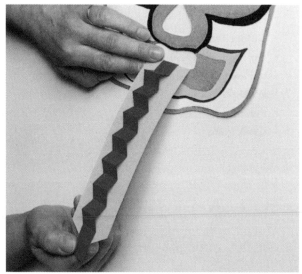

5 Add painted or natural lollipop sticks, and stick painted pulp shapes, fondant cases, or scrunched tissue paper on to them. Stick these to the top of the head-dress. Make paper rolls out of translucent paper or tissue paper, and stick these to the sides.

7 Hook the folded end of the tongue into the dragon's mouth and stick with tape, from behind. Stick a metallic fondant case or other decoration to the bottom of the tongue. This forms a basic tongue, but you could always add further decoration to it. For fastening use method 5 or 4A (see methods section p.425).

MOON

The full-face masks of the moon and the sun are made out of flat card.

> ### TOOLS AND MATERIALS
> * **Medium-weight white card 12 in. (30 cm) square**
> * **White paper doilies**
> * **White tissue paper**
> * **Silver and gold glitter**
> * **Silver spray paint**
> * **Dark-blue and black paint**
> * **Paint brush**
> * **Gold and silver star-shaped stickers**
> * **Glue**
> * **Pencil**
> * **Craft knife and scissors**

PREPARATION

1 *Draw round the template on to the card and cut out the moon shape. Cut out the eyes, nose, and mouth. Draw in the arc to make the crescent. Scrunch and tear tissue paper and doilies, and stick on to the crescent shape of the card to make a rich—but not too thick—textured surface.*

2 *Spray the crescent with silver paint.*

3 *Paint the rest of the card dark-blue/black for the night, and when dry put the star stickers on. Use method 5 for fixing (see methods section p.425).*

441

SUN

TOOLS AND MATERIALS

* **Medium-weight white card 12 in. (30 cm) square**
* **Medium-weight white card 8 x 24 in. (20 x 60 cm)**
* **Gold-crinkle foil paper 8 x 24 in. (20 x 60 cm)**
* **Pale-yellow and light-orange tissue paper**
* **Gold spray paint**
* **Pencil**
* **Craft knife and scissors**
* **Glue and adhesive tape**

PREPARATION

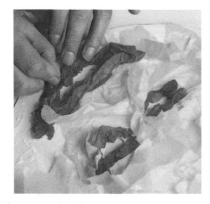

1 *Draw round the template on to the white card and cut out the sun shape. Cut out the features. Make a collage on the sun's face, as in the moon mask, using the yellow tissue paper. Outline the smiling eyes and mouth with a thin row of scrunched, orange tissue paper. Arrange the yellow tissue paper so it covers the nose.*

2 *Gently spray with a thin layer of gold paint, retaining some of the yellow and orange colors beneath. Trim round the edge of the face.*

3 *Cut out the sun rays in white card, three of the smallest shape and six each of the larger shapes. Cover the sun rays with gold-crinkle foil paper.*

4 *Place the smallest three rays at the bottom of the face and tape from behind. They should slightly overlap and be taped to each other as well as to the card. Repeat this process around the sun with the other rays, alternating their shapes. By overlapping they will support each other and not flop when in position. Use method 5 for fixing (see methods section p.425).*

GLOSSARY

B

Burnish: To make smooth or glossy by rubbing with a tool

C

Chinoiserie: A style of art marked by extensive decoration and intricate patterns, indicative of Chinese influence

Coated paper: Paper that has been coated with pigment and its binder, giving a smooth finish

Cold-pressed paper: Paper that has a surface with a slight texture, made by pressing the finished sheet through cold cylinders

Collage: Artistic composition of various materials and objects pasted on a surface, usually marked by thematic lines and colors

Cornucopia: Cone-shaped ornament or receptacle

Corrugated: Shaped into a series of folds or a set of alternating ridges and grooves

D

Deckle: A plastic or wooden frame used when making paper by hand; it rests on top of a mold and helps make paper pulp into sheets of a specific size

Deckle edge: Rough, irregular edge of a paper, typical of handmade papers; can be made on machine-made paper by tearing the paper using a sharp steel ruler

Decoupage: The art of decorating a surface with cutouts

Dowel: A pin that fits closely into a corresponding hole, used to fasten or align

G

Gesso: A mixture of plaster of Paris and glue, can be used as a base for low relief as well as a surface for painting

Grain: The direction in which the fibres lie in wood, leather, stone, or woven fabric

H

Harbin, Robert: 1908-1978; British magician who wrote a number of books on origami, including *Paper Magic*, and also presented television programs on the subject; first president of the British Origami Society

Hexahedron: Solid figure with six plane polygons or faces

Hot-pressed paper: Paper with smooth surface, made by pressing the finished sheet through hot cylinders

I

Ingres paper: Named after the French painter Jean Auguste Dominique (1780-1867); also called Paris paper. It is a coarse paper used in bookbinding as lining paper

M

Mold: A ridged frame with wire mesh or screen on which the deckle is placed when making paper by hand

Mountain fold: Fold behind along the line on a piece of paper

O

Origami: The art of folding paper to create shapes representing objects

Outside-reverse fold: Created by folding back one side of the paper over the main body, forming a hood or collar

P

Papier mâchè: Material made from paper pulp or paper mixed with glue or paste, so it can be molded into various shapes when wet, later becoming solid when dry

Polygon: A closed plane figure bounded by straight lines

Polystyrene: Very light soft plastic, used especially in containers that prevent heat loss and can also be molded into objects

Polyvinyl acetate (PVA): Strong plastic compound used especially in paints and adhesives

Poster paint: Paint in which the color is mixed with egg and water

R

Reverse fold: Inverting an existing fold, in a way that the tips of the paper lie in between different layers

Rough paper: Paper with heavily textured surface

S

Sieve: Tool for sifting solids from liquids, or larger solids from smaller ones, consisting of a wire or plastic net

Squash fold: Made by opening out a part of the paper, and then flattening it

Straightedge: Hand tool with a flat rectangular bar, of metal or wood, used to draw straight lines

U

Uncoated paper: Paper with no additional layer on the surface

V

Valley fold: Fold in front along the line

Varnish: A preparation that is painted on to surface such as wood and metal to form a hard, glossy, and transparent film when it is dry

W

Watermark: Image or pattern impressed on paper and visible when held up to the light

Y

Yoshizawa, Akira: 1911-2005; Japanese origami artist, considered among the greatest of modern paper folders; wrote a number of books

INDEX